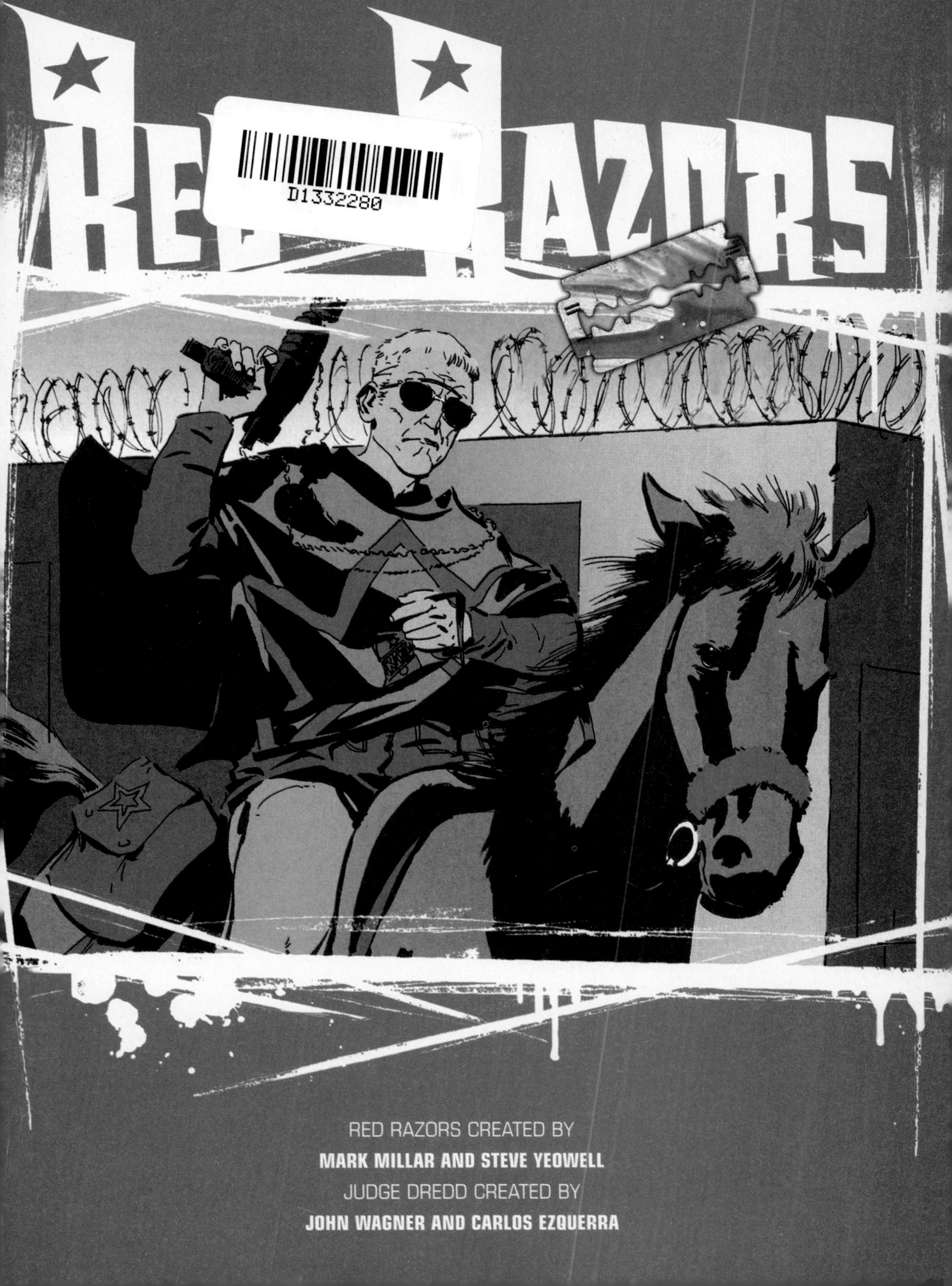

RED RAZORS CREATED BY

MARK MILLAR AND STEVE YEOWELL

JUDGE DREDD CREATED BY

JOHN WAGNER AND CARLOS EZQUERRA

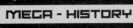
MEGA - HISTORY

- 2031 — COMPLETION OF MEGA-CITY ONE JUDGE SYSTEM ESTABLISHED
- 2070 — ATOMIC WARS DEVASTATE EARTH
- 2072 — JUDGES RESTORE ORDER AND GAIN ABSOLUTE CONTROL
- 2079 — JUDGES RICO AND JOSEPH DREDD GRADUATE FROM THE ACADEMY
- 2088 — ESTABLISHMENT OF LUNA-1 MOON BASE
- 2099 — THE ROBOT REBELLION
- 2100 — DREDD CROSSES THE CURSED EARTH TO SAVE MEGA-CITY TWO
- 2101 — INSANE CHIEF JUDGE CAL ATTEMPTS TO DESTROY THE CITY
- 2102 — FIRST APPEARANCE OF JUDGE DEATH. DREDD SEARCHES FOR THE JUDGE CHILD
- 2104 — FOLLOWING "BLOCK MANIA," THE APOCALYPSE WAR BEGINS
- 2106 — USING A PROTOTYPE TIME MACHINE, DREDD TRAVELS TO 2120 TO STOP THE JUDGE CHILD CALAMITY
- 2109 — SKYSURFER MARLON "CHOPPER" SHAKESPEARE ESCAPES MEGA-CITY ONE FOR OZ, PURSUED BY DREDD
- 2112 — NECROPOLIS: THE DARK JUDGES INVADE AND KILL OVER 60 MILLION
- 2113 — RIOT AT "AQUATRAZ" PENAL COMPLEX
- 2114 — JUDGMENT DAY: SABBAT ARRIVES FROM 2178 AD TO DESTROY THE WORLD
- 2117 — DREDD APPOINTED SECTOR CHIEF, SECTOR 301
- 2121 — CRIMELORD NERO NARCOS LAUNCHES "DOOMSDAY"
- 2126 — THE PRESENT DAY (FOR JUDGE DREDD)
- 2176 — OUR STORY TAKES PLACE

WORLD MAP

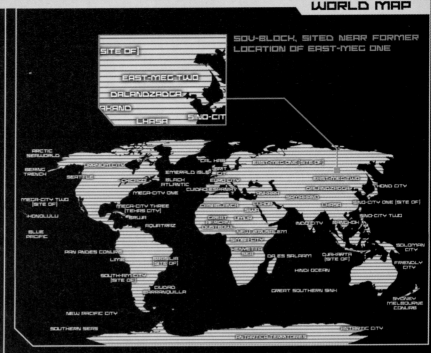

SOV-BLOCK, SITED NEAR FORMER LOCATION OF EAST-MEG ONE

SITE OF] EAST-MEG TWO
DALANDZADGA
AKAND
LHASA SINO-CIT

ARCTIC SEAWORLD
BERING TRENCH
SEATTLE
URANIUM CITY
CHICAGO
CAL HAB
BRIT CIT
EMERALD ISLE
EAST-MEG ONE [SITE OF]
EAST-MEG TWO
DALANDZADGA
HOND CITY
EURO CITY
BLACK ATLANTIC
CIUDAD ESPANA
ANKARA
SAMARKAND
SINO-CITY ONE [SITE OF]
MEGA-CITY ONE
MEGA-CITY TWO [SITE OF]
MEGA-CITY THREE [TEXAS CITY]
CASABLANCA
LUXOR CITY
LHASA
SINO-CITY TWO
HONOLULU
BRIT
INDO CITY
BANGKOK
BLUE PACIFIC
AQUATRAZ
GREAT UTHUR DUSTBOWL
NEW JERUSALEM
SIMBA CITY
SOLOMON CITY
PAN ANDES CONURB
KENYATTA CITY
FRIENDLY CITY
LIMA
BRASILIA [SITE OF]
DA ES SALAAM
DJAKARTA [SITE OF]
HINDI OCEAN
SOUTH-AM CITY [SITE OF]
CIUDAD BARRANQUILLA
GREAT SOUTHERN SINK
SYDNEY MELBOURNE CONURB
NEW PACIFIC CITY
SOUTHERN SEAS
ANTARTIC CITY
ANTARTICA TERRITORIES

LAWMEN OF THE FUTURE

FOLLOWING THE ATOMIC WARS OF 2070, THE BULK OF THE SURVIVORS WERE CROWDED INTO GIGANTIC MEGA-CITIES – VASTLY OVERPOPULATED MELTING POTS, WHERE UNEMPLOYMENT STANDS AT 99% AND CRIME IS RIFE. BEYOND THE CITY WALLS LIES AN IRRADIATED WASTELAND POPULATED BY MUTANTS AND RENEGADES.

A SPECIAL BREED OF POLICE OFFICER WAS REQUIRED TO KEEP ORDER – THE JUDGES. HIGHLY TRAINED INDIVIDUALS EMPOWERED TO DISPENSE INSTANT JUSTICE, THESE LAWMEN ARE JUDGE, JURY AND EXECUTIONER. TOUGHEST OF THEM ALL IS JUDGE DREDD – HE *IS* THE LAW...

WAR IN THE EAST

TOWARDS THE END OF 2103, THE RULING GOVERNMENT OF EAST-MEG ONE BEGAN A NEFARIOUS PLAN TO INVADE MEGA-CITY ONE. THEIR AGENT, AN ASSASSIN NAMED ORLOK, PLANTED A HIGHLY POTENT PSYCHOACTIVE CHEMICAL IN MEGA-CITY ONE'S WATER SUPPLY, CAUSING CITIZENS TO TURN ON THE JUDGES AND ON EACH OTHER IN WHAT CAME TO BE KNOWN AS BLOCK MANIA.

THIS INITIAL ATTACK WAS FOLLOWED UP BY A DIRECT NUCLEAR ASSAULT – KILLING MILLIONS – AND A SUBSEQUENT INVASION AND OCCUPATION, WHICH ACCOUNTED FOR MANY MORE DEATHS. IN A DESPERATE MOVE, JUDGE DREDD LED A SURGICAL STRIKE TEAM TO THE HEART OF EAST-MEG ONE, AND MANAGED TO TURN THE CITY'S OWN NUCLEAR ARSENAL AGAINST ITSELF, CAUSING THE UTTER DESTRUCTION OF THE LARGEST SOV-BLOCK CITY.

NOW, IN 2176, THE SOV-BLOCK STANDS IN DISARRAY, AND WESTERN INFLUENCES HAVE THOROUGHLY PENETRATED THE IRON CURTAIN. ENTER JUDGE RAZORS...

SO 222 563 00200 0 12 5 2000 AD

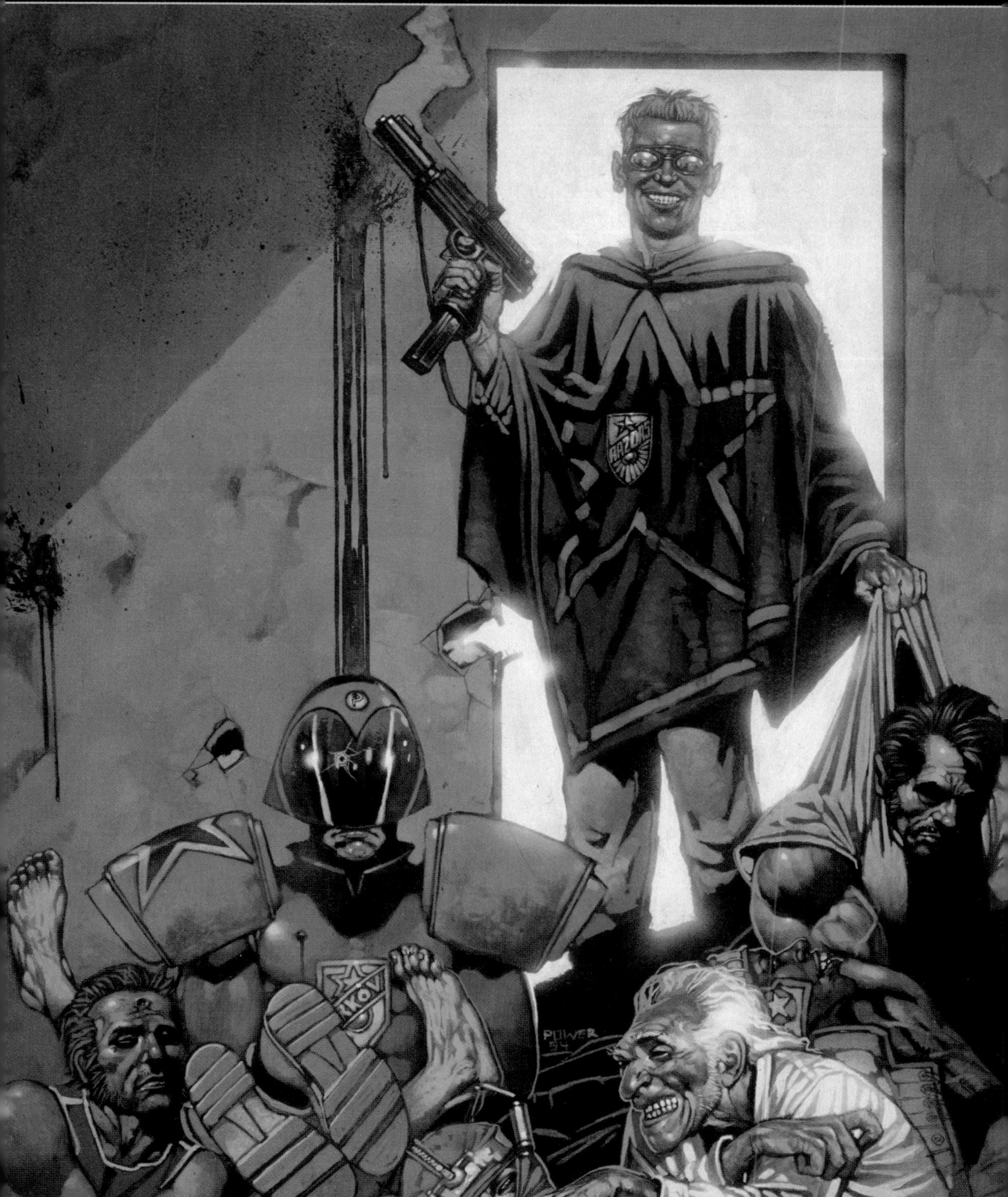
POWER
94

Prog 908 Cover by **Dermot Power**

RED RAZORS

Script: Mark Millar

Art: Steve Yeowell

Colors: Phillip Lynch

Letters: Gordon Robson, Annie Parkhouse

Originally published in *Judge Dredd: The Megazine* 1.08–1.15

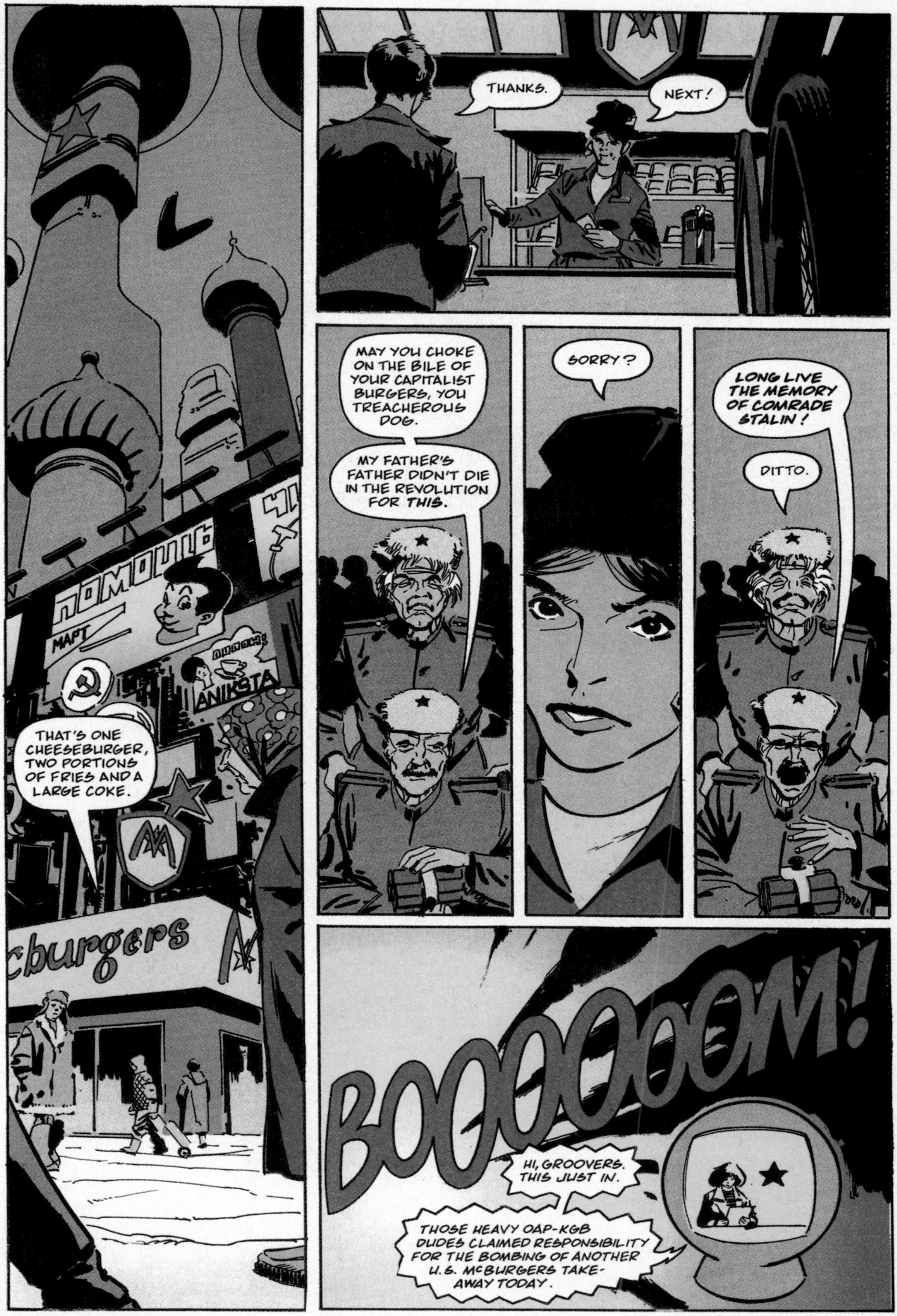

THAT'S ONE CHEESEBURGER, TWO PORTIONS OF FRIES AND A LARGE COKE.
THANKS.
NEXT!
MAY YOU CHOKE ON THE BILE OF YOUR CAPITALIST BURGERS, YOU TREACHEROUS DOG.
MY FATHER'S FATHER DIDN'T DIE IN THE REVOLUTION FOR THIS.
SORRY?
LONG LIVE THE MEMORY OF COMRADE STALIN!
DITTO.
BOOOOOOOM!
HI, GROOVERS. THIS JUST IN.
THOSE HEAVY OAP-KGB DUDES CLAIMED RESPONSIBILITY FOR THE BOMBING OF ANOTHER U.S. McBURGERS TAKE-AWAY TODAY.

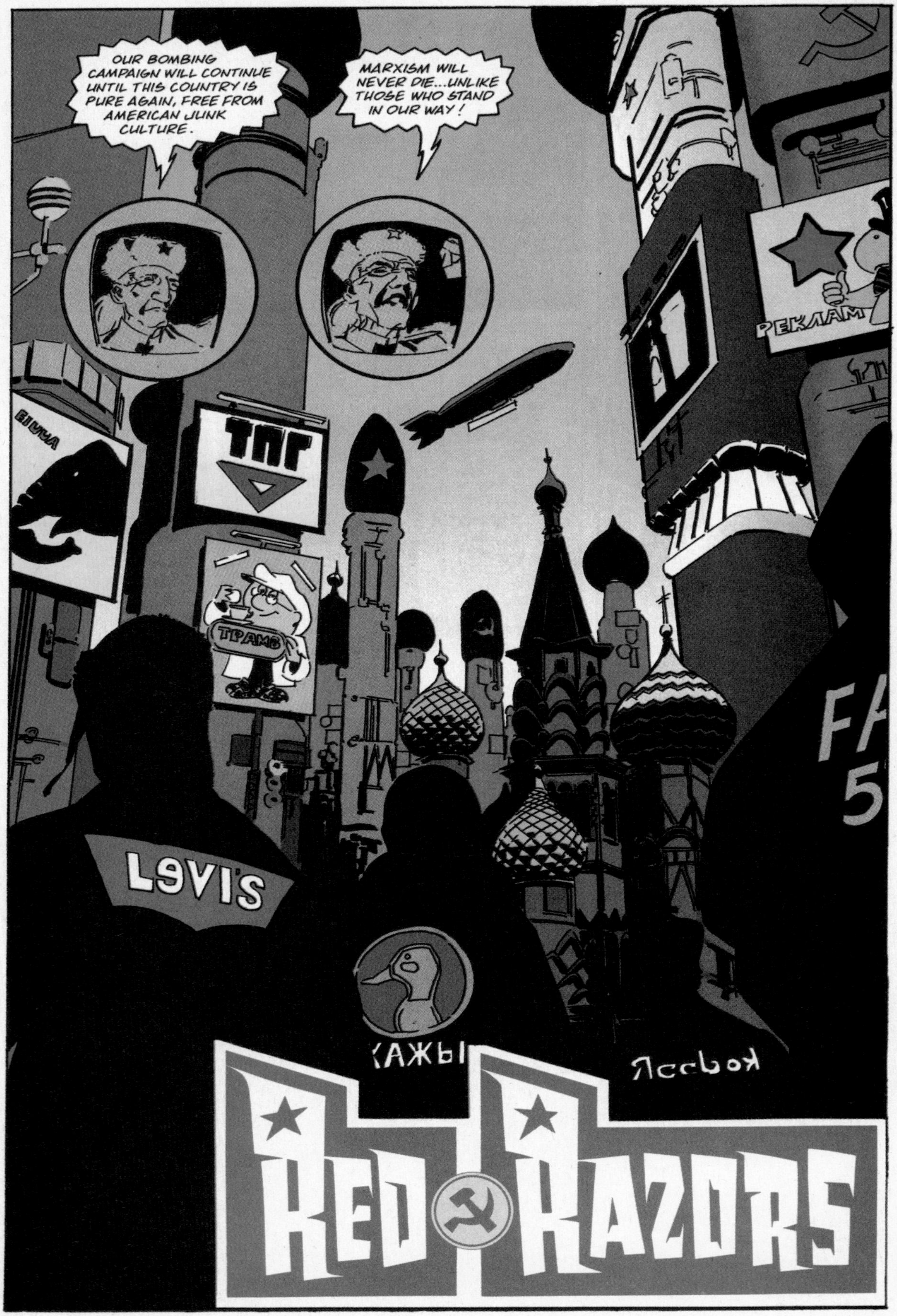
OUR BOMBING CAMPAIGN WILL CONTINUE UNTIL THIS COUNTRY IS PURE AGAIN, FREE FROM AMERICAN JUNK CULTURE.
MARXISM WILL NEVER DIE...UNLIKE THOSE WHO STAND IN OUR WAY!
РЕКЛАМ
ТПГ
ТРАМВ
RED RAZORS

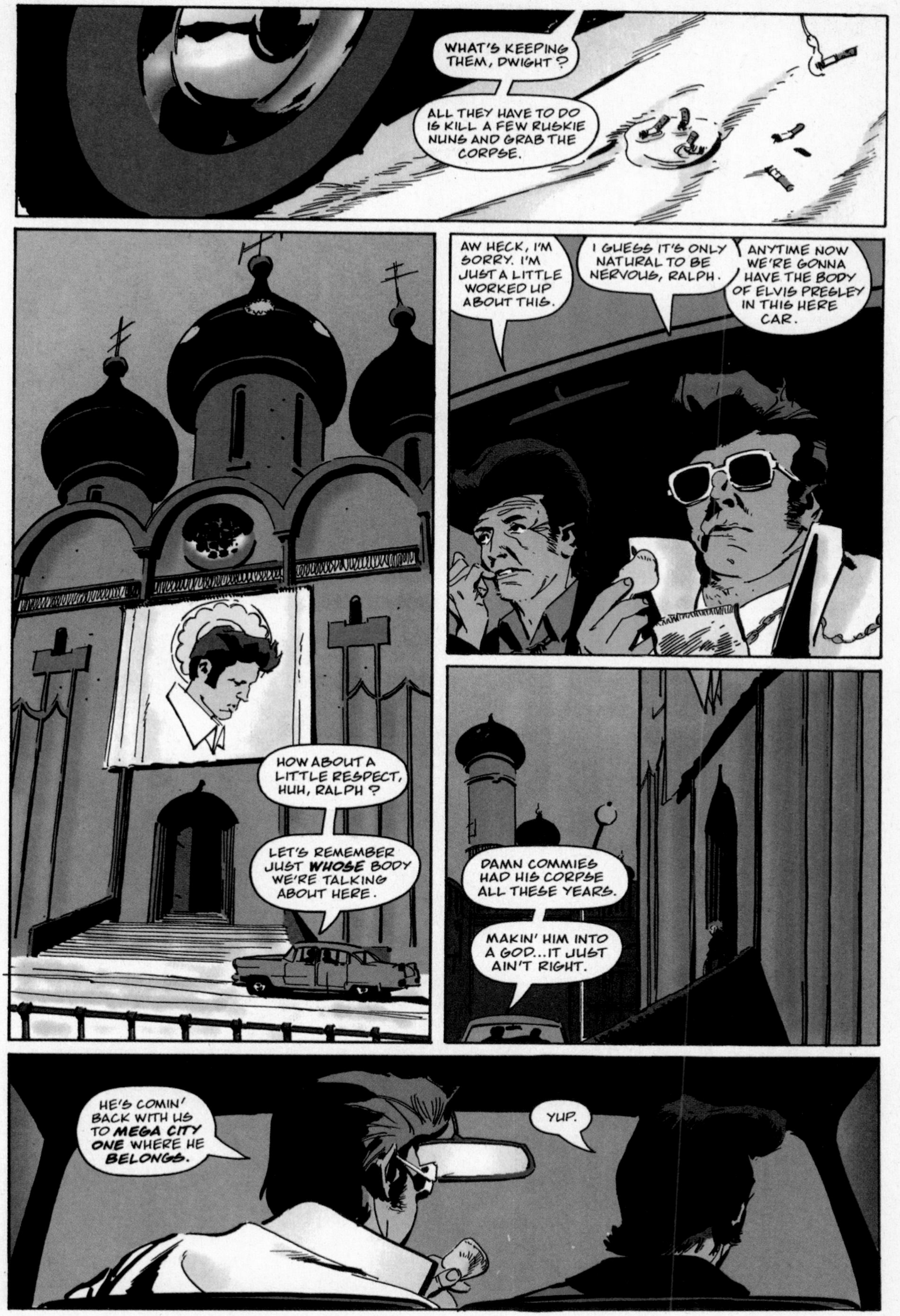
WHAT'S KEEPING THEM, DWIGHT?
ALL THEY HAVE TO DO IS KILL A FEW RUSKIE NUNS AND GRAB THE CORPSE.
AW HECK, I'M SORRY. I'M JUST A LITTLE WORKED UP ABOUT THIS.
I GUESS IT'S ONLY NATURAL TO BE NERVOUS, RALPH.
ANYTIME NOW WE'RE GONNA HAVE THE BODY OF ELVIS PRESLEY IN THIS HERE CAR.
HOW ABOUT A LITTLE RESPECT, HUH, RALPH?
LET'S REMEMBER JUST WHOSE BODY WE'RE TALKING ABOUT HERE.
DAMN COMMIES HAD HIS CORPSE ALL THESE YEARS.
MAKIN' HIM INTO A GOD... IT JUST AIN'T RIGHT.
HE'S COMIN' BACK WITH US TO MEGA CITY ONE WHERE HE BELONGS.
YUP.

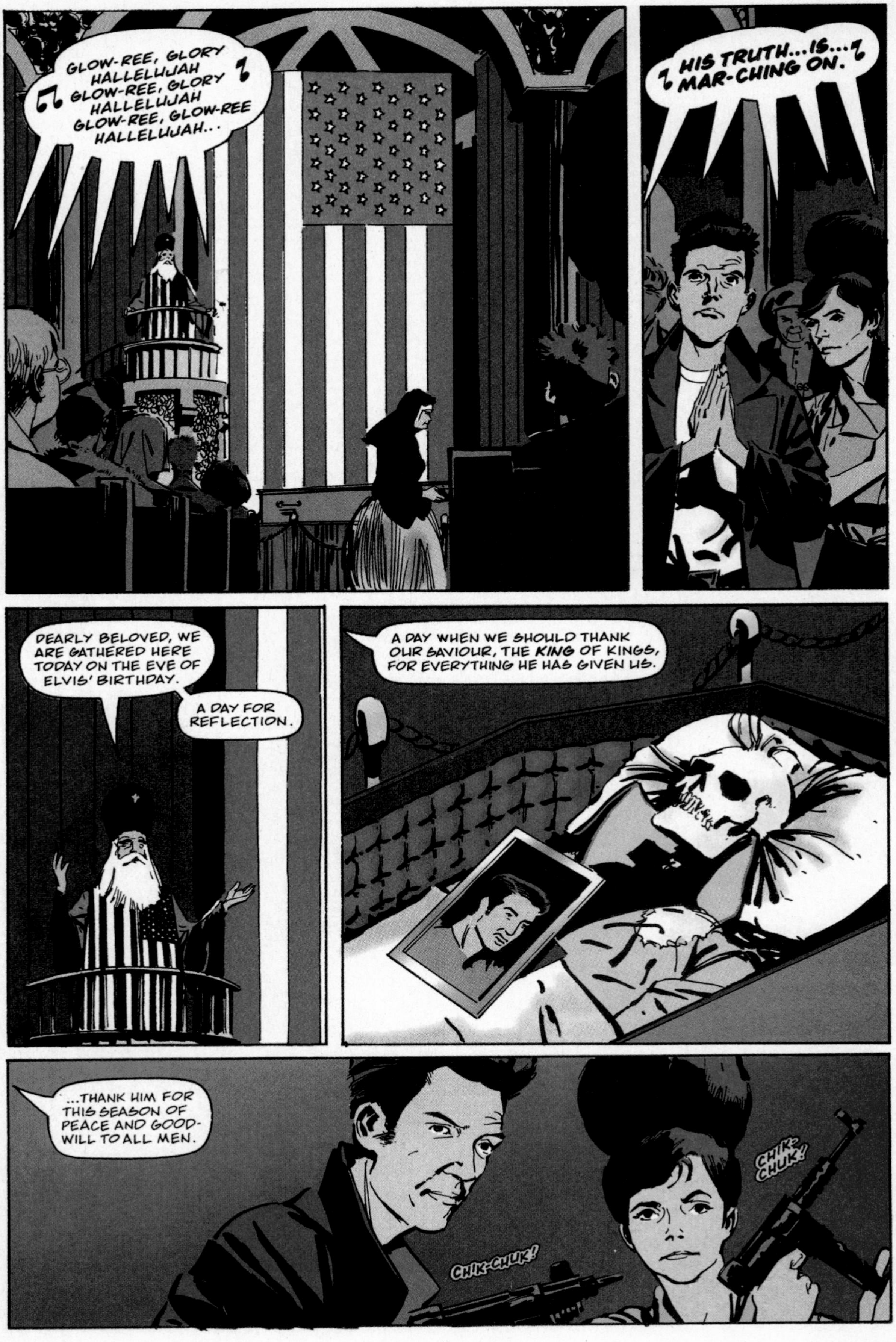
GLOW-REE, GLORY HALLELUJAH GLOW-REE, GLORY HALLELUJAH GLOW-REE, GLOW-REE HALLELUJAH...
HIS TRUTH...IS... MAR-CHING ON.
DEARLY BELOVED, WE ARE GATHERED HERE TODAY ON THE EVE OF ELVIS' BIRTHDAY.
A DAY FOR REFLECTION.
A DAY WHEN WE SHOULD THANK OUR SAVIOUR, THE KING OF KINGS, FOR EVERYTHING HE HAS GIVEN US.
...THANK HIM FOR THIS SEASON OF PEACE AND GOOD-WILL TO ALL MEN.
CHIK-CHUK!
CHIK-CHUK!

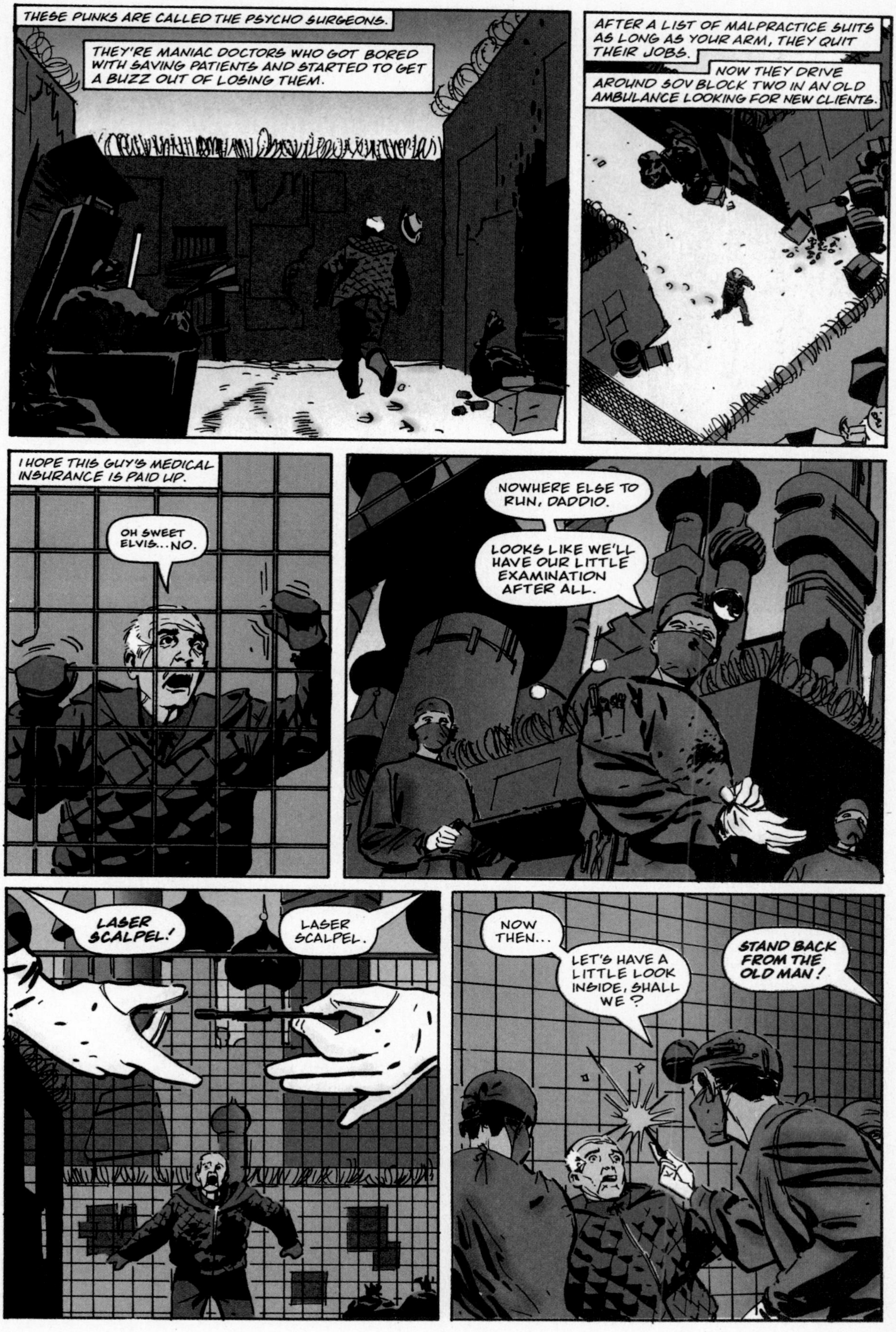
THESE PUNKS ARE CALLED THE PSYCHO SURGEONS.
THEY'RE MANIAC DOCTORS WHO GOT BORED WITH SAVING PATIENTS AND STARTED TO GET A BUZZ OUT OF LOSING THEM.
AFTER A LIST OF MALPRACTICE SUITS AS LONG AS YOUR ARM, THEY QUIT THEIR JOBS.
NOW THEY DRIVE AROUND SOV BLOCK TWO IN AN OLD AMBULANCE LOOKING FOR NEW CLIENTS.
I HOPE THIS GUY'S MEDICAL INSURANCE IS PAID UP.
OH SWEET ELVIS... NO.
NOWHERE ELSE TO RUN, DADDIO.
LOOKS LIKE WE'LL HAVE OUR LITTLE EXAMINATION AFTER ALL.
LASER SCALPEL!
LASER SCALPEL.
NOW THEN...
LET'S HAVE A LITTLE LOOK INSIDE, SHALL WE?
STAND BACK FROM THE OLD MAN!

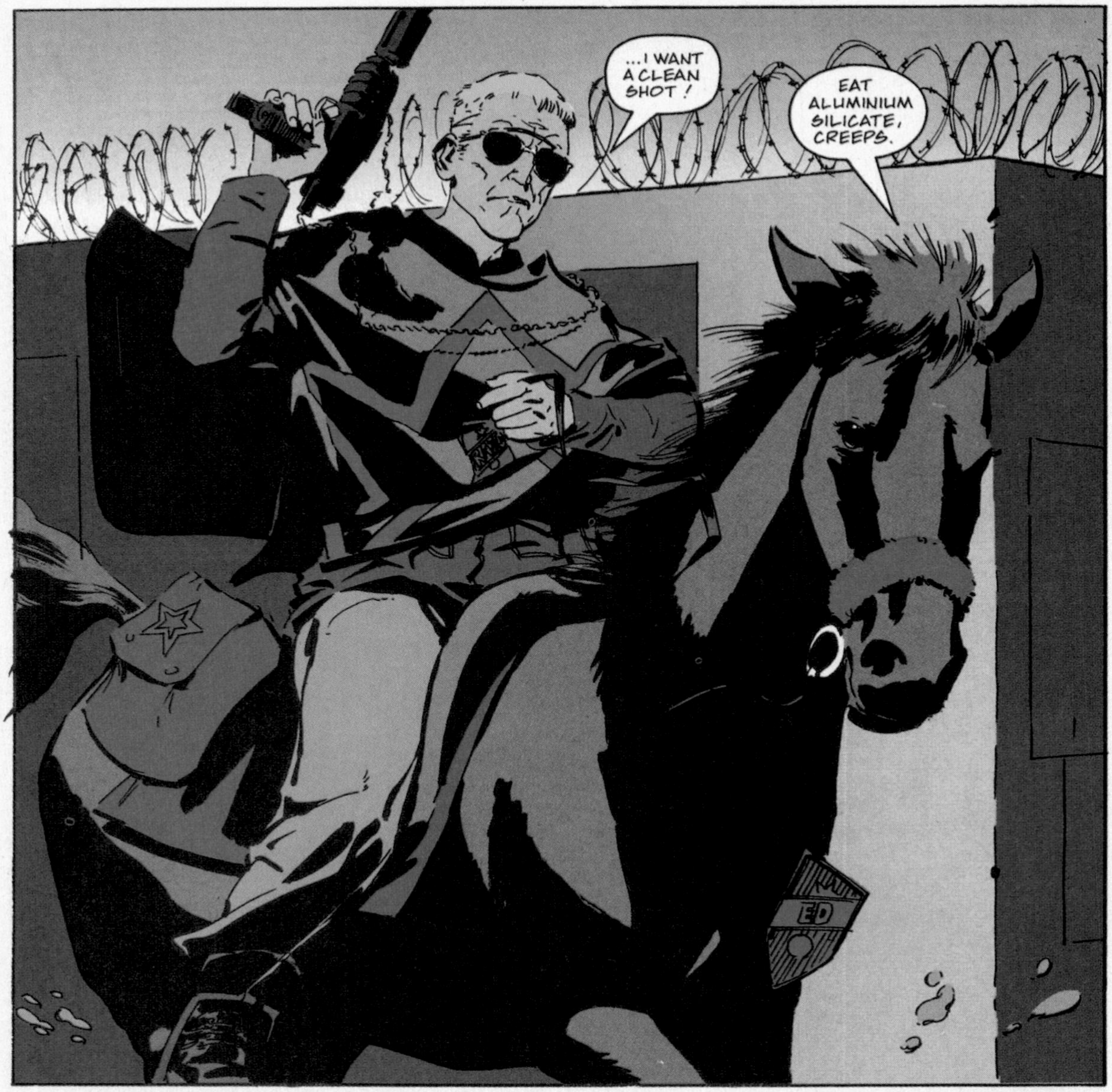
...I WANT A CLEAN SHOT!
EAT ALUMINIUM SILICATE, CREEPS.
ED

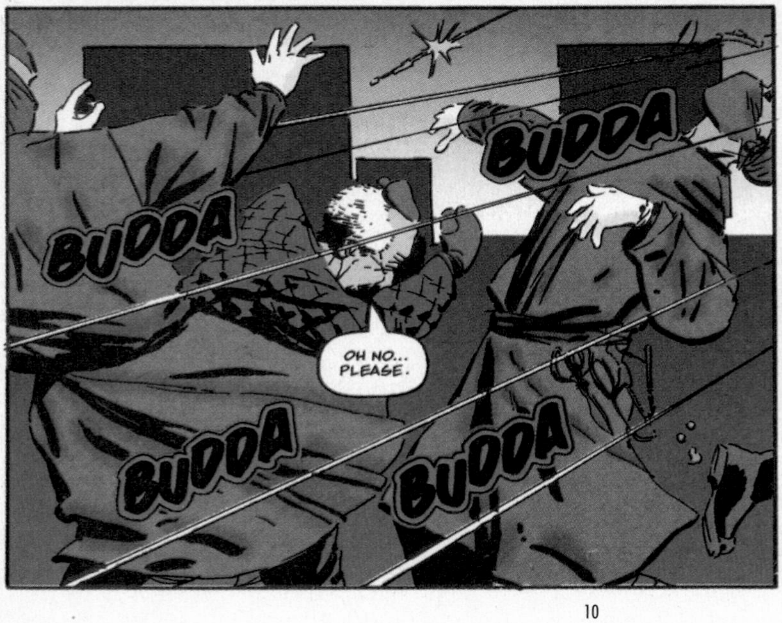
BUDDA
BUDDA
OH NO... PLEASE.
BUDDA
BUDDA

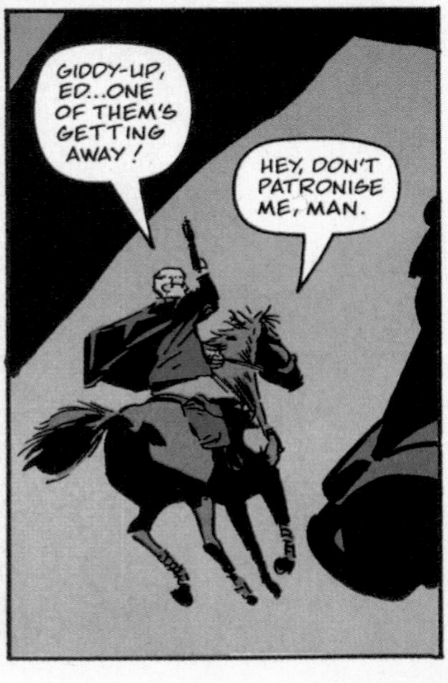
GIDDY-UP, ED...ONE OF THEM'S GETTING AWAY!
HEY, DON'T PATRONISE ME, MAN.

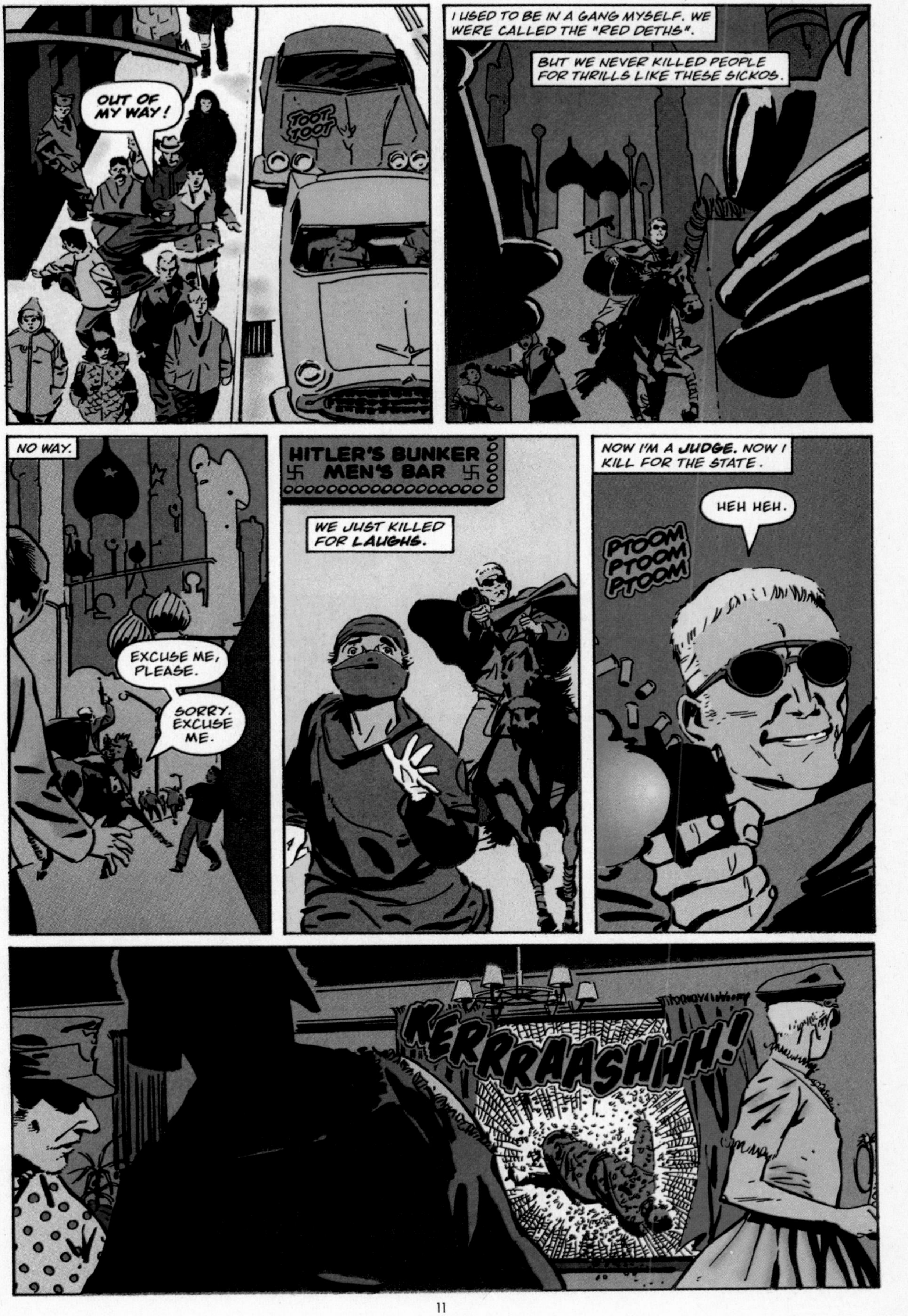
OUT OF MY WAY!
TOOT TOOT
I USED TO BE IN A GANG MYSELF. WE WERE CALLED THE "RED DETHS".
BUT WE NEVER KILLED PEOPLE FOR THRILLS LIKE THESE SICKOS.
NO WAY.
EXCUSE ME, PLEASE.
SORRY. EXCUSE ME.
HITLER'S BUNKER MEN'S BAR
WE JUST KILLED FOR LAUGHS.
NOW I'M A JUDGE. NOW I KILL FOR THE STATE.
HEH HEH.
PTOOM PTOOM PTOOM
KERRRAASHHH!

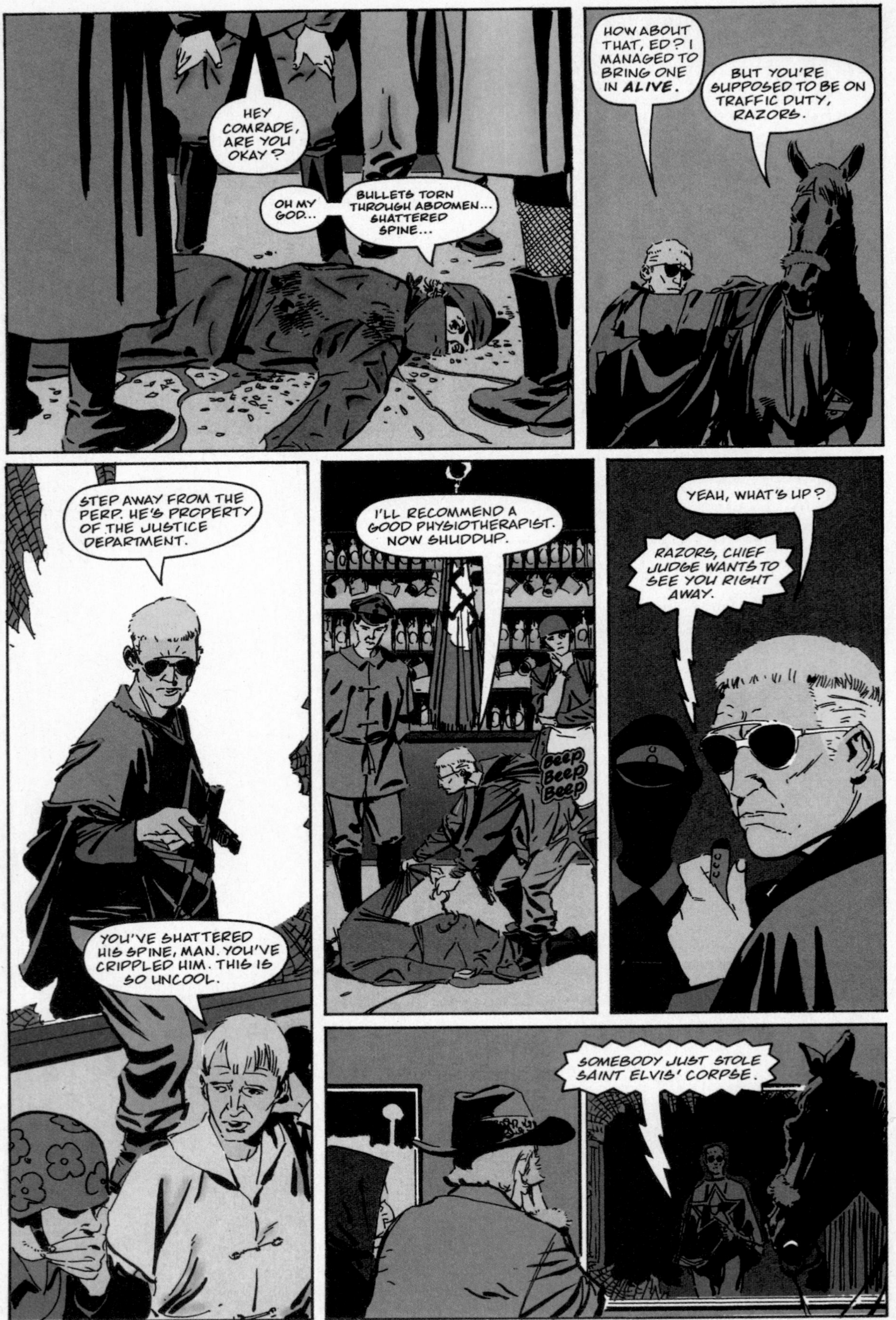
HEY COMRADE, ARE YOU OKAY?
OH MY GOD...
BULLETS TORN THROUGH ABDOMEN... SHATTERED SPINE...
HOW ABOUT THAT, ED? I MANAGED TO BRING ONE IN ALIVE.
BUT YOU'RE SUPPOSED TO BE ON TRAFFIC DUTY, RAZORS.
STEP AWAY FROM THE PERP. HE'S PROPERTY OF THE JUSTICE DEPARTMENT.
YOU'VE SHATTERED HIS SPINE, MAN. YOU'VE CRIPPLED HIM. THIS IS SO UNCOOL.
I'LL RECOMMEND A GOOD PHYSIOTHERAPIST. NOW SHUDDUP.
Beep Beep Beep
YEAH, WHAT'S UP?
RAZORS, CHIEF JUDGE WANTS TO SEE YOU RIGHT AWAY.
SOMEBODY JUST STOLE SAINT ELVIS' CORPSE.

NEXT: ***RED HAWAII!***

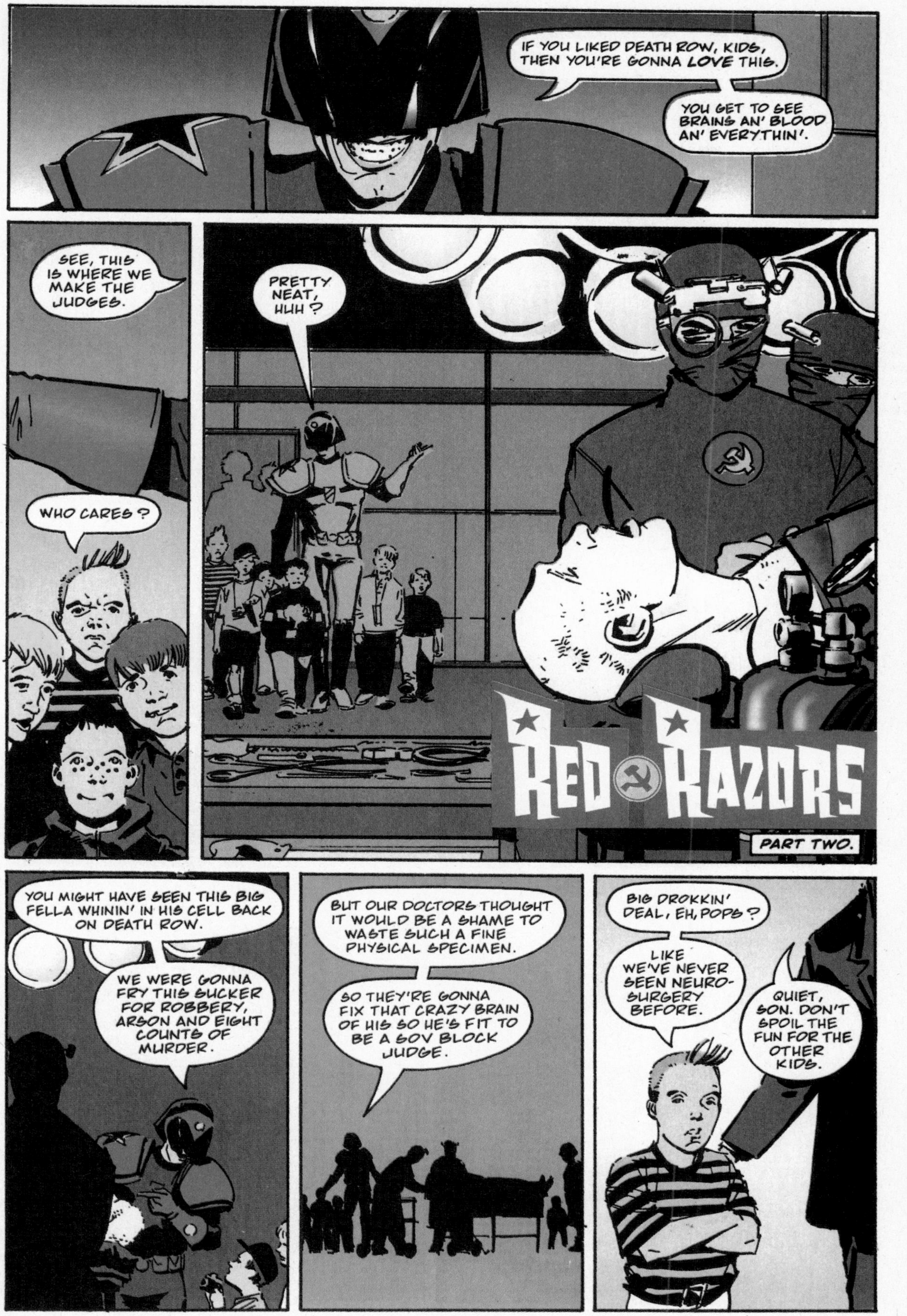
IF YOU LIKED DEATH ROW, KIDS, THEN YOU'RE GONNA LOVE THIS.
YOU GET TO SEE BRAINS AN' BLOOD AN' EVERYTHIN'.
SEE, THIS IS WHERE WE MAKE THE JUDGES.
PRETTY NEAT, HUH ?
WHO CARES ?
RED RAZORS
PART TWO.
YOU MIGHT HAVE SEEN THIS BIG FELLA WHININ' IN HIS CELL BACK ON DEATH ROW.
WE WERE GONNA FRY THIS SUCKER FOR ROBBERY, ARSON AND EIGHT COUNTS OF MURDER.
BUT OUR DOCTORS THOUGHT IT WOULD BE A SHAME TO WASTE SUCH A FINE PHYSICAL SPECIMEN.
SO THEY'RE GONNA FIX THAT CRAZY BRAIN OF HIS SO HE'S FIT TO BE A SOV BLOCK JUDGE.
BIG DROKKIN' DEAL, EH, POPS ?
LIKE WE'VE NEVER SEEN NEURO-SURGERY BEFORE.
QUIET, SON. DON'T SPOIL THE FUN FOR THE OTHER KIDS.

GEE, JUDGE, DOES THAT MEAN THERE'S NO CADET SCHOOL IN THE SOV BLOCKS?

'FRAID SO, KID.

BUT BEING A JUDGE HERE IS A LOT MORE DANGEROUS THAN BACK WHERE YOU COME FROM.

WE DON'T THINK IT'S FAIR TO ASK OUR CITIZENS TO PUT ON A HELMET AND RISK THEIR LIVES.

WE THINK IT MAKES MORE SENSE TO SEND THE FINKS WHO COMMITTED THE CRIMES TO THE FRONT LINE.

WOW. SO ALL YOUR JUDGES ARE EX-CONS?

AW GEEZ, THIS IS THE WORST HOLIDAY WE'VE HAD SINCE BRIT-CIT, POPS. I WISH MOM HAD CUSTODY OF ME THIS YEAR.

YOU MUST REALLY HATE ME TO BRING ME TO A DUMP LIKE THIS.

DON'T SAY THAT, SON. YOU KNOW DADDY LOVES YOU.

WELL, KIDS. THAT WRAPS UP OUR TOUR OF THE JUSTICE DEPARTMENT. WE'D BEST LET THE GOOD DOCTORS GET ON WITH THEIR WORK.

HERE'S A LOLLIPOP FOR EVERYONE FOR BEING SO WELL BEHAVED.

THANKS, JUDGE.

GEE, THIS IS SWELL.

THANKS.

LOLLIPOPS! GEEZ, IS THIS GUY FOR REAL?

THIS DUMP HAS GOTTA BE THE TOILET OF THE WORLD.

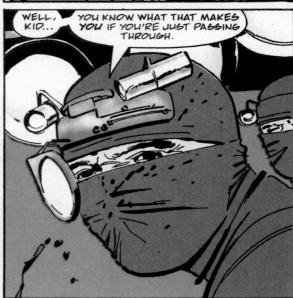

WELL, KID...

YOU KNOW WHAT THAT MAKES YOU IF YOU'RE JUST PASSING THROUGH.

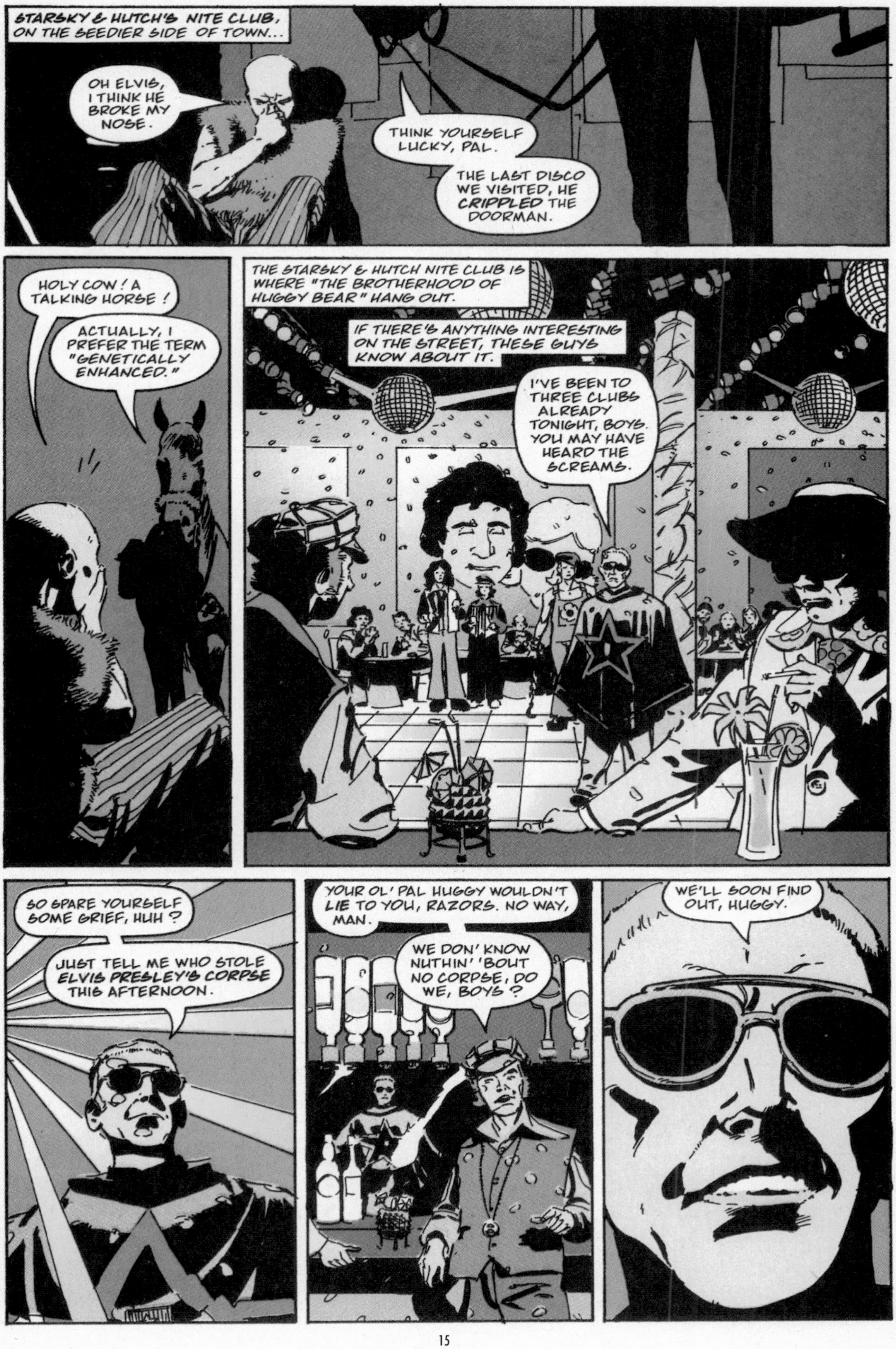
STARSKY & HUTCH'S NITE CLUB, ON THE SEEDIER SIDE OF TOWN...
OH ELVIS, I THINK HE BROKE MY NOSE.
THINK YOURSELF LUCKY, PAL.
THE LAST DISCO WE VISITED, HE CRIPPLED THE DOORMAN.
HOLY COW! A TALKING HORSE!
ACTUALLY, I PREFER THE TERM "GENETICALLY ENHANCED."
THE STARSKY & HUTCH NITE CLUB IS WHERE "THE BROTHERHOOD OF HUGGY BEAR" HANG OUT.
IF THERE'S ANYTHING INTERESTING ON THE STREET, THESE GUYS KNOW ABOUT IT.
I'VE BEEN TO THREE CLUBS ALREADY TONIGHT, BOYS. YOU MAY HAVE HEARD THE SCREAMS.
SO SPARE YOURSELF SOME GRIEF, HUH?
JUST TELL ME WHO STOLE ELVIS PRESLEY'S CORPSE THIS AFTERNOON.
YOUR OL' PAL HUGGY WOULDN'T LIE TO YOU, RAZORS. NO WAY, MAN.
WE DON' KNOW NUTHIN' 'BOUT NO CORPSE, DO WE, BOYS?
WE'LL SOON FIND OUT, HUGGY.

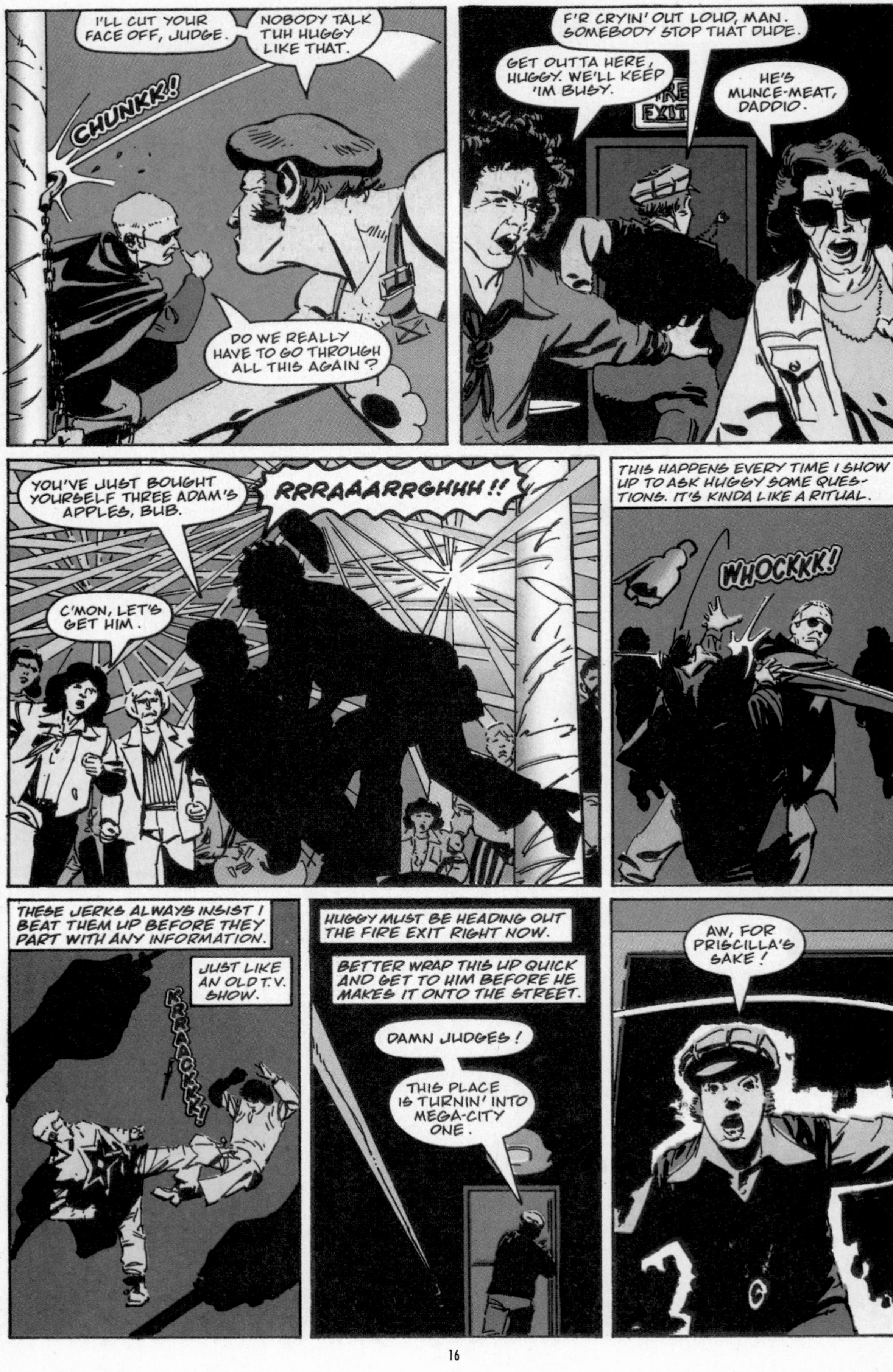
I'LL CUT YOUR FACE OFF, JUDGE.
NOBODY TALK TUH HUGGY LIKE THAT.
CHUNKK!
DO WE REALLY HAVE TO GO THROUGH ALL THIS AGAIN?
F'R CRYIN' OUT LOUD, MAN. SOMEBODY STOP THAT DUDE.
GET OUTTA HERE, HUGGY. WE'LL KEEP 'IM BUSY.
HE'S MUNCE-MEAT, DADDIO.
FIRE EXIT
YOU'VE JUST BOUGHT YOURSELF THREE ADAM'S APPLES, BUB.
RRRAAARRGHHH!!
C'MON, LET'S GET HIM.
THIS HAPPENS EVERY TIME I SHOW UP TO ASK HUGGY SOME QUESTIONS. IT'S KINDA LIKE A RITUAL.
WHOCKKK!
THESE JERKS ALWAYS INSIST I BEAT THEM UP BEFORE THEY PART WITH ANY INFORMATION.
JUST LIKE AN OLD T.V. SHOW.
KRRACKKK!
HUGGY MUST BE HEADING OUT THE FIRE EXIT RIGHT NOW.
BETTER WRAP THIS UP QUICK AND GET TO HIM BEFORE HE MAKES IT ONTO THE STREET.
DAMN JUDGES!
THIS PLACE IS TURNIN' INTO MEGA-CITY ONE.
AW, FOR PRISCILLA'S SAKE!

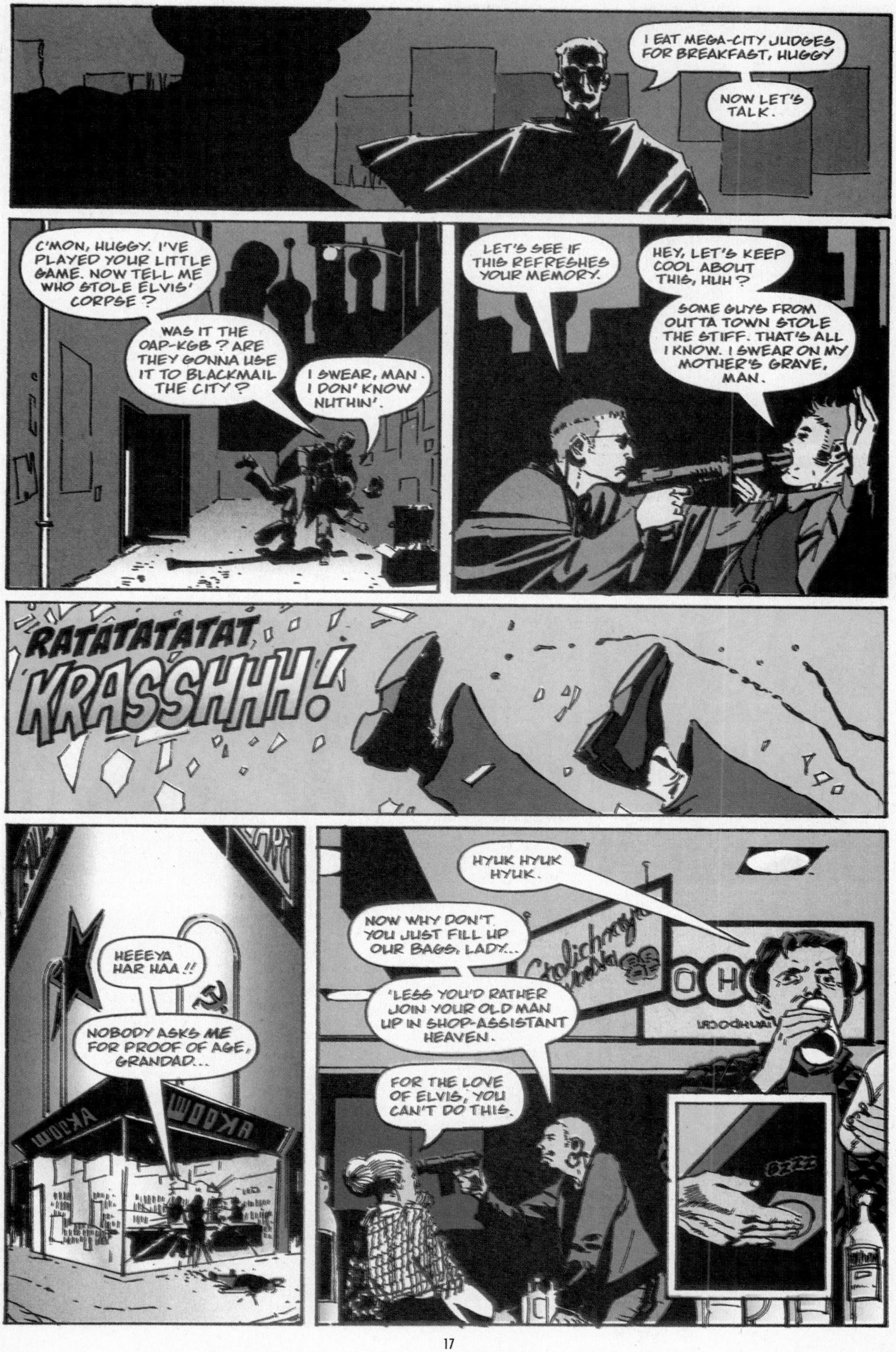
I EAT MEGA-CITY JUDGES FOR BREAKFAST, HUGGY
NOW LET'S TALK.
C'MON, HUGGY. I'VE PLAYED YOUR LITTLE GAME. NOW TELL ME WHO STOLE ELVIS' CORPSE?
WAS IT THE OAP-KGB? ARE THEY GONNA USE IT TO BLACKMAIL THE CITY?
I SWEAR, MAN. I DON' KNOW NUTHIN'.
LET'S SEE IF THIS REFRESHES YOUR MEMORY.
HEY, LET'S KEEP COOL ABOUT THIS, HUH?
SOME GUYS FROM OUTTA TOWN STOLE THE STIFF. THAT'S ALL I KNOW. I SWEAR ON MY MOTHER'S GRAVE, MAN.
RATATATATAT
KRASSHHH!
HEEEYA HAR HAA!!
NOBODY ASKS ME FOR PROOF OF AGE, GRANDAD...
HYUK HYUK HYUK.
NOW WHY DON'T YOU JUST FILL UP OUR BAGS, LADY...
'LESS YOU'D RATHER JOIN YOUR OLD MAN UP IN SHOP-ASSISTANT HEAVEN.
FOR THE LOVE OF ELVIS, YOU CAN'T DO THIS.

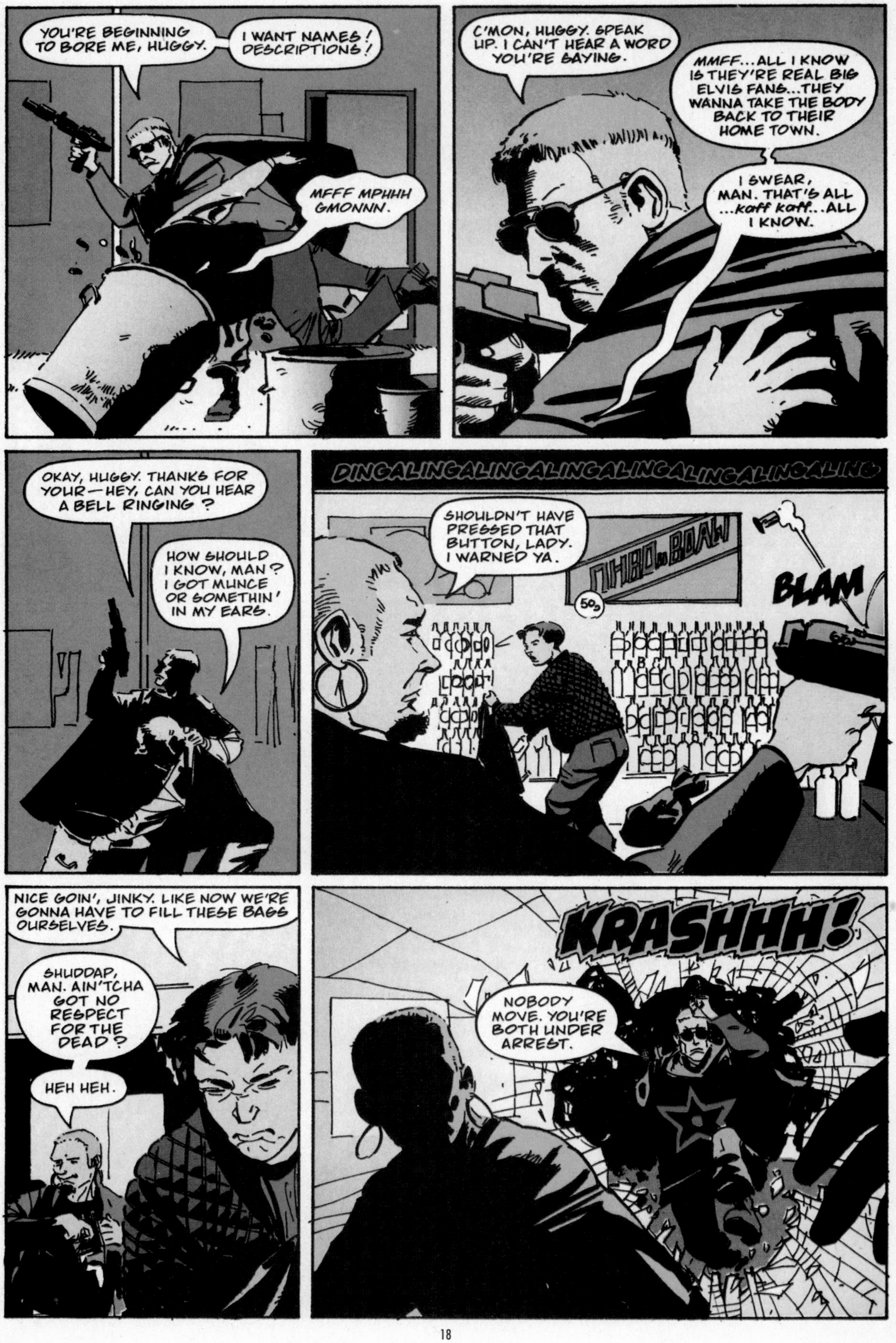

YOU'RE BEGINNING TO BORE ME, HUGGY.
I WANT NAMES! DESCRIPTIONS!
MFFF MPHHH GMONNN.
C'MON, HUGGY. SPEAK UP. I CAN'T HEAR A WORD YOU'RE SAYING.
MMFF...ALL I KNOW IS THEY'RE REAL BIG ELVIS FANS...THEY WANNA TAKE THE BODY BACK TO THEIR HOME TOWN.
I SWEAR, MAN. THAT'S ALL ...kaff kaff...ALL I KNOW.
OKAY, HUGGY. THANKS FOR YOUR—HEY, CAN YOU HEAR A BELL RINGING?
HOW SHOULD I KNOW, MAN? I GOT MUNCE OR SOMETHIN' IN MY EARS.
DINGALINGALINGALINGALINGALINGALINGALING
SHOULDN'T HAVE PRESSED THAT BUTTON, LADY. I WARNED YA.
BLAM
NICE GOIN', JINKY. LIKE NOW WE'RE GONNA HAVE TO FILL THESE BAGS OURSELVES.
SHUDDAP, MAN. AIN'TCHA GOT NO RESPECT FOR THE DEAD?
HEH HEH.
KRASHHH!
NOBODY MOVE. YOU'RE BOTH UNDER ARREST.

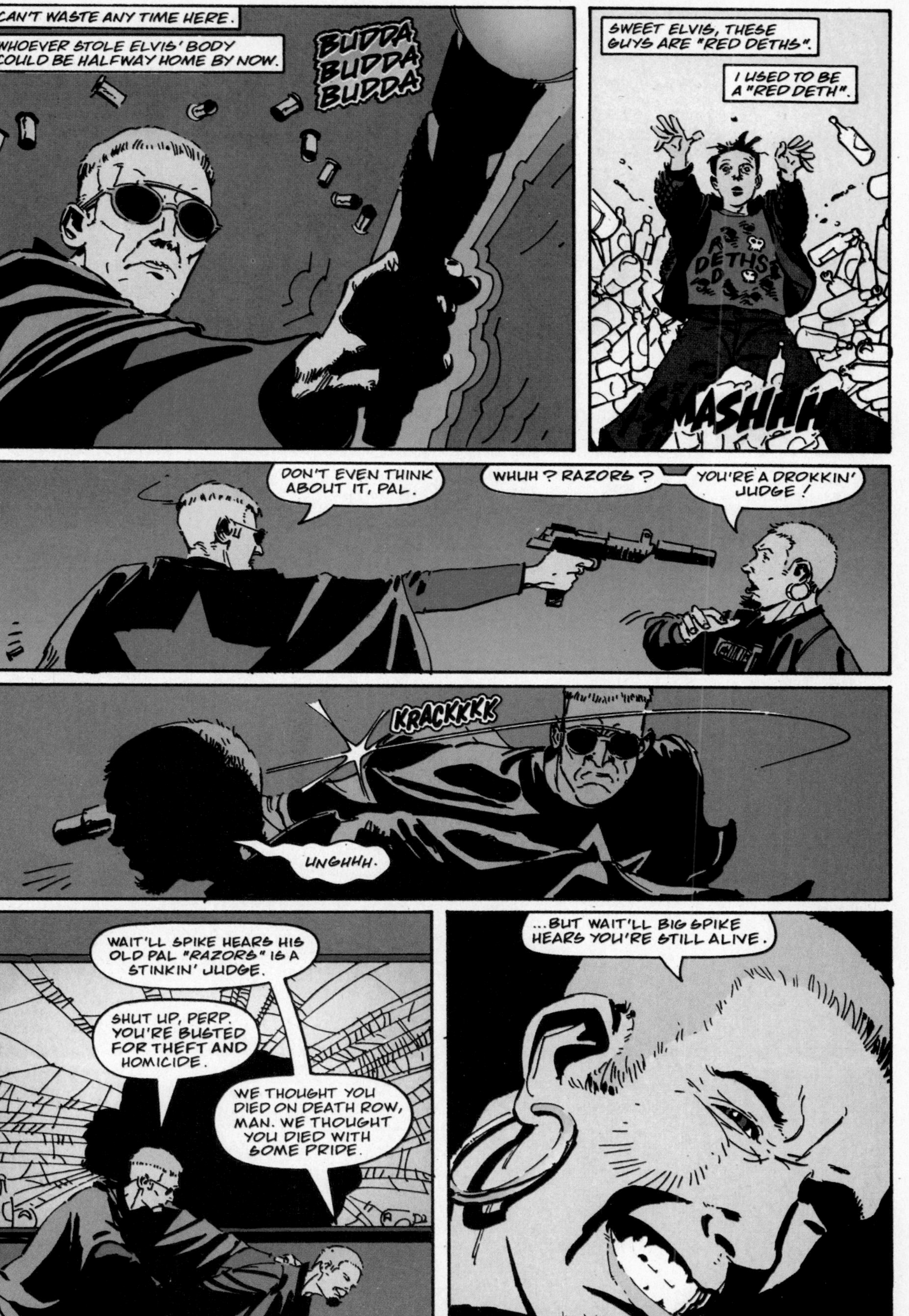

CAN'T WASTE ANY TIME HERE.
WHOEVER STOLE ELVIS' BODY COULD BE HALFWAY HOME BY NOW.
BUDDA BUDDA BUDDA
SWEET ELVIS, THESE GUYS ARE "RED DETHS".
I USED TO BE A "RED DETH".
SMASHHH
DON'T EVEN THINK ABOUT IT, PAL.
WHUH ? RAZORS ?
YOU'RE A DROKKIN' JUDGE !
KRACKKKK
UNGHHH.
WAIT'LL SPIKE HEARS HIS OLD PAL "RAZORS" IS A STINKIN' JUDGE.
SHUT UP, PERP. YOU'RE BUSTED FOR THEFT AND HOMICIDE.
WE THOUGHT YOU DIED ON DEATH ROW, MAN. WE THOUGHT YOU DIED WITH SOME PRIDE.
...BUT WAIT'LL BIG SPIKE HEARS YOU'RE STILL ALIVE.

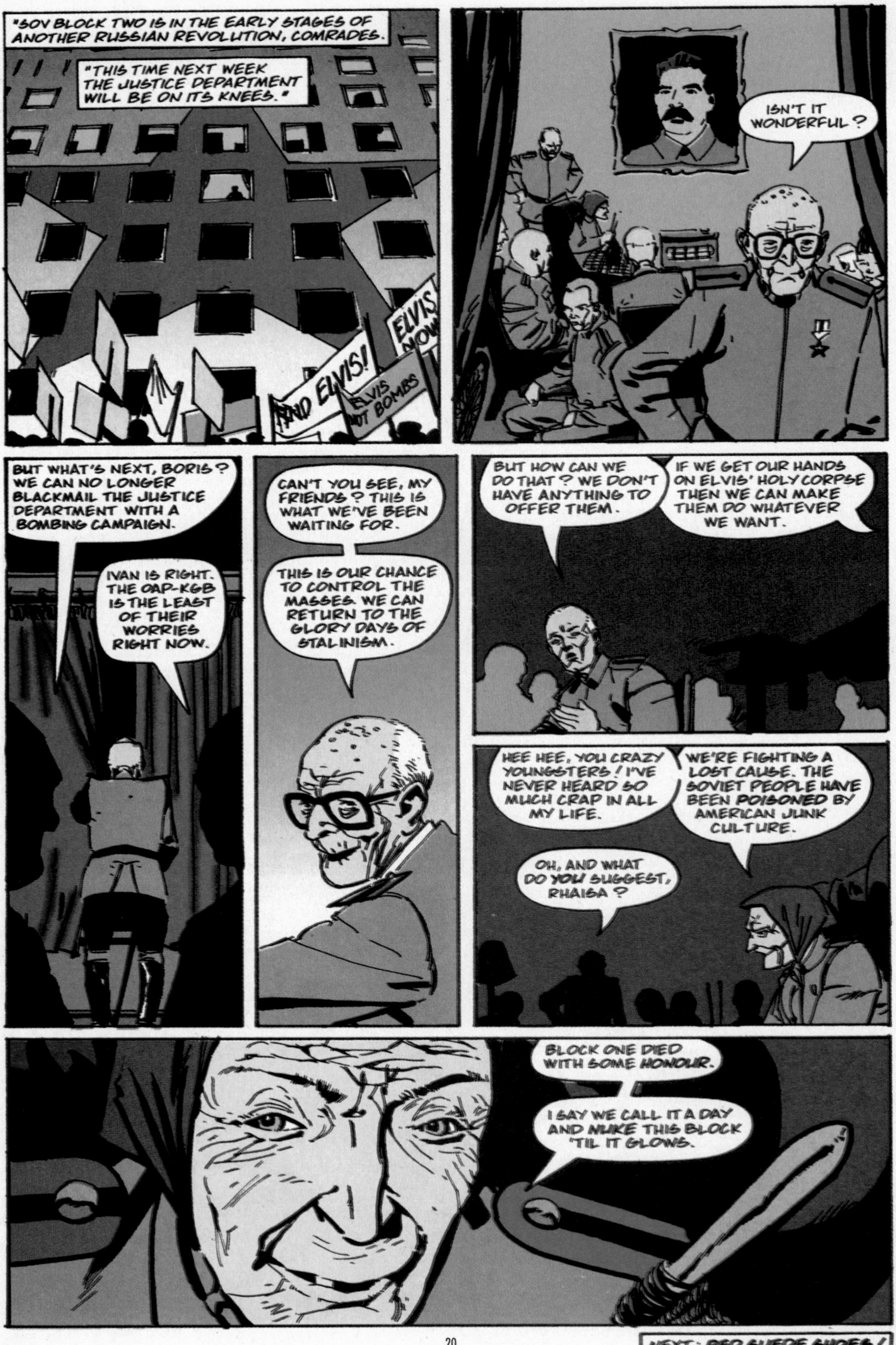
"SOV BLOCK TWO IS IN THE EARLY STAGES OF ANOTHER RUSSIAN REVOLUTION, COMRADES.
"THIS TIME NEXT WEEK THE JUSTICE DEPARTMENT WILL BE ON ITS KNEES."
ELVIS NOW
AND ELVIS!
ELVIS NOT BOMBS
ISN'T IT WONDERFUL?
BUT WHAT'S NEXT, BORIS? WE CAN NO LONGER BLACKMAIL THE JUSTICE DEPARTMENT WITH A BOMBING CAMPAIGN.
IVAN IS RIGHT. THE OAP-KGB IS THE LEAST OF THEIR WORRIES RIGHT NOW.
CAN'T YOU SEE, MY FRIENDS? THIS IS WHAT WE'VE BEEN WAITING FOR.
THIS IS OUR CHANCE TO CONTROL THE MASSES. WE CAN RETURN TO THE GLORY DAYS OF STALINISM.
BUT HOW CAN WE DO THAT? WE DON'T HAVE ANYTHING TO OFFER THEM.
IF WE GET OUR HANDS ON ELVIS' HOLY CORPSE THEN WE CAN MAKE THEM DO WHATEVER WE WANT.
HEE HEE, YOU CRAZY YOUNGSTERS! I'VE NEVER HEARD SO MUCH CRAP IN ALL MY LIFE.
WE'RE FIGHTING A LOST CAUSE. THE SOVIET PEOPLE HAVE BEEN POISONED BY AMERICAN JUNK CULTURE.
OH, AND WHAT DO YOU SUGGEST, RHAISA?
BLOCK ONE DIED WITH SOME HONOUR.
I SAY WE CALL IT A DAY AND NUKE THIS BLOCK 'TIL IT GLOWS.

NEXT: RED SUEDE SHOES!

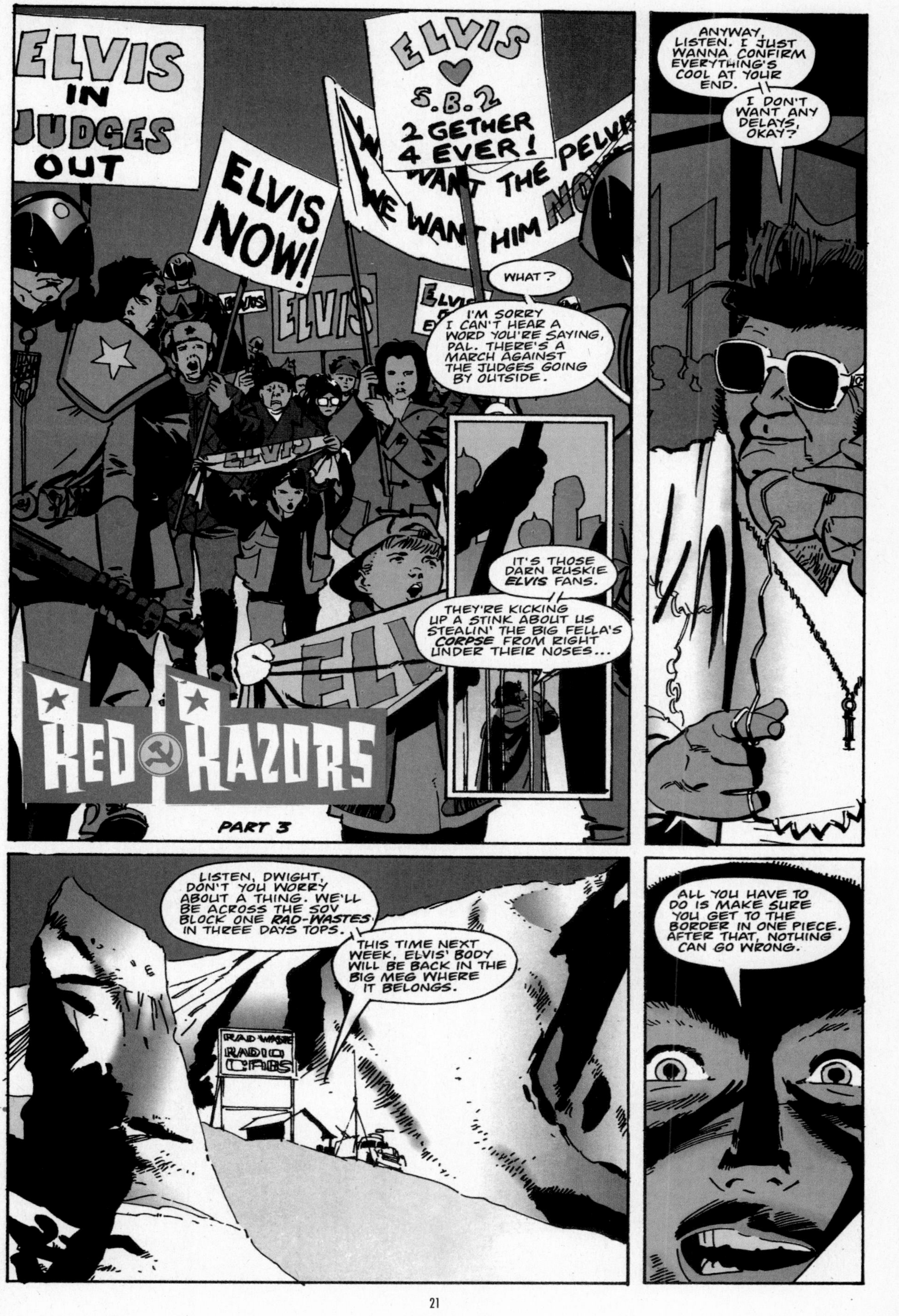

ELVIS IN JUDGES OUT
ELVIS ♥ S.B.2 2 GETHER 4 EVER!
WANT THE PELV
WE WANT HIM
ELVIS NOW!
ELVIS
WHAT?
I'M SORRY I CAN'T HEAR A WORD YOU'RE SAYING, PAL. THERE'S A MARCH AGAINST THE JUDGES GOING BY OUTSIDE.
IT'S THOSE DARN RUSKIE ELVIS FANS.
THEY'RE KICKING UP A STINK ABOUT US STEALIN' THE BIG FELLA'S CORPSE FROM RIGHT UNDER THEIR NOSES...
RED RAZORS
PART 3
ANYWAY, LISTEN. I JUST WANNA CONFIRM EVERYTHING'S COOL AT YOUR END.
I DON'T WANT ANY DELAYS, OKAY?
LISTEN, DWIGHT, DON'T YOU WORRY ABOUT A THING. WE'LL BE ACROSS THE SOV BLOCK ONE RAD-WASTES IN THREE DAYS TOPS.
THIS TIME NEXT WEEK, ELVIS' BODY WILL BE BACK IN THE BIG MEG WHERE IT BELONGS.
RAD WASTE RADIO CABS
ALL YOU HAVE TO DO IS MAKE SURE YOU GET TO THE BORDER IN ONE PIECE. AFTER THAT, NOTHING CAN GO WRONG.

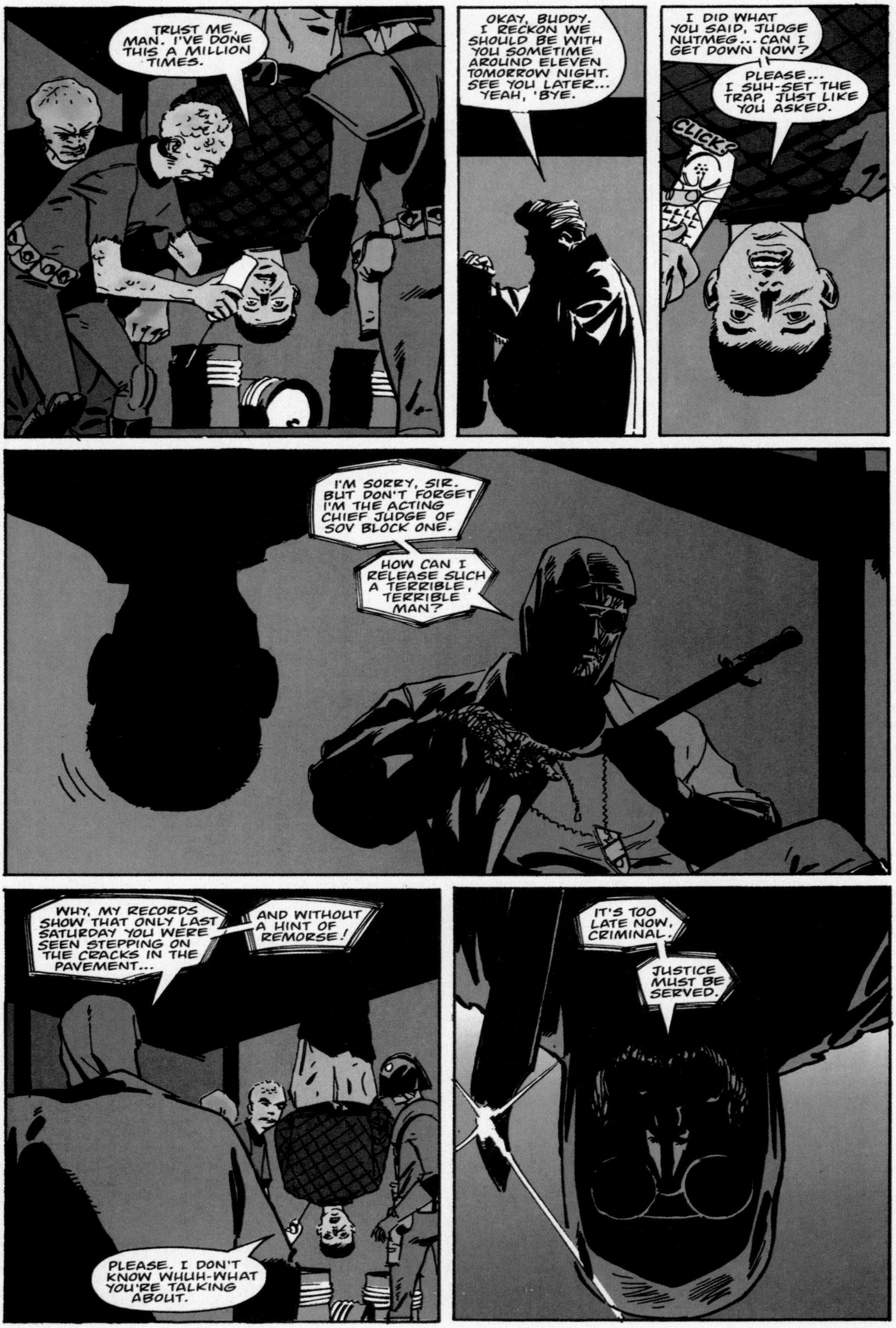
TRUST ME, MAN. I'VE DONE THIS A MILLION TIMES.
OKAY, BUDDY. I RECKON WE SHOULD BE WITH YOU SOMETIME AROUND ELEVEN TOMORROW NIGHT. SEE YOU LATER... YEAH, 'BYE.
I DID WHAT YOU SAID, JUDGE NUTMEG... CAN I GET DOWN NOW?
PLEASE... I SUH-SET THE TRAP, JUST LIKE YOU ASKED.
CLICK!
I'M SORRY, SIR. BUT DON'T FORGET I'M THE ACTING CHIEF JUDGE OF SOV BLOCK ONE.
HOW CAN I RELEASE SUCH A TERRIBLE, TERRIBLE MAN?
WHY, MY RECORDS SHOW THAT ONLY LAST SATURDAY YOU WERE SEEN STEPPING ON THE CRACKS IN THE PAVEMENT...
AND WITHOUT A HINT OF REMORSE!
PLEASE. I DON'T KNOW WHUH-WHAT YOU'RE TALKING ABOUT.
IT'S TOO LATE NOW, CRIMINAL.
JUSTICE MUST BE SERVED.

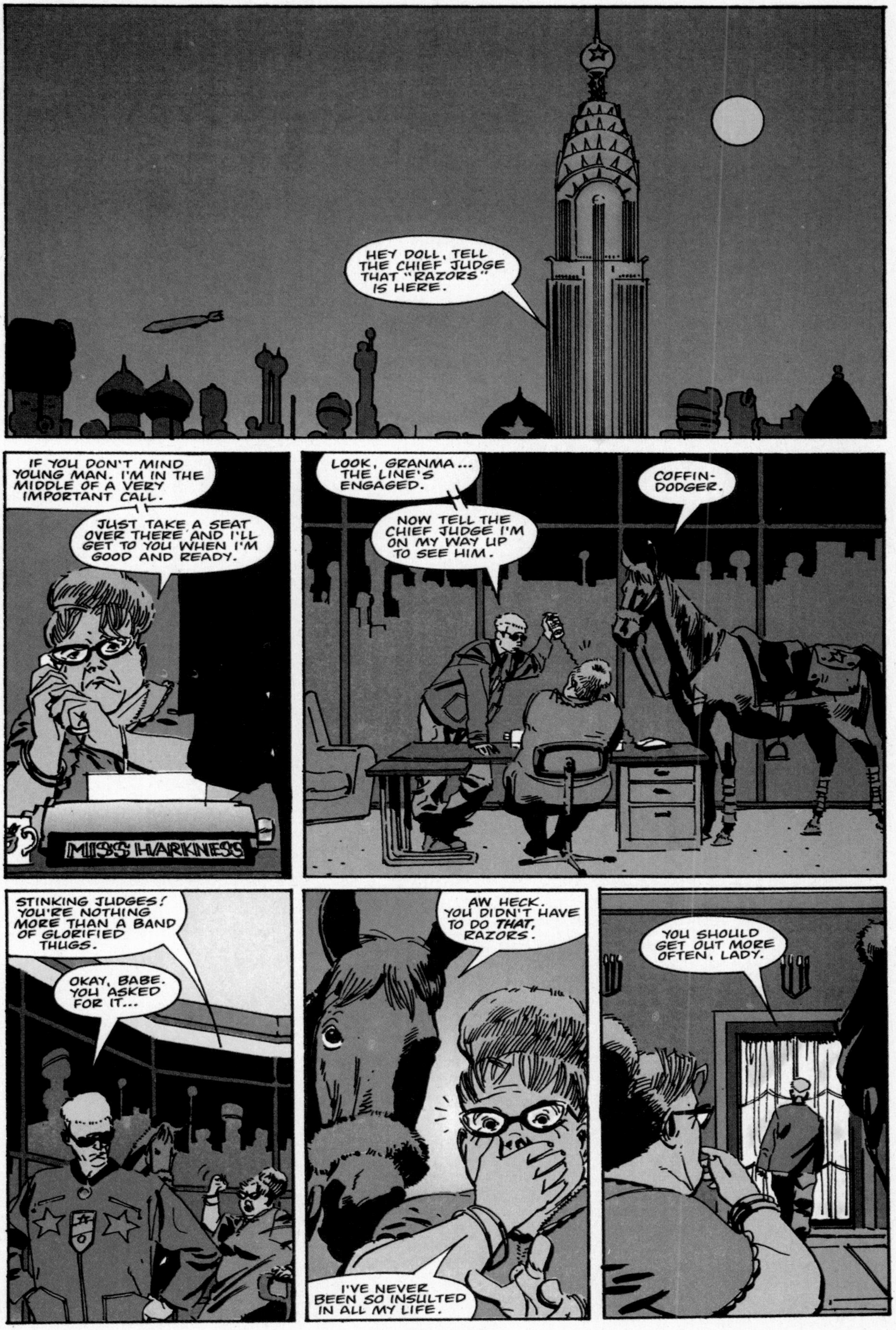
HEY DOLL, TELL THE CHIEF JUDGE THAT "RAZORS" IS HERE.
IF YOU DON'T MIND YOUNG MAN. I'M IN THE MIDDLE OF A VERY IMPORTANT CALL.
JUST TAKE A SEAT OVER THERE AND I'LL GET TO YOU WHEN I'M GOOD AND READY.
MISS HARKNESS
LOOK, GRANMA... THE LINE'S ENGAGED.
NOW TELL THE CHIEF JUDGE I'M ON MY WAY UP TO SEE HIM.
COFFIN-DODGER.
STINKING JUDGES! YOU'RE NOTHING MORE THAN A BAND OF GLORIFIED THUGS.
OKAY, BABE. YOU ASKED FOR IT...
AW HECK. YOU DIDN'T HAVE TO DO *THAT*, RAZORS.
I'VE NEVER BEEN SO INSULTED IN ALL MY LIFE.
YOU SHOULD GET OUT MORE OFTEN, LADY.

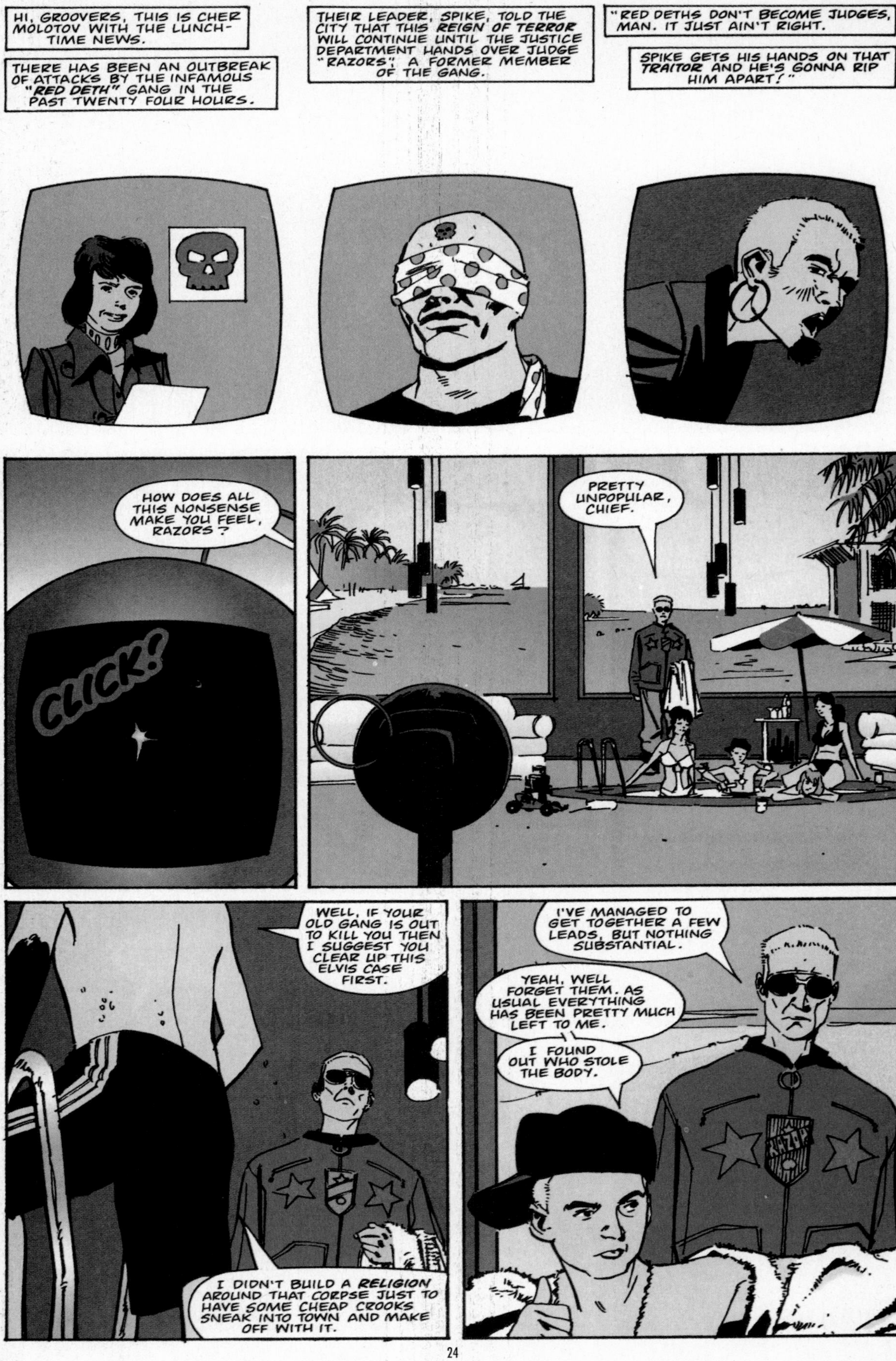

HI, GROOVERS, THIS IS CHER MOLOTOV WITH THE LUNCH-TIME NEWS.
THERE HAS BEEN AN OUTBREAK OF ATTACKS BY THE INFAMOUS "RED DETH" GANG IN THE PAST TWENTY FOUR HOURS.
THEIR LEADER, SPIKE, TOLD THE CITY THAT THIS REIGN OF TERROR WILL CONTINUE UNTIL THE JUSTICE DEPARTMENT HANDS OVER JUDGE "RAZORS", A FORMER MEMBER OF THE GANG.
"RED DETHS DON'T BECOME JUDGES, MAN. IT JUST AIN'T RIGHT.
SPIKE GETS HIS HANDS ON THAT TRAITOR AND HE'S GONNA RIP HIM APART!"
HOW DOES ALL THIS NONSENSE MAKE YOU FEEL, RAZORS?
CLICK!
PRETTY UNPOPULAR, CHIEF.
WELL, IF YOUR OLD GANG IS OUT TO KILL YOU THEN I SUGGEST YOU CLEAR UP THIS ELVIS CASE FIRST.
I DIDN'T BUILD A RELIGION AROUND THAT CORPSE JUST TO HAVE SOME CHEAP CROOKS SNEAK INTO TOWN AND MAKE OFF WITH IT.
I'VE MANAGED TO GET TOGETHER A FEW LEADS, BUT NOTHING SUBSTANTIAL.
YEAH, WELL FORGET THEM. AS USUAL EVERYTHING HAS BEEN PRETTY MUCH LEFT TO ME.
I FOUND OUT WHO STOLE THE BODY.

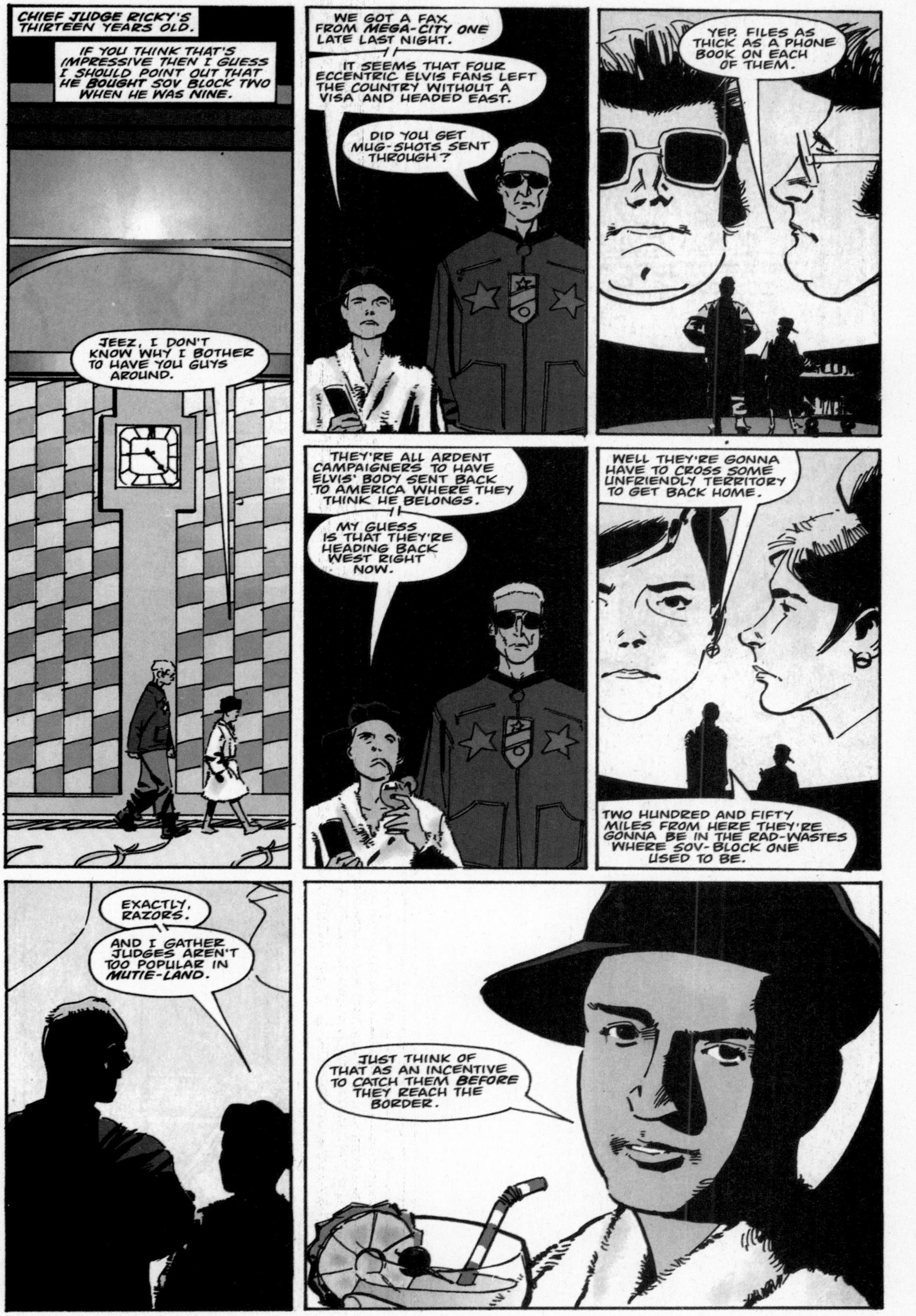

CHIEF JUDGE RICKY'S THIRTEEN YEARS OLD.
IF YOU THINK THAT'S IMPRESSIVE THEN I GUESS I SHOULD POINT OUT THAT HE BOUGHT SOV BLOCK TWO WHEN HE WAS NINE.
JEEZ, I DON'T KNOW WHY I BOTHER TO HAVE YOU GUYS AROUND.
WE GOT A FAX FROM MEGA-CITY ONE LATE LAST NIGHT.
IT SEEMS THAT FOUR ECCENTRIC ELVIS FANS LEFT THE COUNTRY WITHOUT A VISA AND HEADED EAST.
DID YOU GET MUG-SHOTS SENT THROUGH?
YEP. FILES AS THICK AS A PHONE BOOK ON EACH OF THEM.
THEY'RE ALL ARDENT CAMPAIGNERS TO HAVE ELVIS' BODY SENT BACK TO AMERICA WHERE THEY THINK HE BELONGS.
MY GUESS IS THAT THEY'RE HEADING BACK WEST RIGHT NOW.
WELL THEY'RE GONNA HAVE TO CROSS SOME UNFRIENDLY TERRITORY TO GET BACK HOME.
TWO HUNDRED AND FIFTY MILES FROM HERE THEY'RE GONNA BE IN THE RAD-WASTES WHERE SOV-BLOCK ONE USED TO BE.
EXACTLY, RAZORS.
AND I GATHER JUDGES AREN'T TOO POPULAR IN MUTIE-LAND.
JUST THINK OF THAT AS AN INCENTIVE TO CATCH THEM BEFORE THEY REACH THE BORDER.

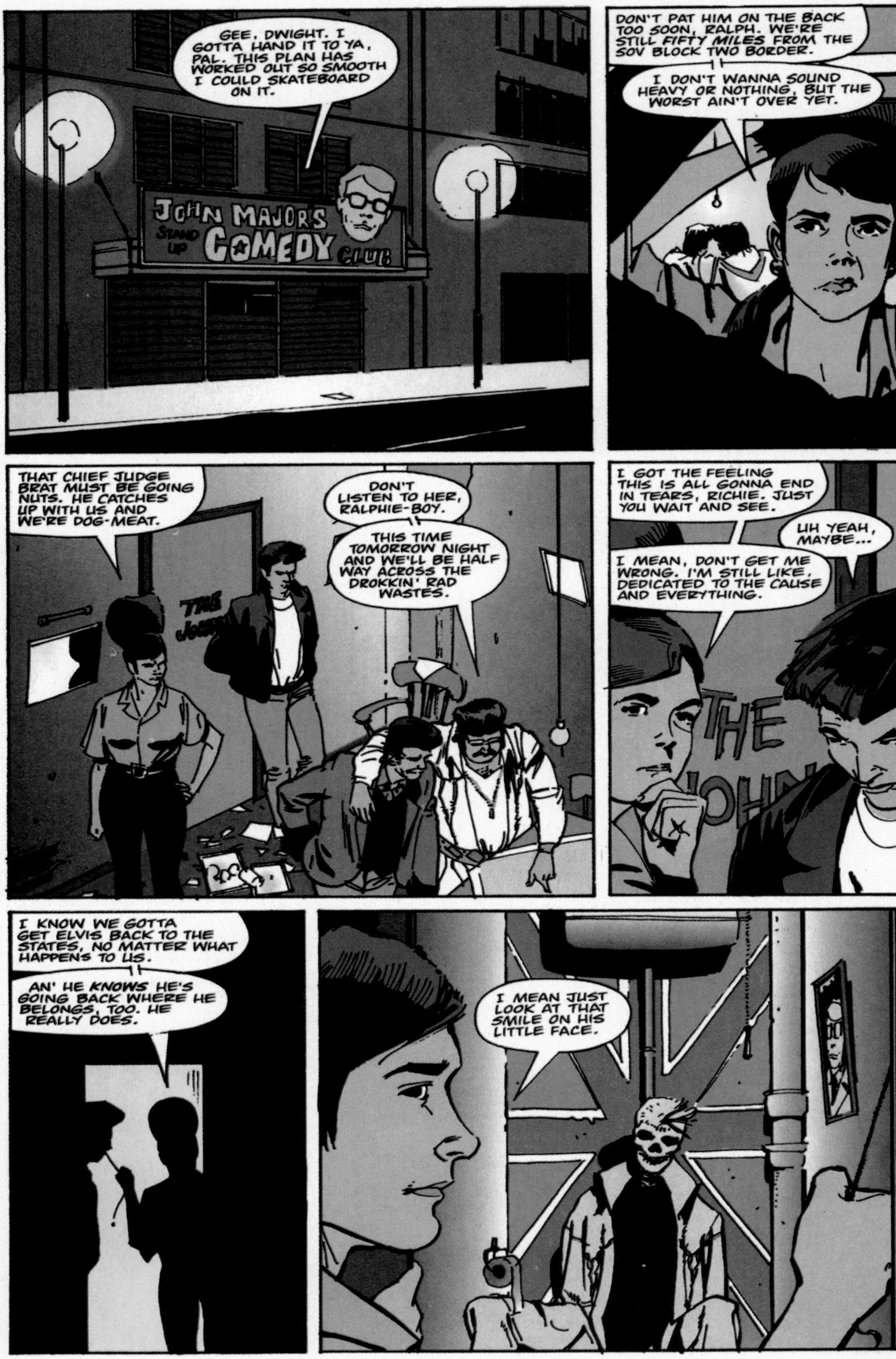
GEE, DWIGHT. I GOTTA HAND IT TO YA, PAL. THIS PLAN HAS WORKED OUT SO SMOOTH I COULD SKATEBOARD ON IT.
JOHN MAJORS STAND UP COMEDY CLUB
DON'T PAT HIM ON THE BACK TOO SOON, RALPH. WE'RE STILL FIFTY MILES FROM THE SOV BLOCK TWO BORDER.
I DON'T WANNA SOUND HEAVY OR NOTHING, BUT THE WORST AIN'T OVER YET.
THAT CHIEF JUDGE BRAT MUST BE GOING NUTS. HE CATCHES UP WITH US AND WE'RE DOG-MEAT.
DON'T LISTEN TO HER, RALPHIE-BOY.
THIS TIME TOMORROW NIGHT AND WE'LL BE HALF WAY ACROSS THE DROKKIN' RAD WASTES.
I GOT THE FEELING THIS IS ALL GONNA END IN TEARS, RICHIE. JUST YOU WAIT AND SEE.
UH YEAH, MAYBE...
I MEAN, DON'T GET ME WRONG. I'M STILL LIKE, DEDICATED TO THE CAUSE AND EVERYTHING.
I KNOW WE GOTTA GET ELVIS BACK TO THE STATES, NO MATTER WHAT HAPPENS TO US.
AN' HE KNOWS HE'S GOING BACK WHERE HE BELONGS, TOO. HE REALLY DOES.
I MEAN JUST LOOK AT THAT SMILE ON HIS LITTLE FACE.

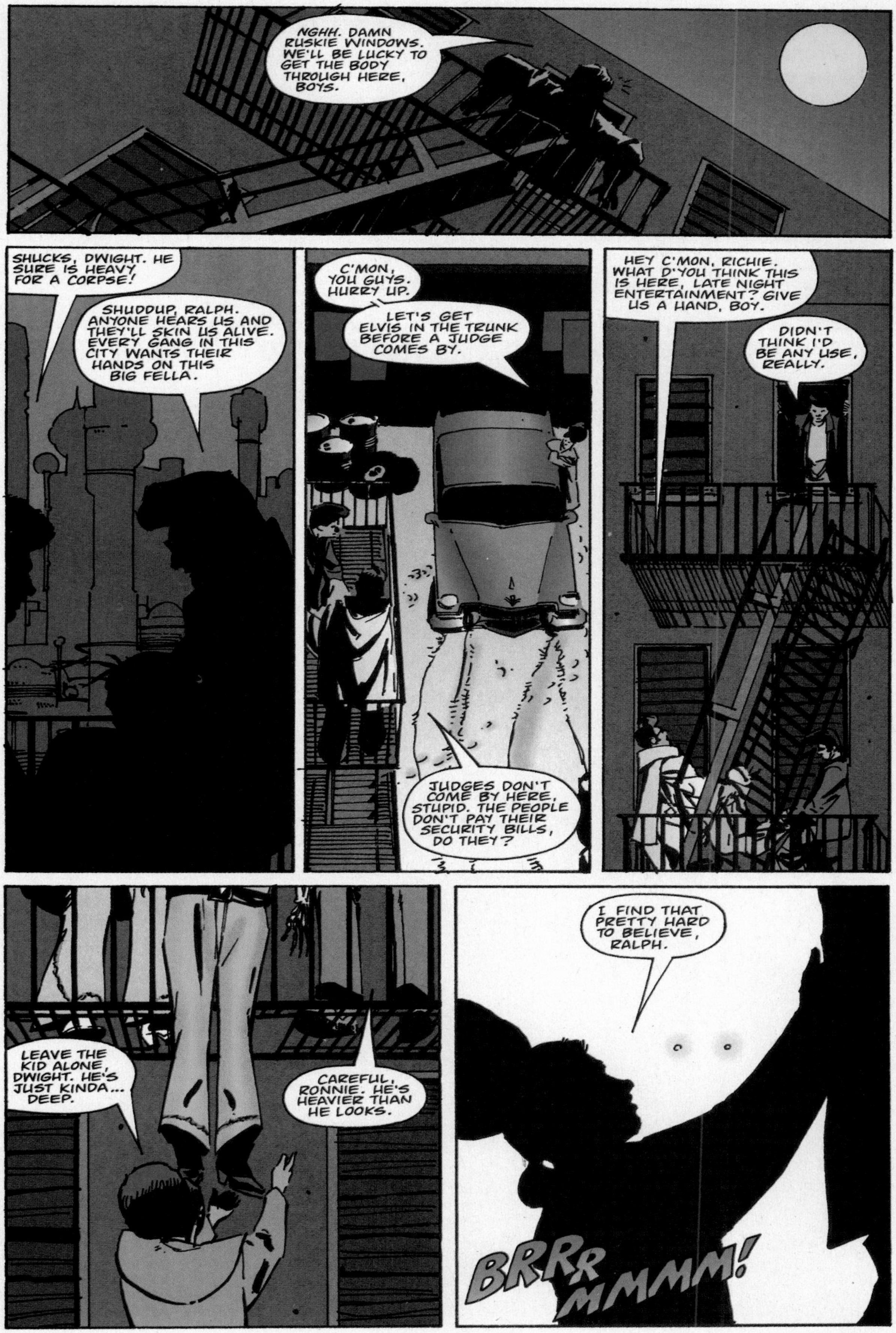
NGHH. DAMN RUSKIE WINDOWS. WE'LL BE LUCKY TO GET THE BODY THROUGH HERE, BOYS.
SHUCKS, DWIGHT. HE SURE IS HEAVY FOR A CORPSE!
SHUDDUP, RALPH. ANYONE HEARS US AND THEY'LL SKIN US ALIVE. EVERY GANG IN THIS CITY WANTS THEIR HANDS ON THIS BIG FELLA.
C'MON, YOU GUYS. HURRY UP.
LET'S GET ELVIS IN THE TRUNK BEFORE A JUDGE COMES BY.
JUDGES DON'T COME BY HERE, STUPID. THE PEOPLE DON'T PAY THEIR SECURITY BILLS, DO THEY?
HEY C'MON, RICHIE. WHAT D'YOU THINK THIS IS HERE, LATE NIGHT ENTERTAINMENT? GIVE US A HAND, BOY.
DIDN'T THINK I'D BE ANY USE, REALLY.
LEAVE THE KID ALONE, DWIGHT. HE'S JUST KINDA... DEEP.
CAREFUL, RONNIE. HE'S HEAVIER THAN HE LOOKS.
I FIND THAT PRETTY HARD TO BELIEVE, RALPH.
BRRR MMMM!

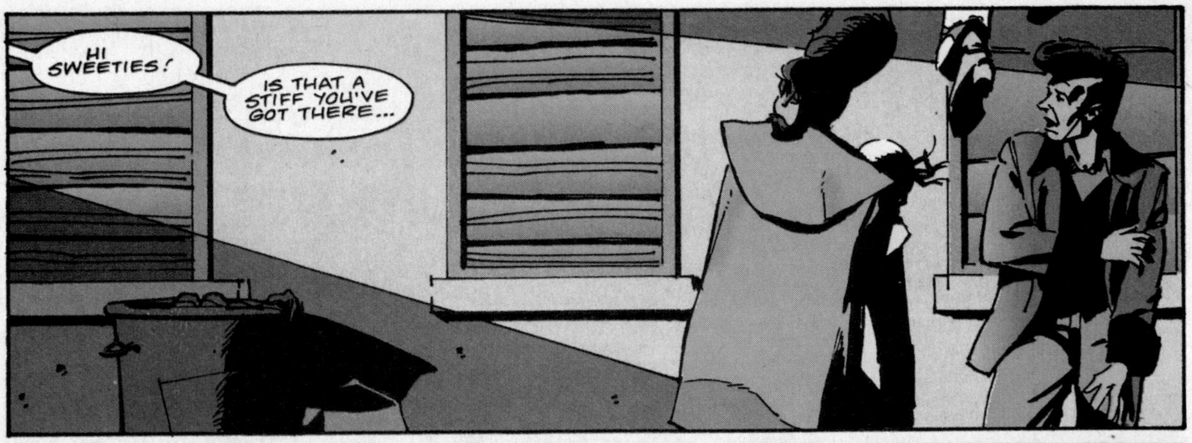
HI SWEETIES!
IS THAT A STIFF YOU'VE GOT THERE...

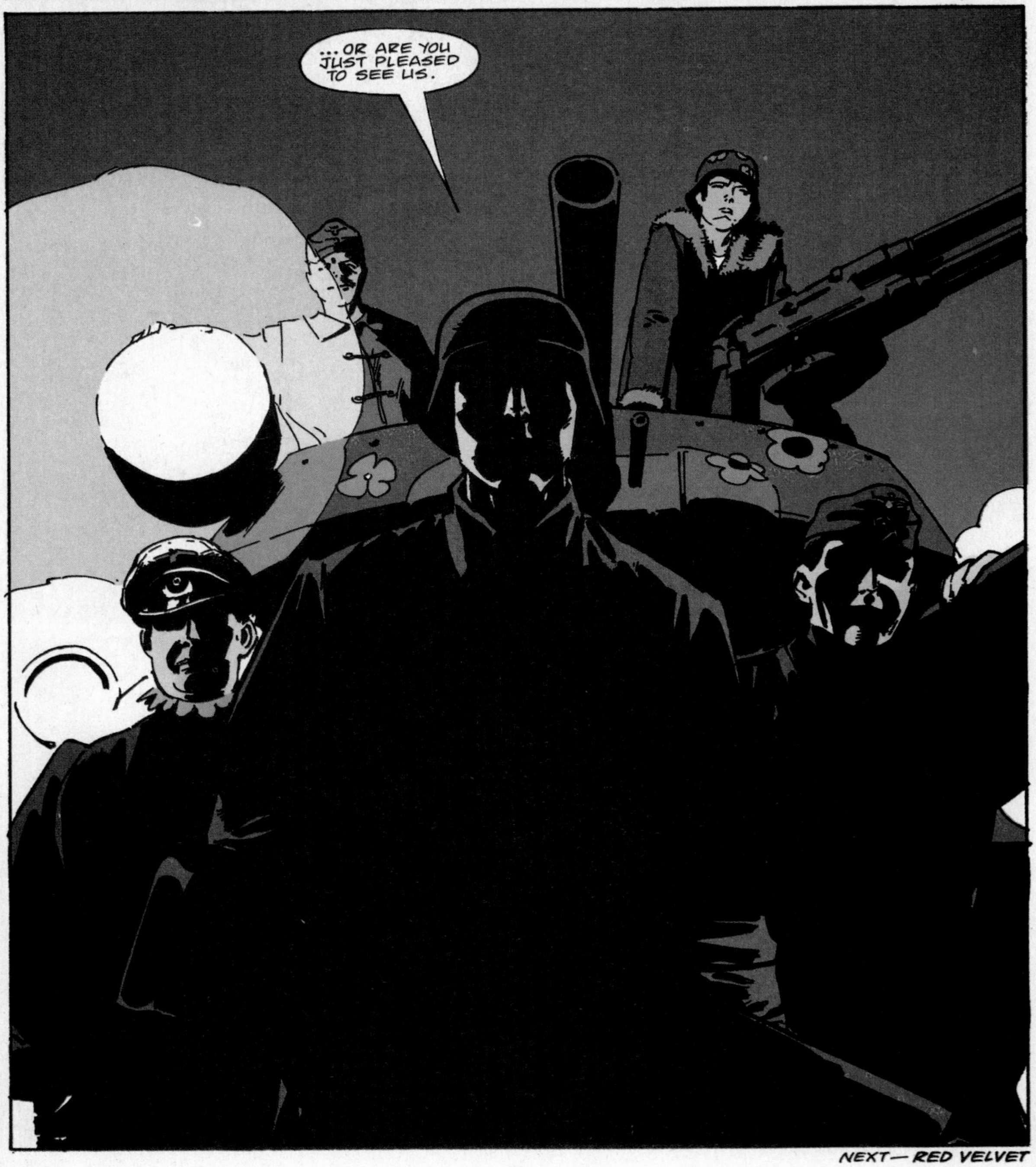
...OR ARE YOU JUST PLEASED TO SEE US.

NEXT— RED VELVET

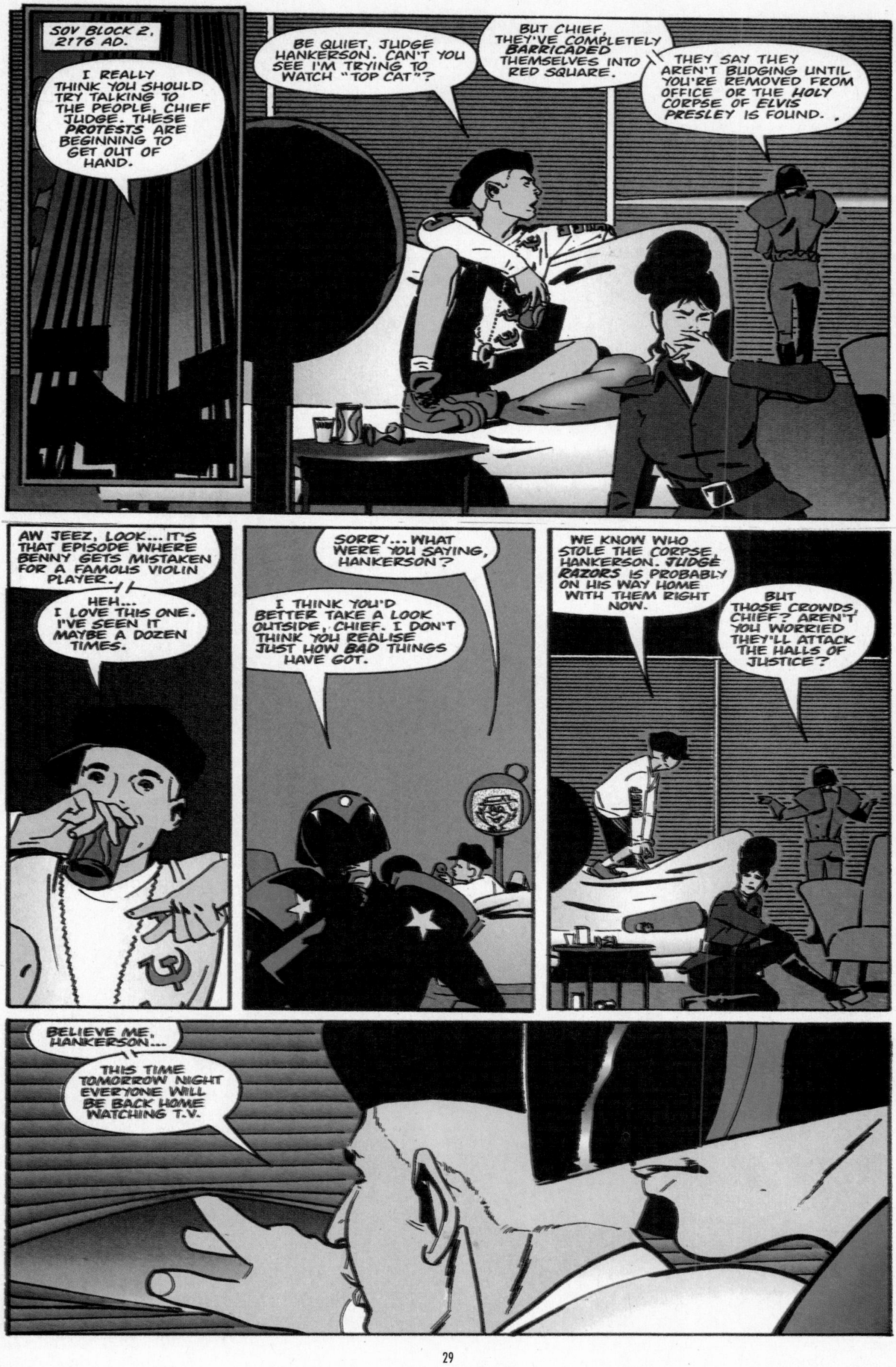
SOV BLOCK 2, 2176 AD.
I REALLY THINK YOU SHOULD TRY TALKING TO THE PEOPLE, CHIEF JUDGE. THESE PROTESTS ARE BEGINNING TO GET OUT OF HAND.
BE QUIET, JUDGE HANKERSON. CAN'T YOU SEE I'M TRYING TO WATCH "TOP CAT"?
BUT CHIEF, THEY'VE COMPLETELY BARRICADED THEMSELVES INTO RED SQUARE.
THEY SAY THEY AREN'T BUDGING UNTIL YOU'RE REMOVED FROM OFFICE OR THE HOLY CORPSE OF ELVIS PRESLEY IS FOUND.
AW JEEZ, LOOK... IT'S THAT EPISODE WHERE BENNY GETS MISTAKEN FOR A FAMOUS VIOLIN PLAYER.
HEH... I LOVE THIS ONE. I'VE SEEN IT MAYBE A DOZEN TIMES.
SORRY... WHAT WERE YOU SAYING, HANKERSON?
I THINK YOU'D BETTER TAKE A LOOK OUTSIDE, CHIEF. I DON'T THINK YOU REALISE JUST HOW BAD THINGS HAVE GOT.
WE KNOW WHO STOLE THE CORPSE, HANKERSON. JUDGE RAZORS IS PROBABLY ON HIS WAY HOME WITH THEM RIGHT NOW.
BUT THOSE CROWDS, CHIEF? AREN'T YOU WORRIED THEY'LL ATTACK THE HALLS OF JUSTICE?
BELIEVE ME, HANKERSON...
THIS TIME TOMORROW NIGHT EVERYONE WILL BE BACK HOME WATCHING T.V.

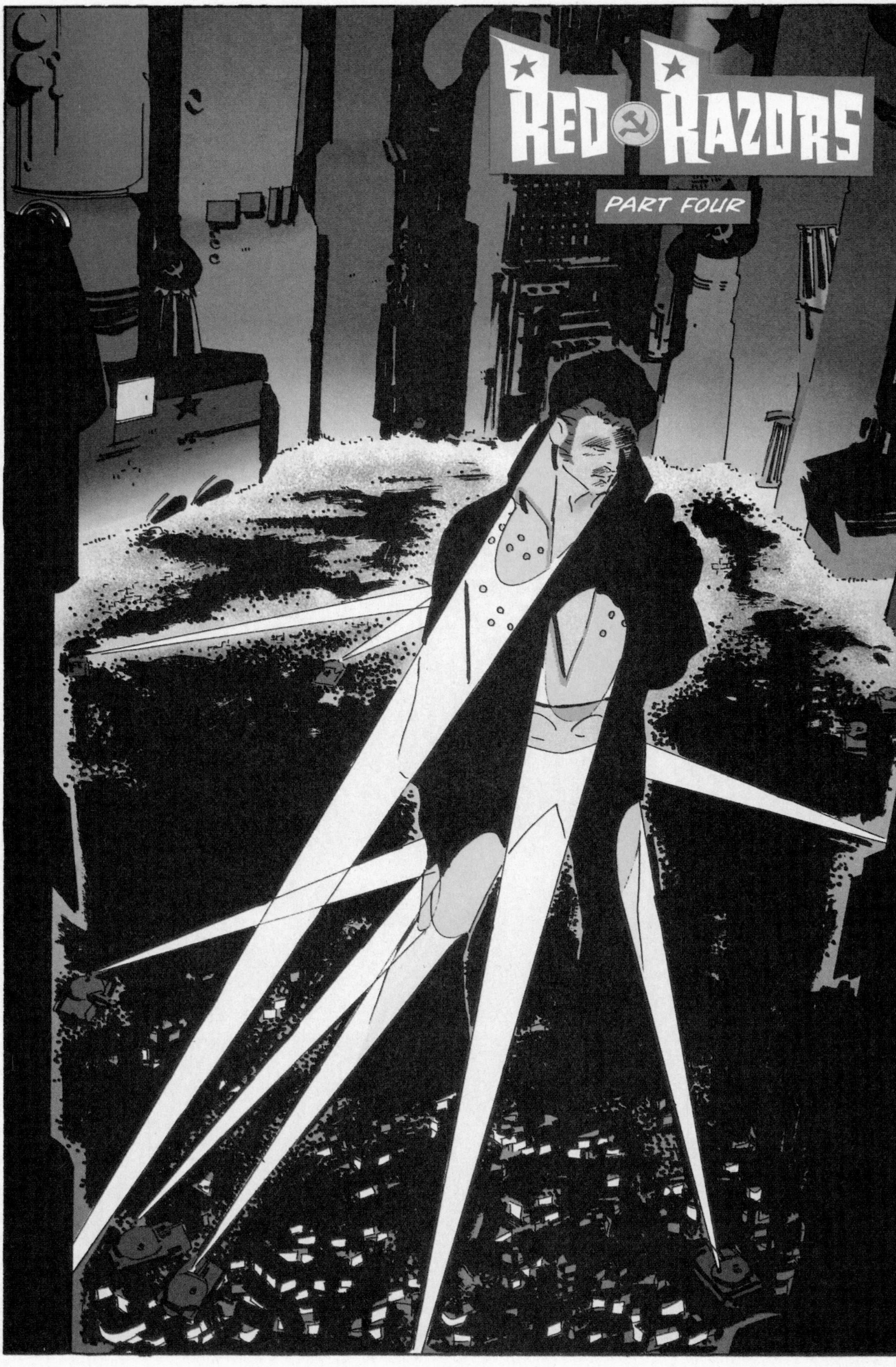
RED RAZORS
PART FOUR

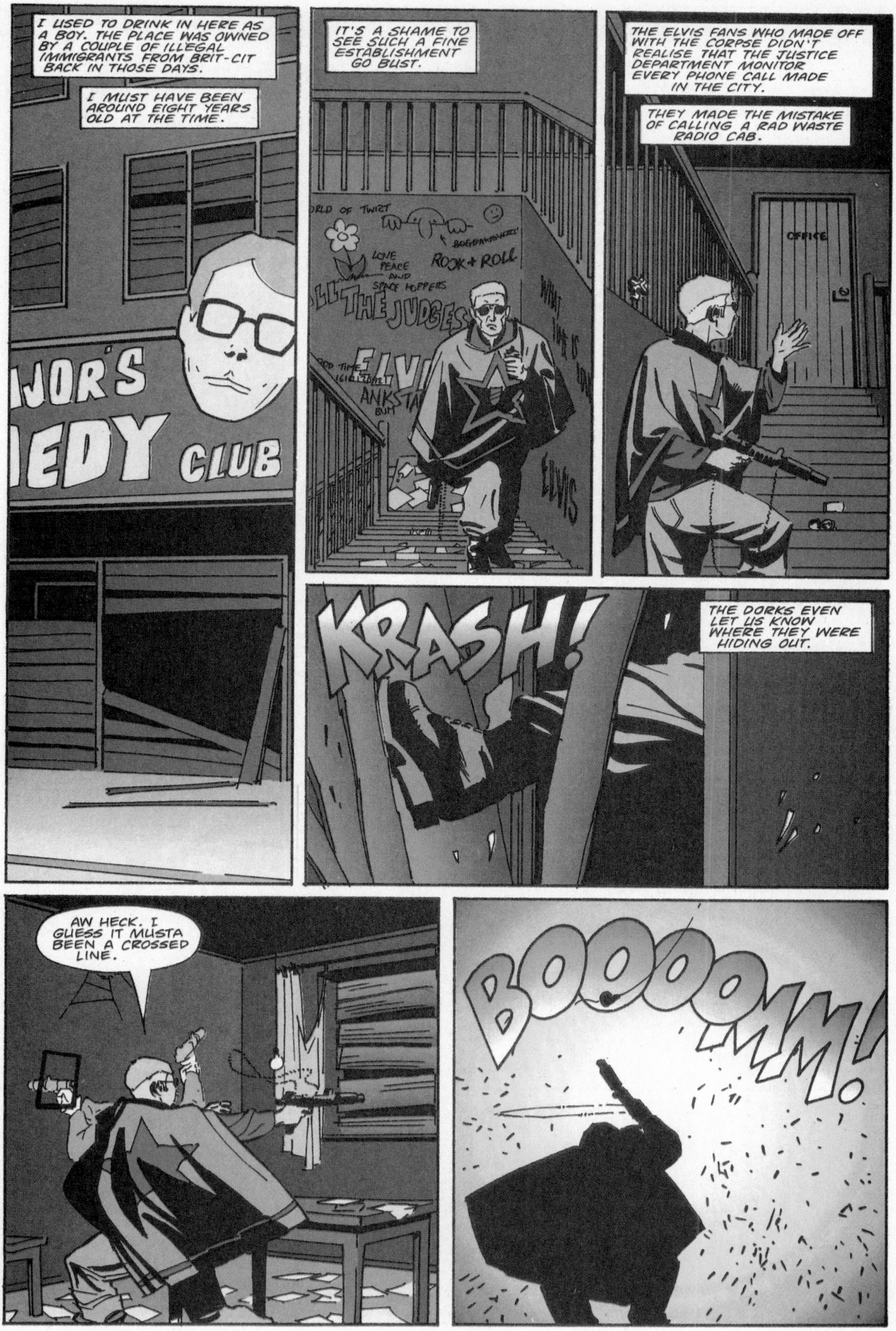
I USED TO DRINK IN HERE AS A BOY. THE PLACE WAS OWNED BY A COUPLE OF ILLEGAL IMMIGRANTS FROM BRIT-CIT BACK IN THOSE DAYS.
I MUST HAVE BEEN AROUND EIGHT YEARS OLD AT THE TIME.
CLUB
IT'S A SHAME TO SEE SUCH A FINE ESTABLISHMENT GO BUST.
ROCK + ROLL
LOVE PEACE AND SPACE HOPPERS
THE JUDGES
ELVIS
THE ELVIS FANS WHO MADE OFF WITH THE CORPSE DIDN'T REALISE THAT THE JUSTICE DEPARTMENT MONITOR EVERY PHONE CALL MADE IN THE CITY.
THEY MADE THE MISTAKE OF CALLING A RAD WASTE RADIO CAB.
OFFICE
KRASH!
THE DORKS EVEN LET US KNOW WHERE THEY WERE HIDING OUT.
AW HECK. I GUESS IT MUSTA BEEN A CROSSED LINE.
BOOOOOMM!

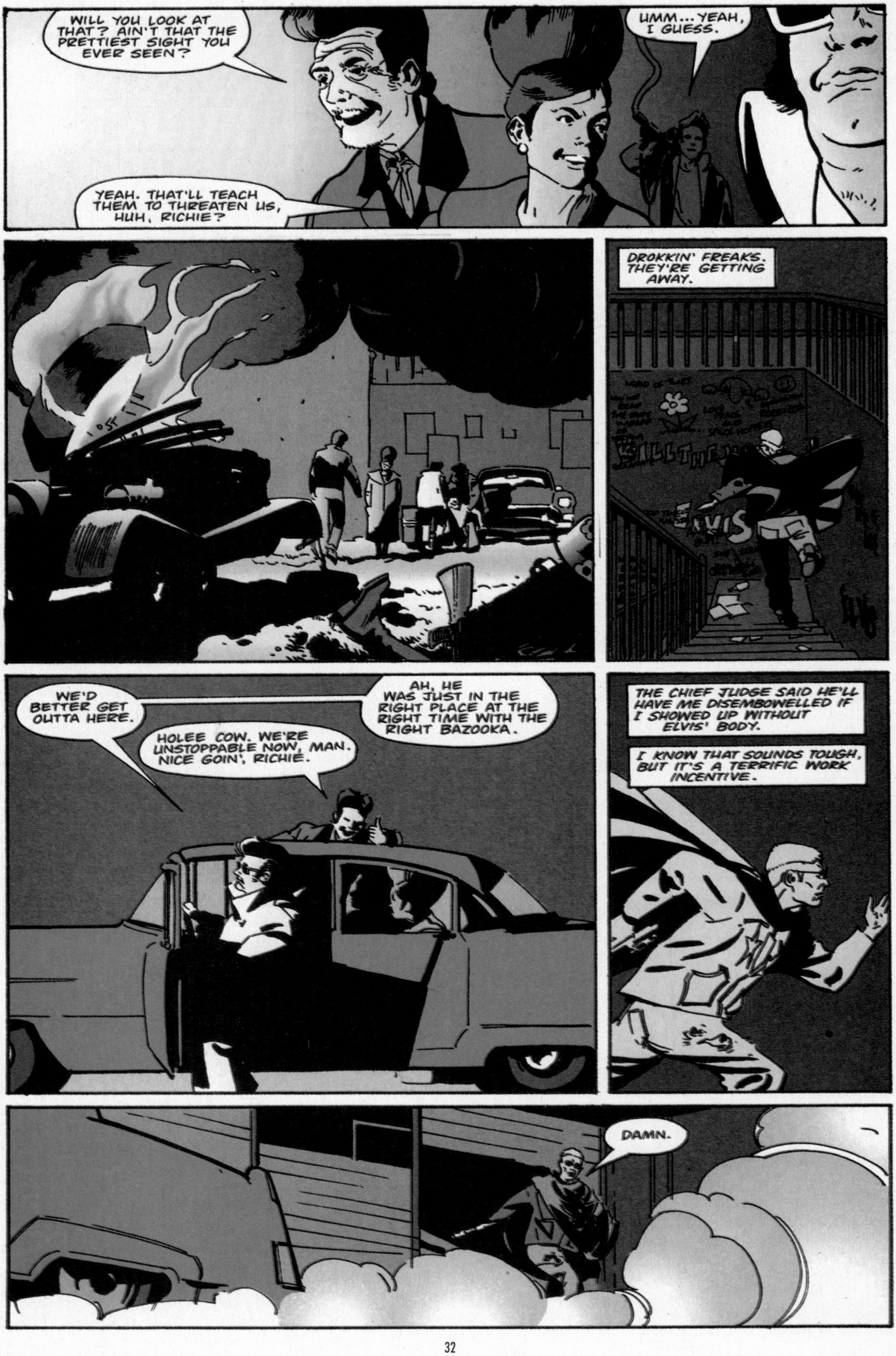
WILL YOU LOOK AT THAT? AIN'T THAT THE PRETTIEST SIGHT YOU EVER SEEN?
UMM... YEAH, I GUESS.
YEAH. THAT'LL TEACH THEM TO THREATEN US, HUH, RICHIE?
DROKKIN' FREAKS. THEY'RE GETTING AWAY.
ELVIS
WE'D BETTER GET OUTTA HERE.
AH, HE WAS JUST IN THE RIGHT PLACE AT THE RIGHT TIME WITH THE RIGHT BAZOOKA.
HOLEE COW. WE'RE UNSTOPPABLE NOW, MAN. NICE GOIN', RICHIE.
THE CHIEF JUDGE SAID HE'LL HAVE ME DISEMBOWELLED IF I SHOWED UP WITHOUT ELVIS' BODY.
I KNOW THAT SOUNDS TOUGH, BUT IT'S A TERRIFIC WORK INCENTIVE.
DAMN.

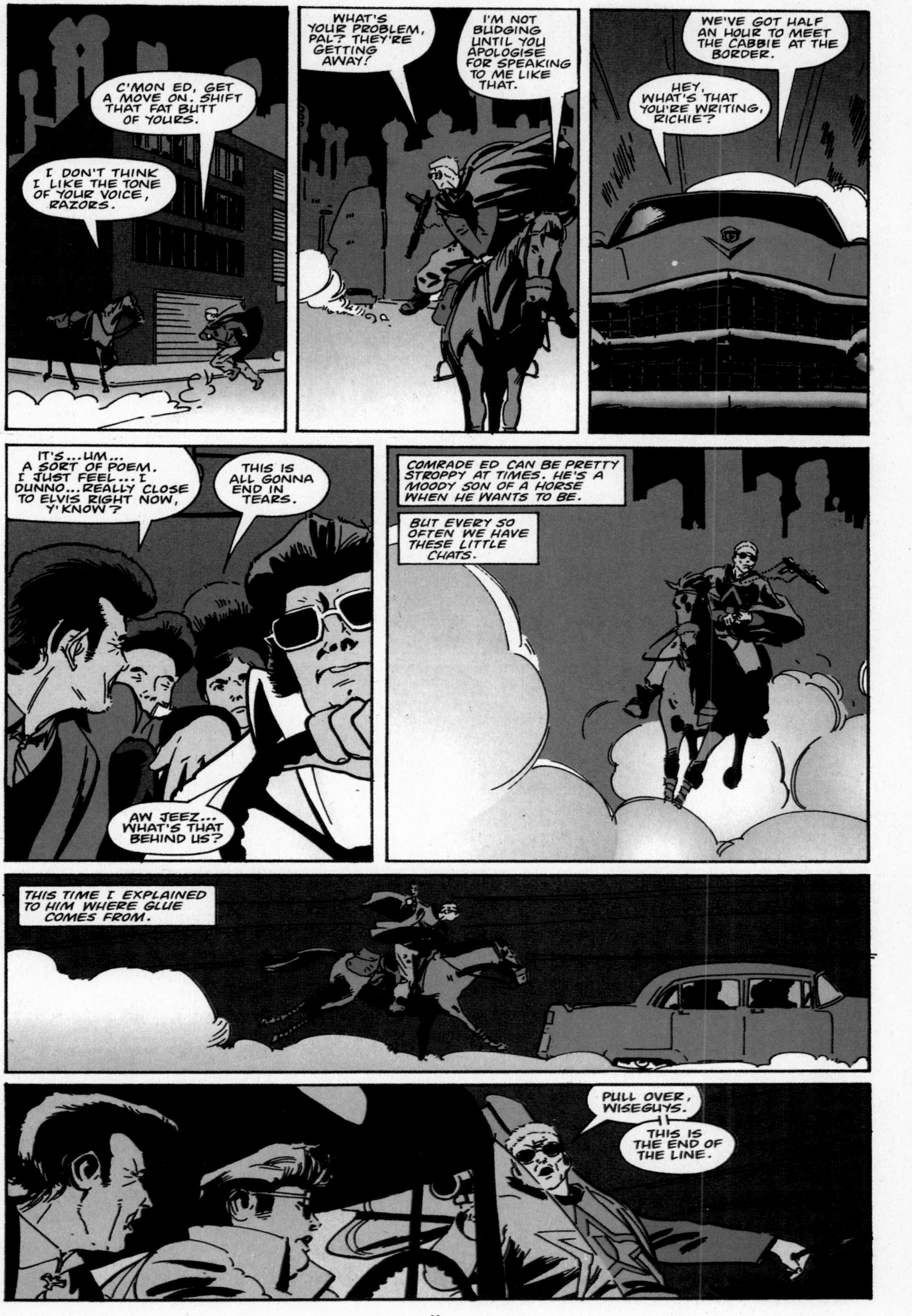
C'MON ED, GET A MOVE ON. SHIFT THAT FAT BUTT OF YOURS.
I DON'T THINK I LIKE THE TONE OF YOUR VOICE, RAZORS.
WHAT'S YOUR PROBLEM, PAL? THEY'RE GETTING AWAY!
I'M NOT BUDGING UNTIL YOU APOLOGISE FOR SPEAKING TO ME LIKE THAT.
WE'VE GOT HALF AN HOUR TO MEET THE CABBIE AT THE BORDER.
HEY, WHAT'S THAT YOU'RE WRITING, RICHIE?
IT'S...UM... A SORT OF POEM. I JUST FEEL... I DUNNO...REALLY CLOSE TO ELVIS RIGHT NOW, Y'KNOW?
THIS IS ALL GONNA END IN TEARS.
AW JEEZ... WHAT'S THAT BEHIND US?
COMRADE ED CAN BE PRETTY STROPPY AT TIMES. HE'S A MOODY SON OF A HORSE WHEN HE WANTS TO BE.
BUT EVERY SO OFTEN WE HAVE THESE LITTLE CHATS.
THIS TIME I EXPLAINED TO HIM WHERE GLUE COMES FROM.
PULL OVER, WISEGUYS.
THIS IS THE END OF THE LINE.

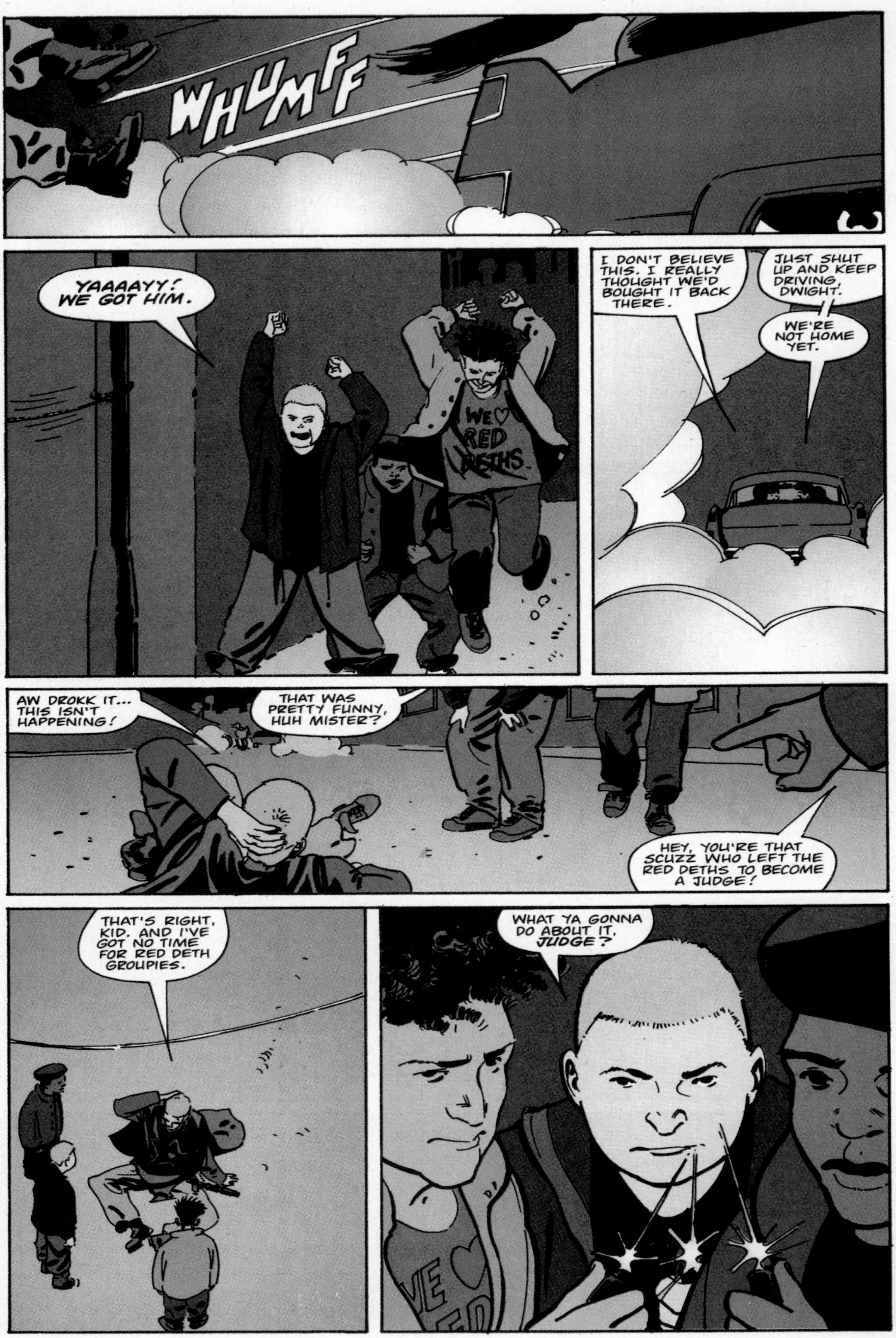
WHUMFF
YAAAAYY! WE GOT HIM.
I DON'T BELIEVE THIS. I REALLY THOUGHT WE'D BOUGHT IT BACK THERE.
JUST SHUT UP AND KEEP DRIVING, DWIGHT.
WE'RE NOT HOME YET.
AW DROKK IT... THIS ISN'T HAPPENING!
THAT WAS PRETTY FUNNY, HUH MISTER?
HEY, YOU'RE THAT SCUZZ WHO LEFT THE RED DETHS TO BECOME A JUDGE!
THAT'S RIGHT, KID. AND I'VE GOT NO TIME FOR RED DETH GROUPIES.
WHAT YA GONNA DO ABOUT IT, JUDGE?

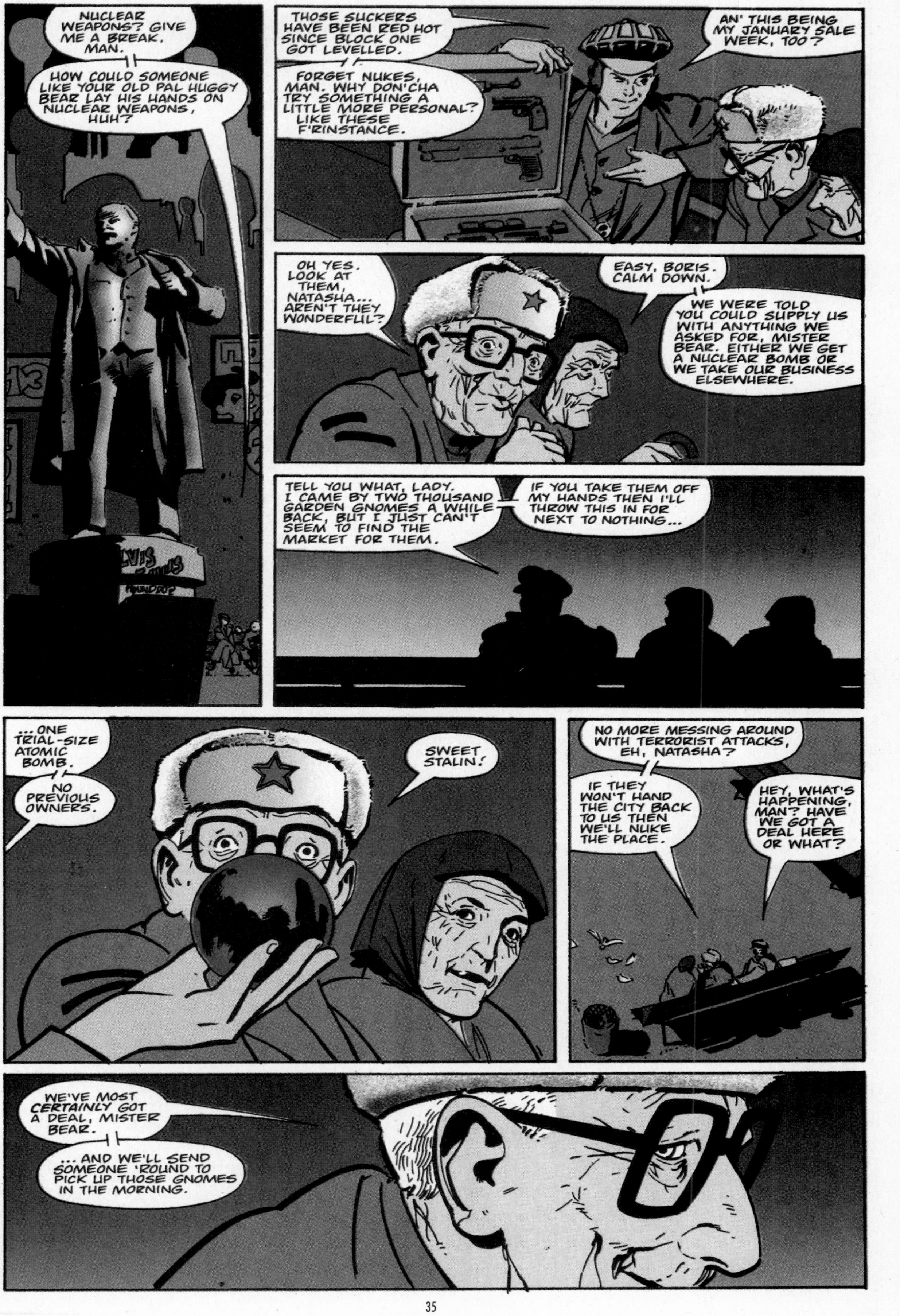
NUCLEAR WEAPONS? GIVE ME A BREAK, MAN.
HOW COULD SOMEONE LIKE YOUR OLD PAL HUGGY BEAR LAY HIS HANDS ON NUCLEAR WEAPONS, HUH?
THOSE SUCKERS HAVE BEEN RED HOT SINCE BLOCK ONE GOT LEVELLED.
FORGET NUKES, MAN. WHY DON'CHA TRY SOMETHING A LITTLE MORE PERSONAL? LIKE THESE F'RINSTANCE.
AN' THIS BEING MY JANUARY SALE WEEK, TOO?
OH YES. LOOK AT THEM, NATASHA... AREN'T THEY WONDERFUL?
EASY, BORIS. CALM DOWN.
WE WERE TOLD YOU COULD SUPPLY US WITH ANYTHING WE ASKED FOR, MISTER BEAR. EITHER WE GET A NUCLEAR BOMB OR WE TAKE OUR BUSINESS ELSEWHERE.
TELL YOU WHAT, LADY. I CAME BY TWO THOUSAND GARDEN GNOMES A WHILE BACK, BUT I JUST CAN'T SEEM TO FIND THE MARKET FOR THEM.
IF YOU TAKE THEM OFF MY HANDS THEN I'LL THROW THIS IN FOR NEXT TO NOTHING...
... ONE TRIAL-SIZE ATOMIC BOMB.
NO PREVIOUS OWNERS.
SWEET STALIN!
NO MORE MESSING AROUND WITH TERRORIST ATTACKS, EH, NATASHA?
IF THEY WON'T HAND THE CITY BACK TO US THEN WE'LL NUKE THE PLACE.
HEY, WHAT'S HAPPENING, MAN? HAVE WE GOT A DEAL HERE OR WHAT?
WE'VE MOST CERTAINLY GOT A DEAL, MISTER BEAR.
... AND WE'LL SEND SOMEONE 'ROUND TO PICK UP THOSE GNOMES IN THE MORNING.

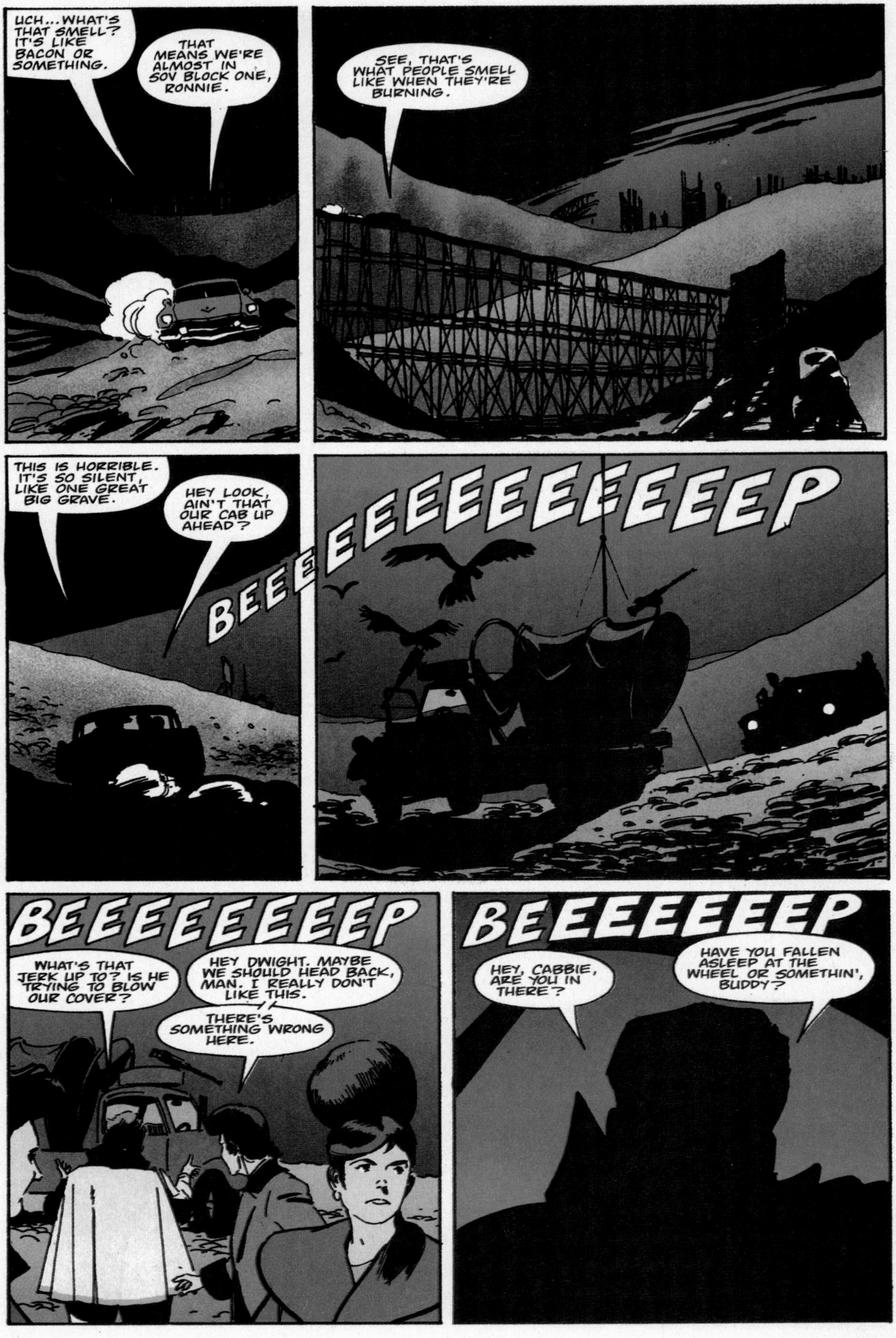
UCH... WHAT'S THAT SMELL? IT'S LIKE BACON OR SOMETHING.
THAT MEANS WE'RE ALMOST IN SOV BLOCK ONE, RONNIE.
SEE, THAT'S WHAT PEOPLE SMELL LIKE WHEN THEY'RE BURNING.
THIS IS HORRIBLE. IT'S SO SILENT, LIKE ONE GREAT BIG GRAVE.
HEY LOOK, AIN'T THAT OUR CAB UP AHEAD?
BEEEEEEEEEEEEEEP
BEEEEEEEEEP
WHAT'S THAT JERK UP TO? IS HE TRYING TO BLOW OUR COVER?
HEY DWIGHT. MAYBE WE SHOULD HEAD BACK, MAN. I REALLY DON'T LIKE THIS.
THERE'S SOMETHING WRONG HERE.
BEEEEEEEEP
HEY, CABBIE, ARE YOU IN THERE?
HAVE YOU FALLEN ASLEEP AT THE WHEEL OR SOMETHIN', BUDDY?

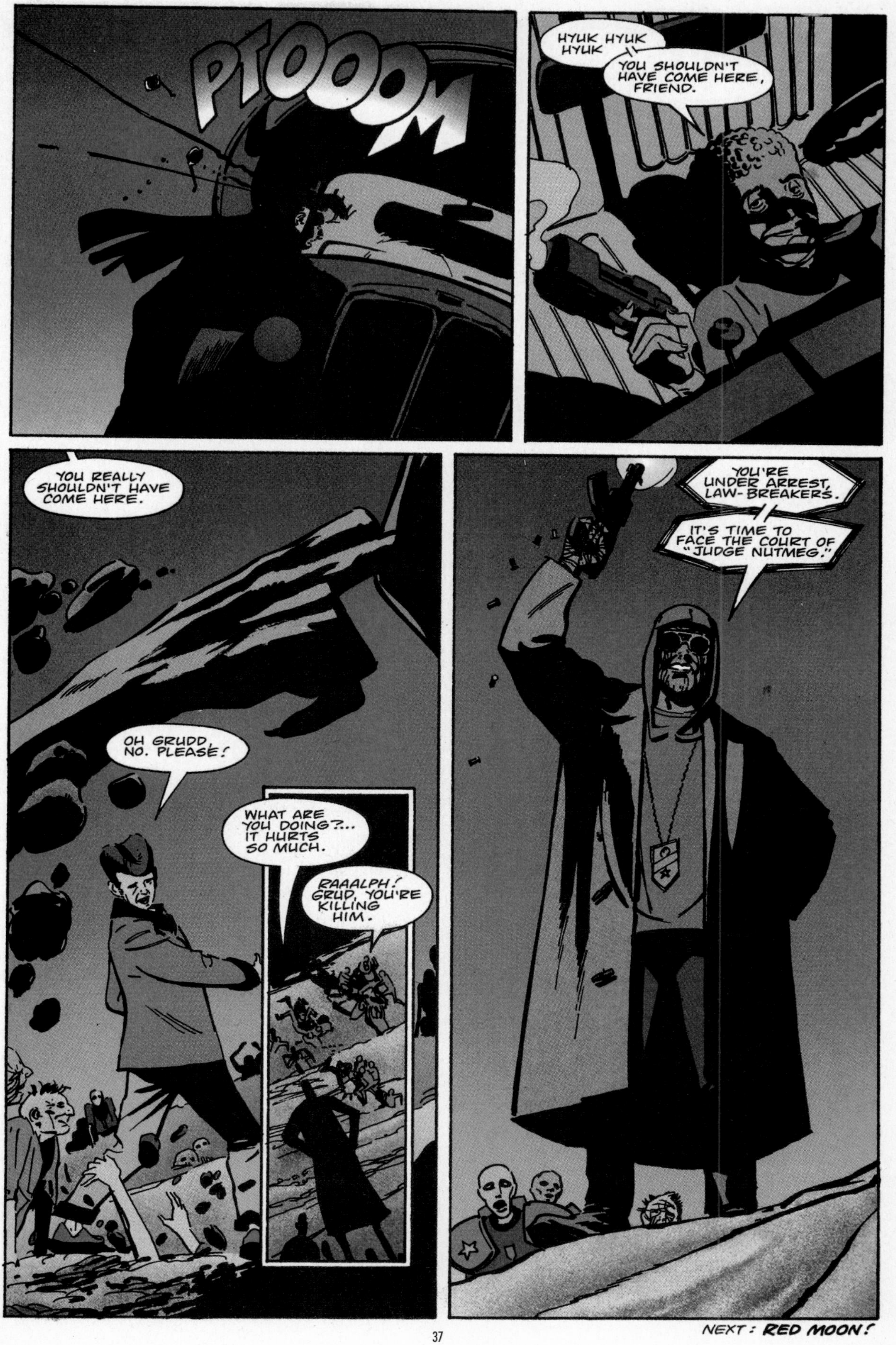
PTOOOM
HYUK HYUK HYUK
YOU SHOULDN'T HAVE COME HERE, FRIEND.
YOU REALLY SHOULDN'T HAVE COME HERE.
OH GRUDD, NO. PLEASE!
WHAT ARE YOU DOING?... IT HURTS SO MUCH.
RAAALPH! GRUD, YOU'RE KILLING HIM.
YOU'RE UNDER ARREST, LAW-BREAKERS.
IT'S TIME TO FACE THE COURT OF "JUDGE NUTMEG."

NEXT: **RED MOON!**

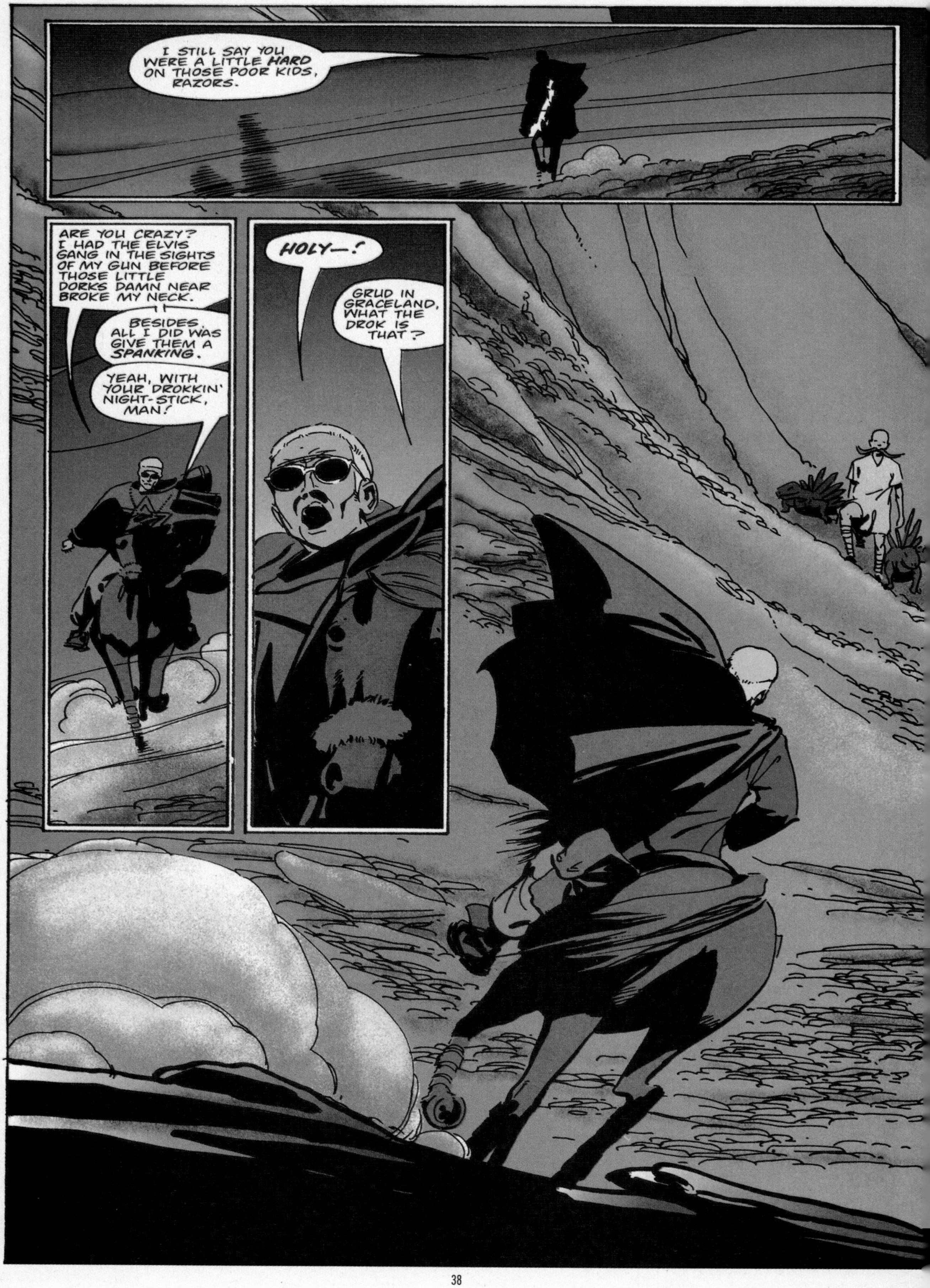
I STILL SAY YOU WERE A LITTLE HARD ON THOSE POOR KIDS, RAZORS.
ARE YOU CRAZY? I HAD THE ELVIS GANG IN THE SIGHTS OF MY GUN BEFORE THOSE LITTLE DORKS DAMN NEAR BROKE MY NECK.
BESIDES, ALL I DID WAS GIVE THEM A SPANKING.
YEAH, WITH YOUR 'DROKKIN' NIGHT-STICK, MAN!
HOLY—!
GRUD IN GRACELAND, WHAT THE DROK IS THAT?

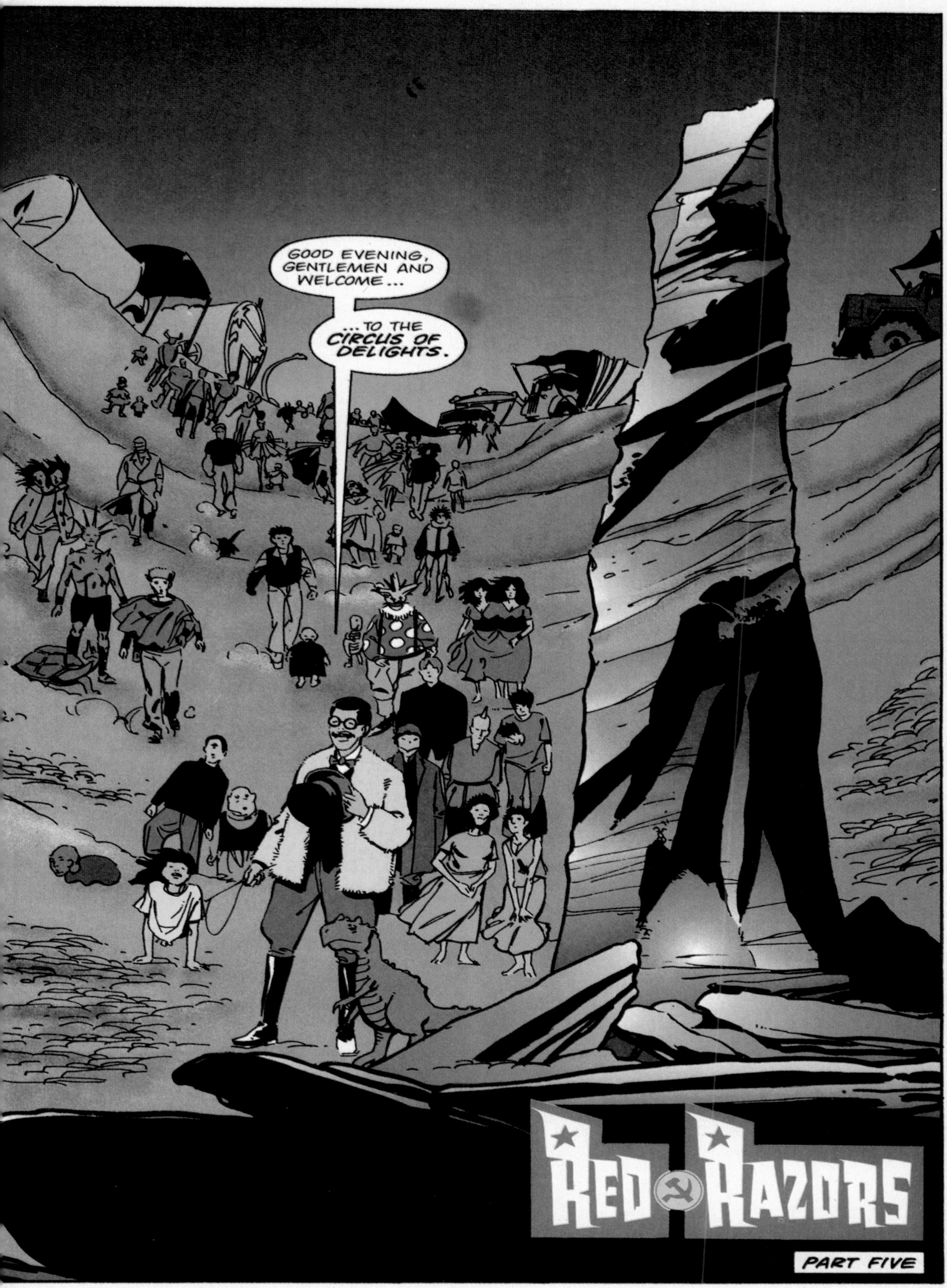
GOOD EVENING, GENTLEMEN AND WELCOME...
...TO THE CIRCUS OF DELIGHTS.
RED RAZORS
PART FIVE

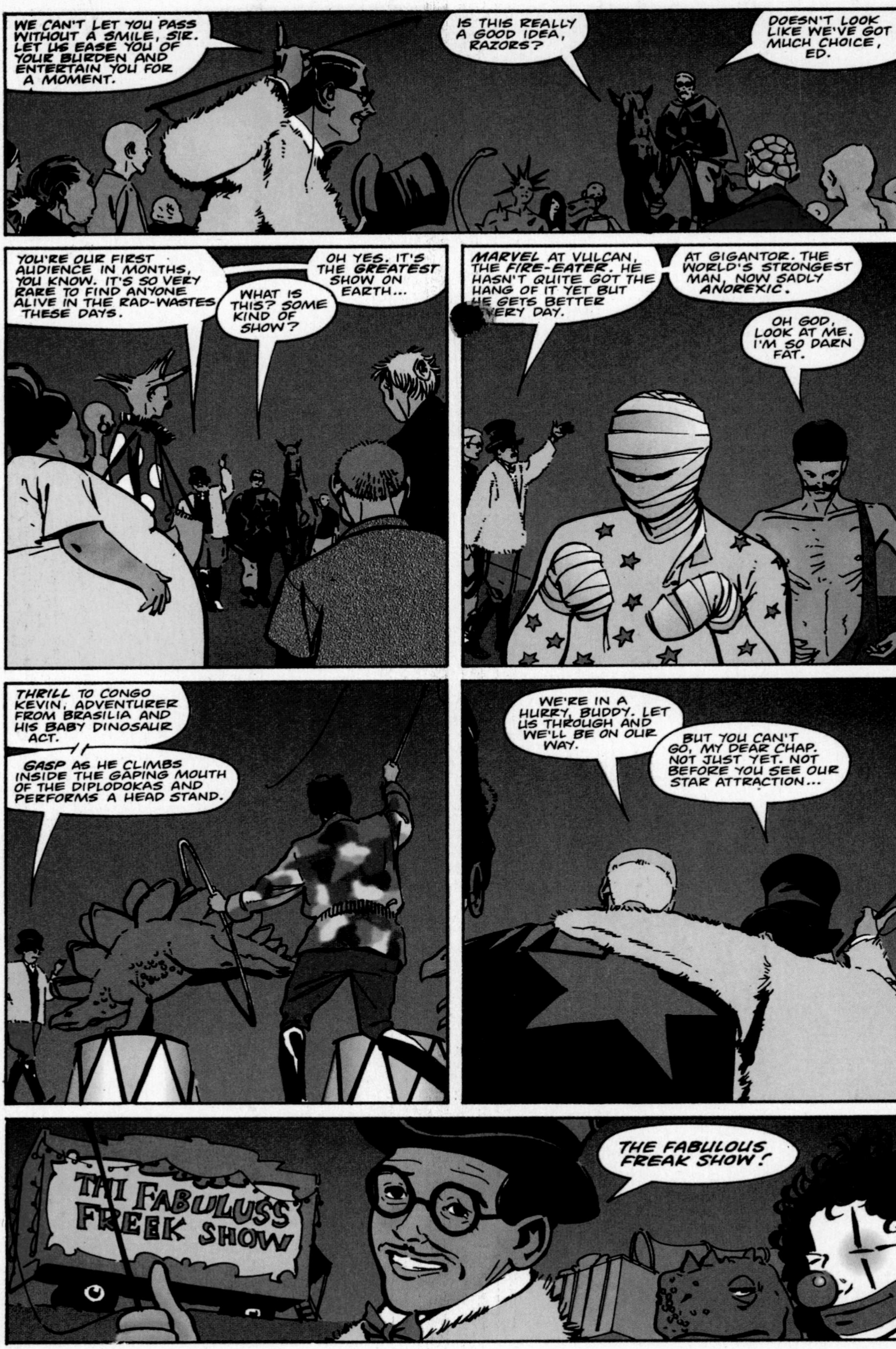
WE CAN'T LET YOU PASS WITHOUT A SMILE, SIR. LET US EASE YOU OF YOUR BURDEN AND ENTERTAIN YOU FOR A MOMENT.
IS THIS REALLY A GOOD IDEA, RAZORS?
DOESN'T LOOK LIKE WE'VE GOT MUCH CHOICE, ED.
YOU'RE OUR FIRST AUDIENCE IN MONTHS, YOU KNOW. IT'S SO VERY RARE TO FIND ANYONE ALIVE IN THE RAD-WASTES THESE DAYS.
WHAT IS THIS? SOME KIND OF SHOW?
OH YES. IT'S THE GREATEST SHOW ON EARTH...
MARVEL AT VULCAN, THE FIRE-EATER. HE HASN'T QUITE GOT THE HANG OF IT YET BUT HE GETS BETTER EVERY DAY.
AT GIGANTOR. THE WORLD'S STRONGEST MAN, NOW SADLY ANOREXIC.
OH GOD, LOOK AT ME. I'M SO DARN FAT.
THRILL TO CONGO KEVIN, ADVENTURER FROM BRASILIA AND HIS BABY DINOSAUR ACT.
GASP AS HE CLIMBS INSIDE THE GAPING MOUTH OF THE DIPLODOKAS AND PERFORMS A HEAD STAND.
WE'RE IN A HURRY, BUDDY. LET US THROUGH AND WE'LL BE ON OUR WAY.
BUT YOU CAN'T GO, MY DEAR CHAP. NOT JUST YET. NOT BEFORE YOU SEE OUR STAR ATTRACTION...
THI FABULUSS FREEK SHOW
THE FABULOUS FREAK SHOW!

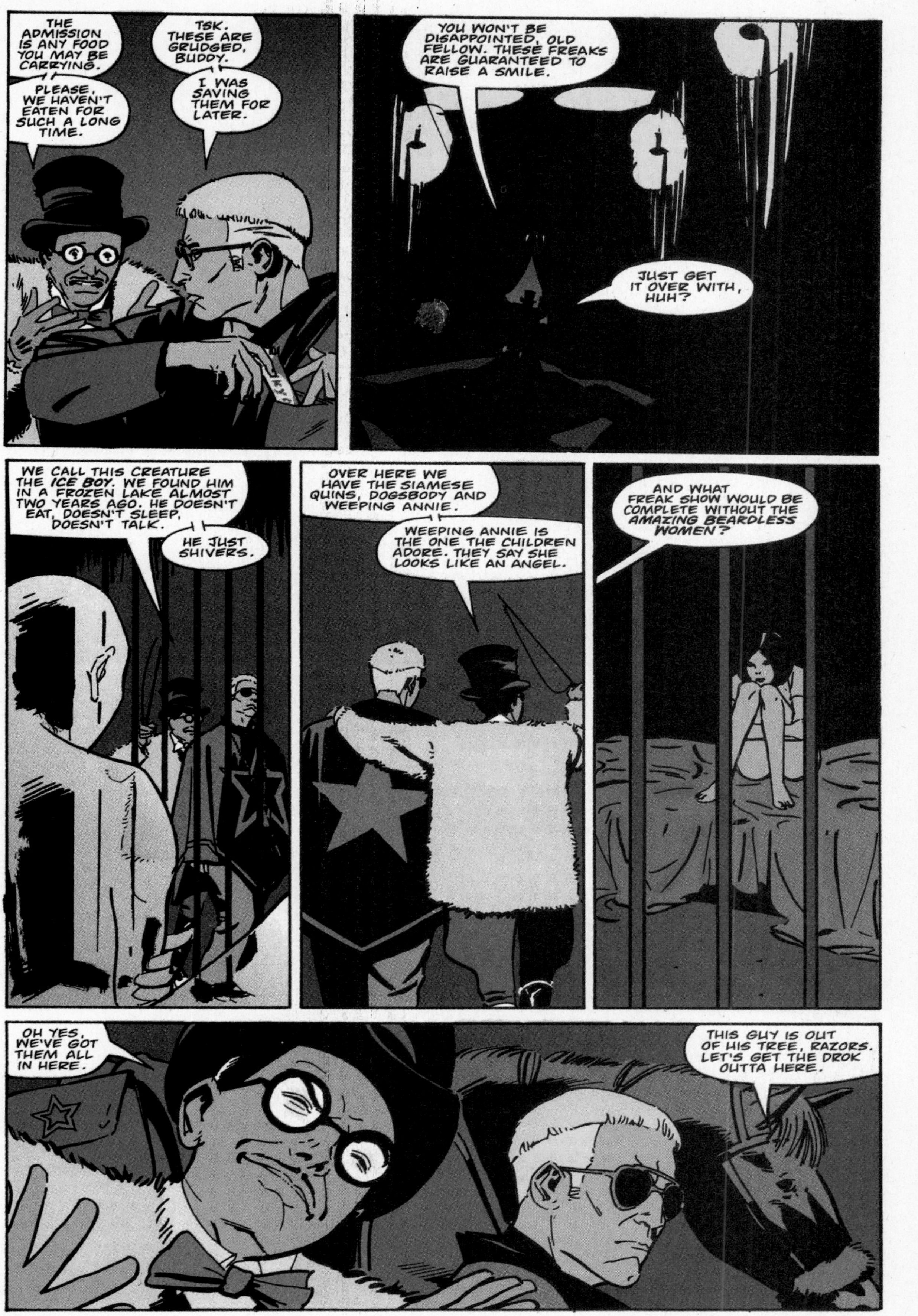
THE ADMISSION IS ANY FOOD YOU MAY BE CARRYING.
PLEASE, WE HAVEN'T EATEN FOR SUCH A LONG TIME.
TSK. THESE ARE GRUDGED, BUDDY.
I WAS SAVING THEM FOR LATER.
YOU WON'T BE DISAPPOINTED, OLD FELLOW. THESE FREAKS ARE GUARANTEED TO RAISE A SMILE.
JUST GET IT OVER WITH, HUH?
WE CALL THIS CREATURE THE *ICE BOY*. WE FOUND HIM IN A FROZEN LAKE ALMOST TWO YEARS AGO. HE DOESN'T EAT, DOESN'T SLEEP, DOESN'T TALK.
HE JUST SHIVERS.
OVER HERE WE HAVE THE SIAMESE QUINS, DOGSBODY AND WEEPING ANNIE.
WEEPING ANNIE IS THE ONE THE CHILDREN ADORE. THEY SAY SHE LOOKS LIKE AN ANGEL.
AND WHAT FREAK SHOW WOULD BE COMPLETE WITHOUT THE *AMAZING BEARDLESS WOMEN*?
OH YES, WE'VE GOT THEM ALL IN HERE.
THIS GUY IS OUT OF HIS TREE, RAZORS. LET'S GET THE DROK OUTTA HERE.

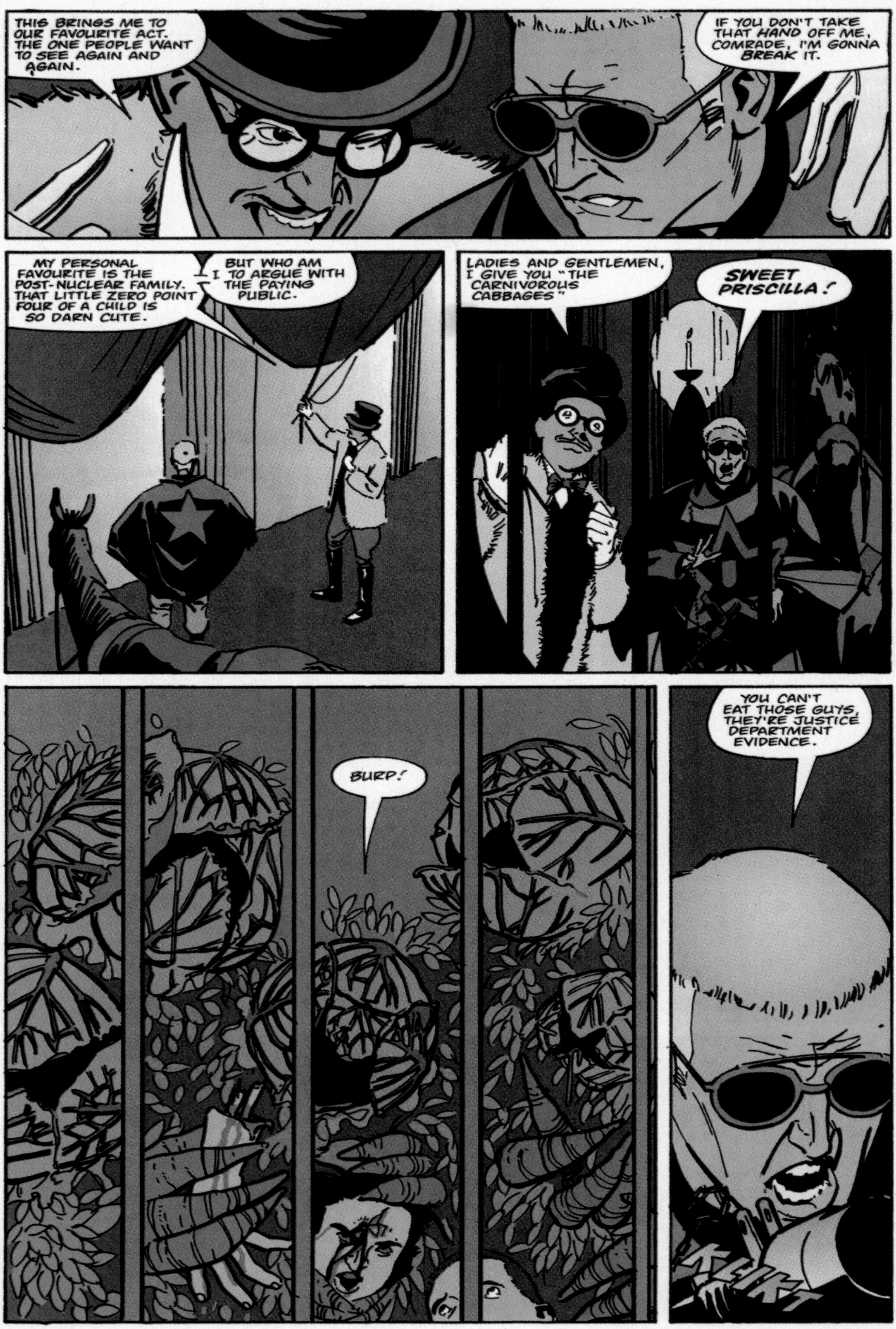
THIS BRINGS ME TO OUR FAVOURITE ACT. THE ONE PEOPLE WANT TO SEE AGAIN AND AGAIN.
IF YOU DON'T TAKE THAT HAND OFF ME, COMRADE, I'M GONNA BREAK IT.
MY PERSONAL FAVOURITE IS THE POST-NUCLEAR FAMILY. THAT LITTLE ZERO POINT FOUR OF A CHILD IS SO DARN CUTE.
BUT WHO AM I TO ARGUE WITH THE PAYING PUBLIC.
LADIES AND GENTLEMEN, I GIVE YOU "THE CARNIVOROUS CABBAGES"
SWEET PRISCILLA!
BURP!
YOU CAN'T EAT THOSE GUYS, THEY'RE JUSTICE DEPARTMENT EVIDENCE.

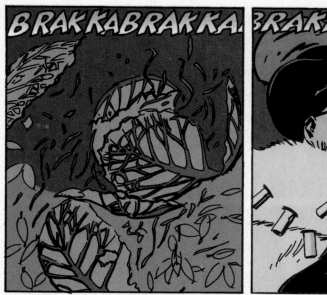

BRAKKABRAKKA...BRAKKA...

NO. DON'T KILL THEM. THE CABBAGES ARE OUR MOST POPULAR ACT.

TOUCHING A SOV BLOCK JUDGE IS AN OFFENCE, CREEP.

KKKRASH!

THOSE STIFFS BELONGED TO A GANG I'VE BEEN TRACKING FOR NEARLY THREE DAYS.

WHAT DID YOU DO WITH THE OTHERS?

I NEVER TOUCHED THEM. I SWEAR.

THE BLOCK ONE JUDGES TOOK THEM AWAY TO THEIR NEW HALLS OF JUSTICE. DEEP IN THE RAD-WASTES.

NOBODY GETS OUT OF THAT PLACE ALIVE. YOU'LL NEVER FIND THEM NOW.

MAYBE SO.

GOOD THING I'VE GOT YOU TO SHOW ME THE WAY, HUH?

CLICK

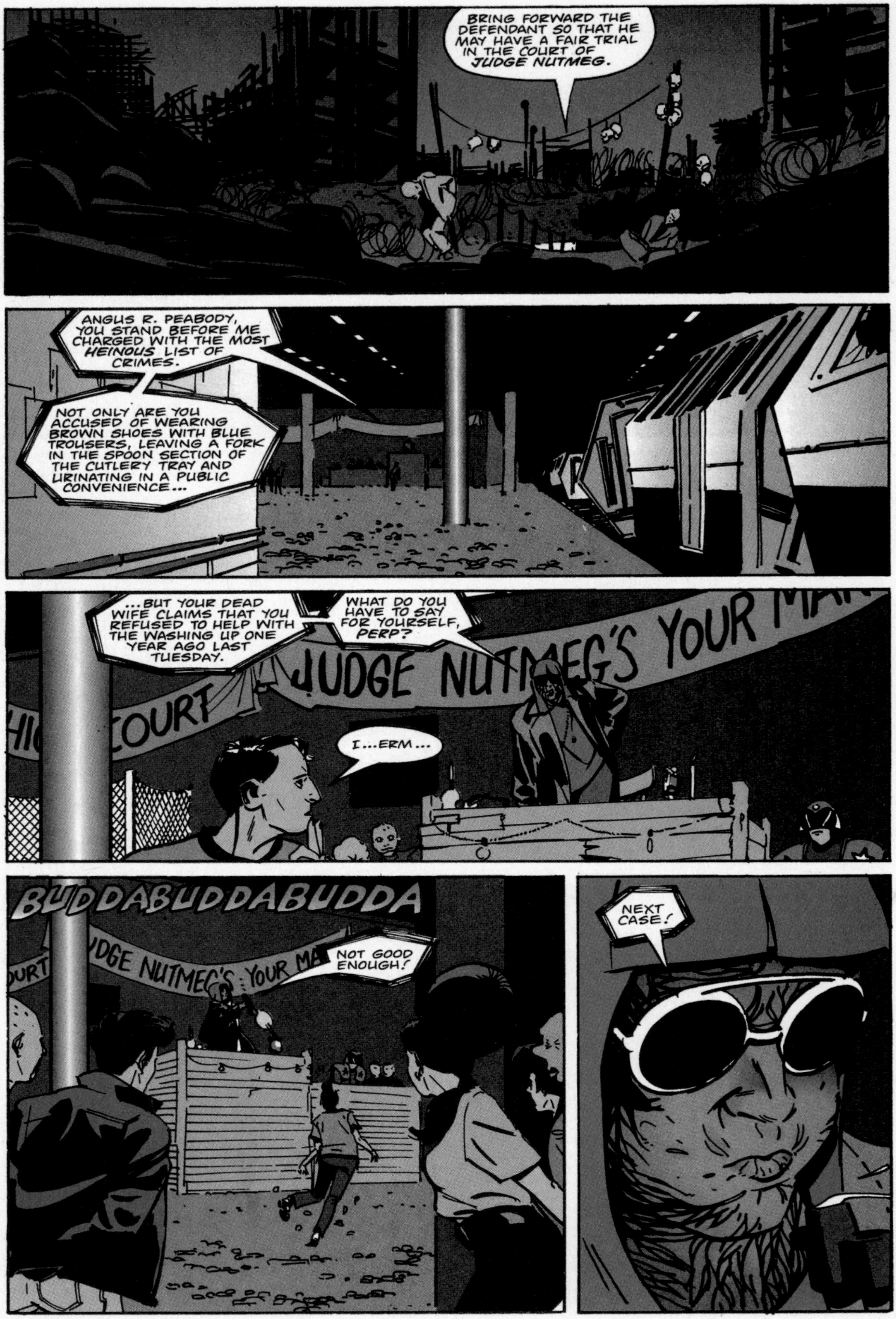
BRING FORWARD THE DEFENDANT SO THAT HE MAY HAVE A FAIR TRIAL IN THE COURT OF JUDGE NUTMEG.
ANGUS R. PEABODY, YOU STAND BEFORE ME CHARGED WITH THE MOST HEINOUS LIST OF CRIMES.
NOT ONLY ARE YOU ACCUSED OF WEARING BROWN SHOES WITH BLUE TROUSERS, LEAVING A FORK IN THE SPOON SECTION OF THE CUTLERY TRAY AND URINATING IN A PUBLIC CONVENIENCE...
...BUT YOUR DEAD WIFE CLAIMS THAT YOU REFUSED TO HELP WITH THE WASHING UP ONE YEAR AGO LAST TUESDAY.
WHAT DO YOU HAVE TO SAY FOR YOURSELF, PERP?
JUDGE NUTMEG'S YOUR MA
COURT
I...ERM...
BUDDABUDDABUDDA
JUDGE NUTMEG'S YOUR MA
NOT GOOD ENOUGH!
NEXT CASE!

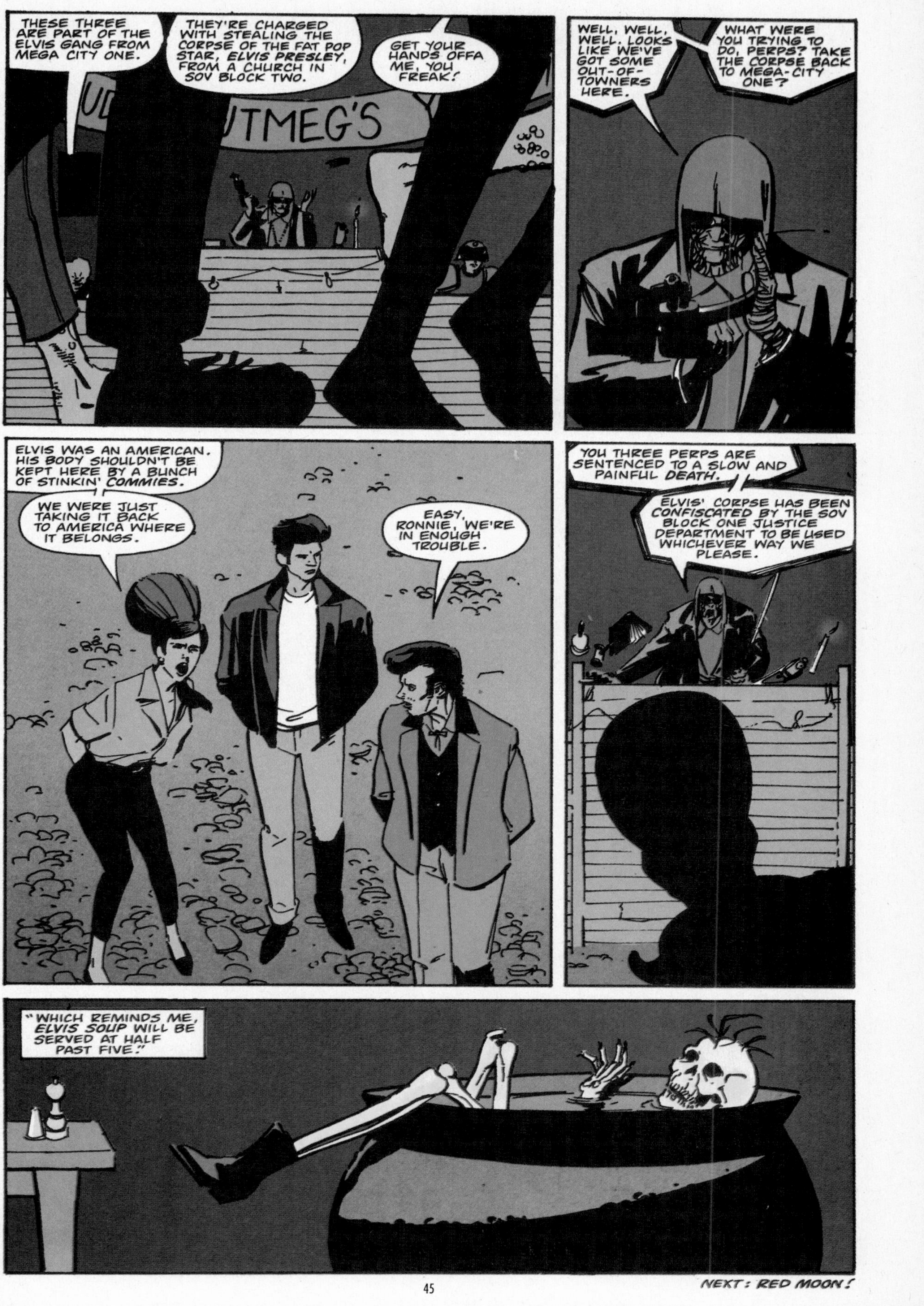
THESE THREE ARE PART OF THE ELVIS GANG FROM MEGA CITY ONE.
THEY'RE CHARGED WITH STEALING THE CORPSE OF THE FAT POP STAR, ELVIS PRESLEY, FROM A CHURCH IN SOV BLOCK TWO.
GET YOUR HANDS OFFA ME, YOU FREAK!
UTMEG'S
WELL, WELL, WELL. LOOKS LIKE WE'VE GOT SOME OUT-OF-TOWNERS HERE.
WHAT WERE YOU TRYING TO DO, PERPS? TAKE THE CORPSE BACK TO MEGA-CITY ONE?
ELVIS WAS AN AMERICAN. HIS BODY SHOULDN'T BE KEPT HERE BY A BUNCH OF STINKIN' COMMIES.
WE WERE JUST TAKING IT BACK TO AMERICA WHERE IT BELONGS.
EASY, RONNIE, WE'RE IN ENOUGH TROUBLE.
YOU THREE PERPS ARE SENTENCED TO A SLOW AND PAINFUL DEATH.
ELVIS' CORPSE HAS BEEN CONFISCATED BY THE SOV BLOCK ONE JUSTICE DEPARTMENT TO BE USED WHICHEVER WAY WE PLEASE.
"WHICH REMINDS ME, ELVIS SOUP WILL BE SERVED AT HALF PAST FIVE."
NEXT: RED MOON!

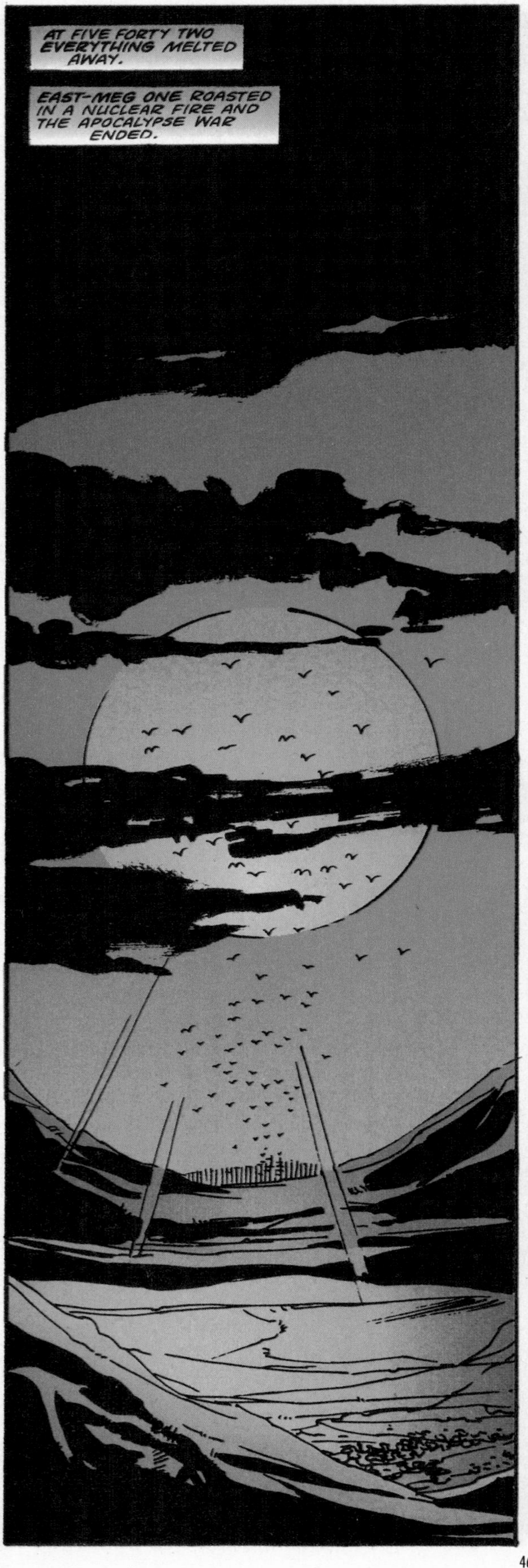
AT FIVE FORTY TWO EVERYTHING MELTED AWAY.
EAST-MEG ONE ROASTED IN A NUCLEAR FIRE AND THE APOCALYPSE WAR ENDED.

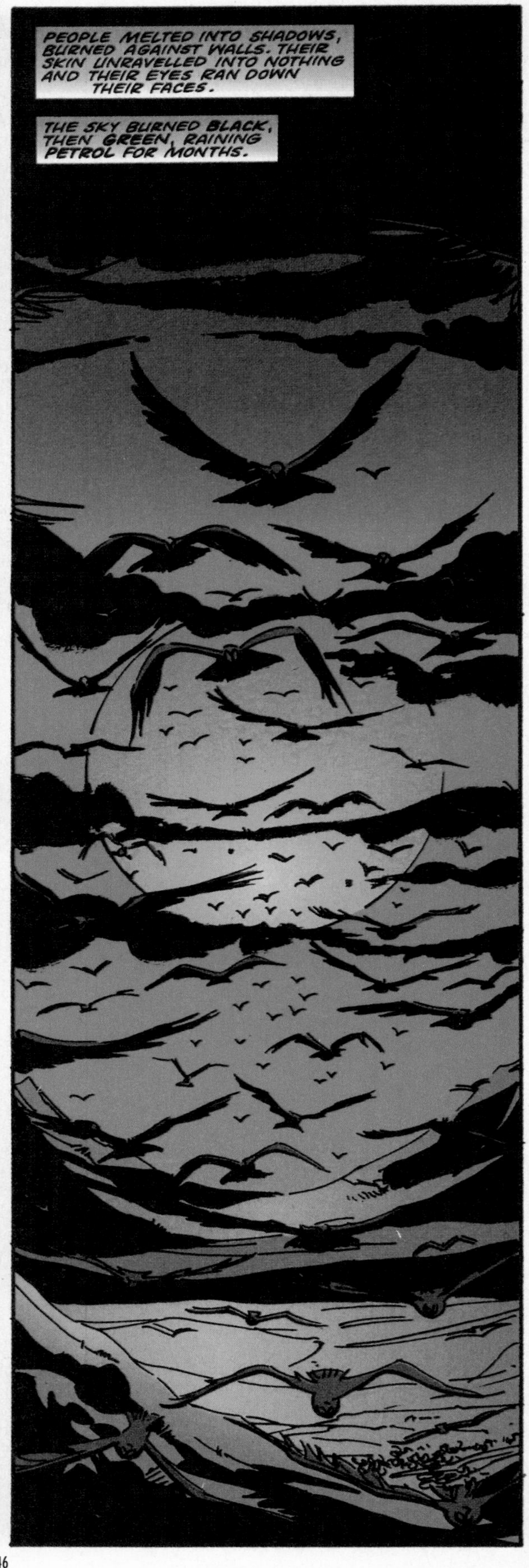
PEOPLE MELTED INTO SHADOWS, BURNED AGAINST WALLS. THEIR SKIN UNRAVELLED INTO NOTHING AND THEIR EYES RAN DOWN THEIR FACES.
THE SKY BURNED BLACK, THEN GREEN, RAINING PETROL FOR MONTHS.

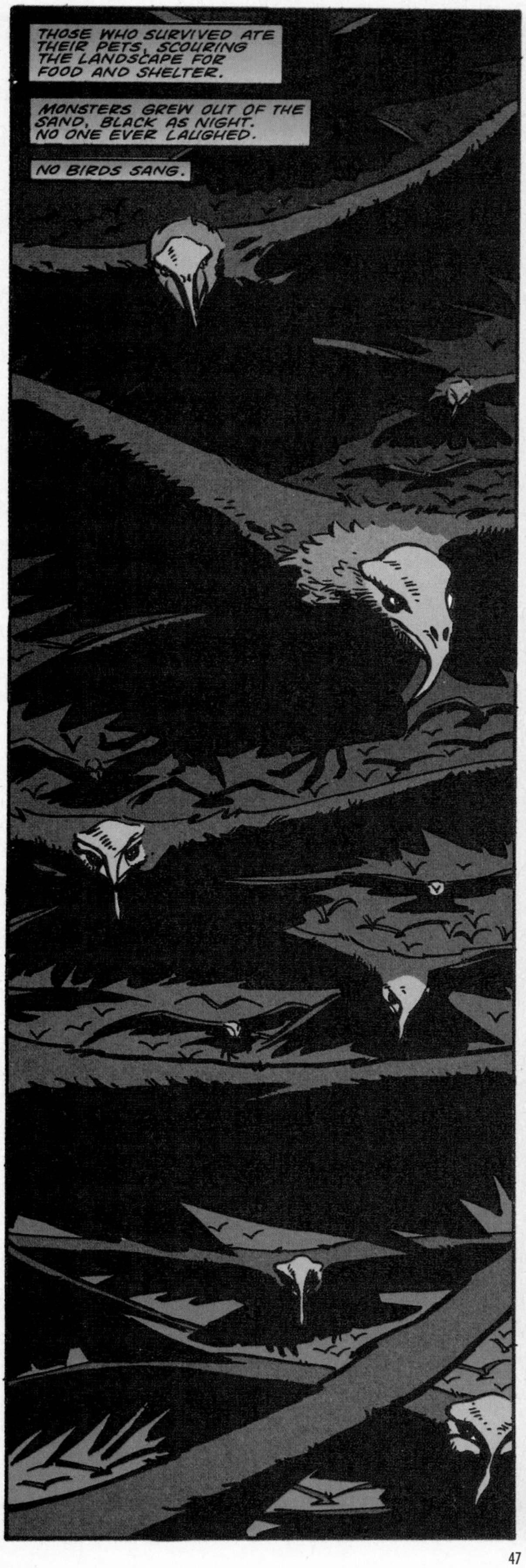
THOSE WHO SURVIVED ATE THEIR PETS, SCOURING THE LANDSCAPE FOR FOOD AND SHELTER.
MONSTERS GREW OUT OF THE SAND, BLACK AS NIGHT. NO ONE EVER LAUGHED.
NO BIRDS SANG.

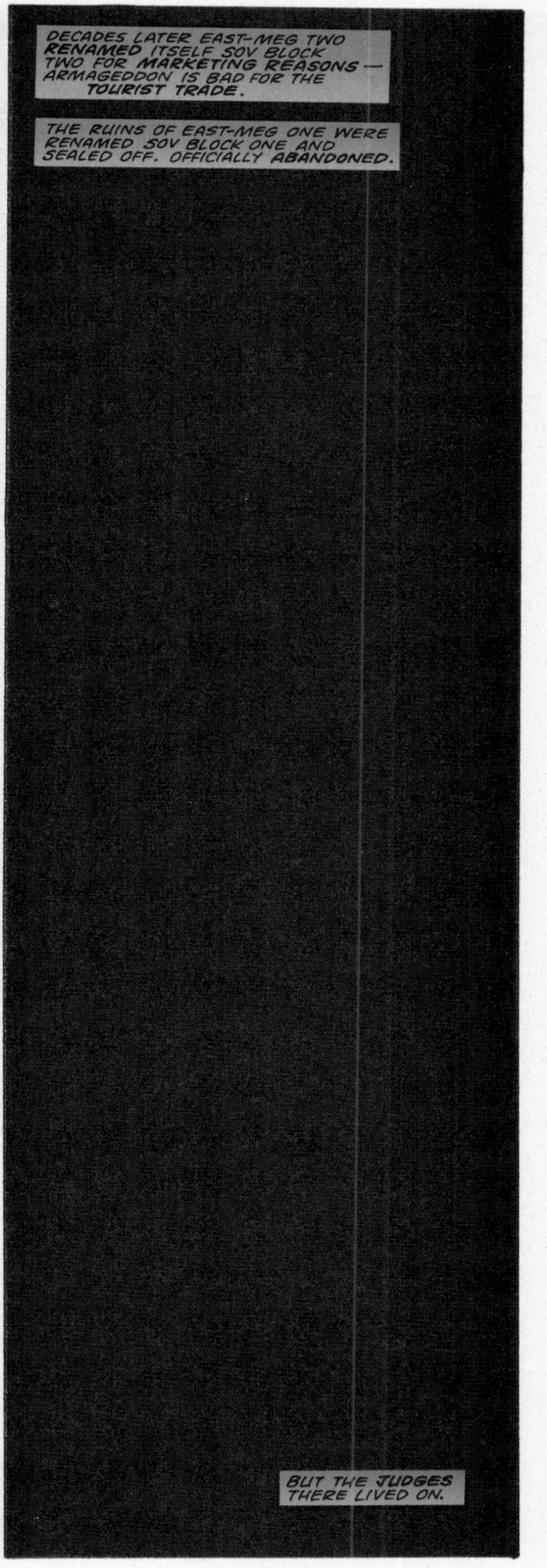
DECADES LATER EAST-MEG TWO RENAMED ITSELF SOV BLOCK TWO FOR MARKETING REASONS — ARMAGEDDON IS BAD FOR THE TOURIST TRADE.
THE RUINS OF EAST-MEG ONE WERE RENAMED SOV BLOCK ONE AND SEALED OFF. OFFICIALLY ABANDONED.
BUT THE JUDGES THERE LIVED ON.

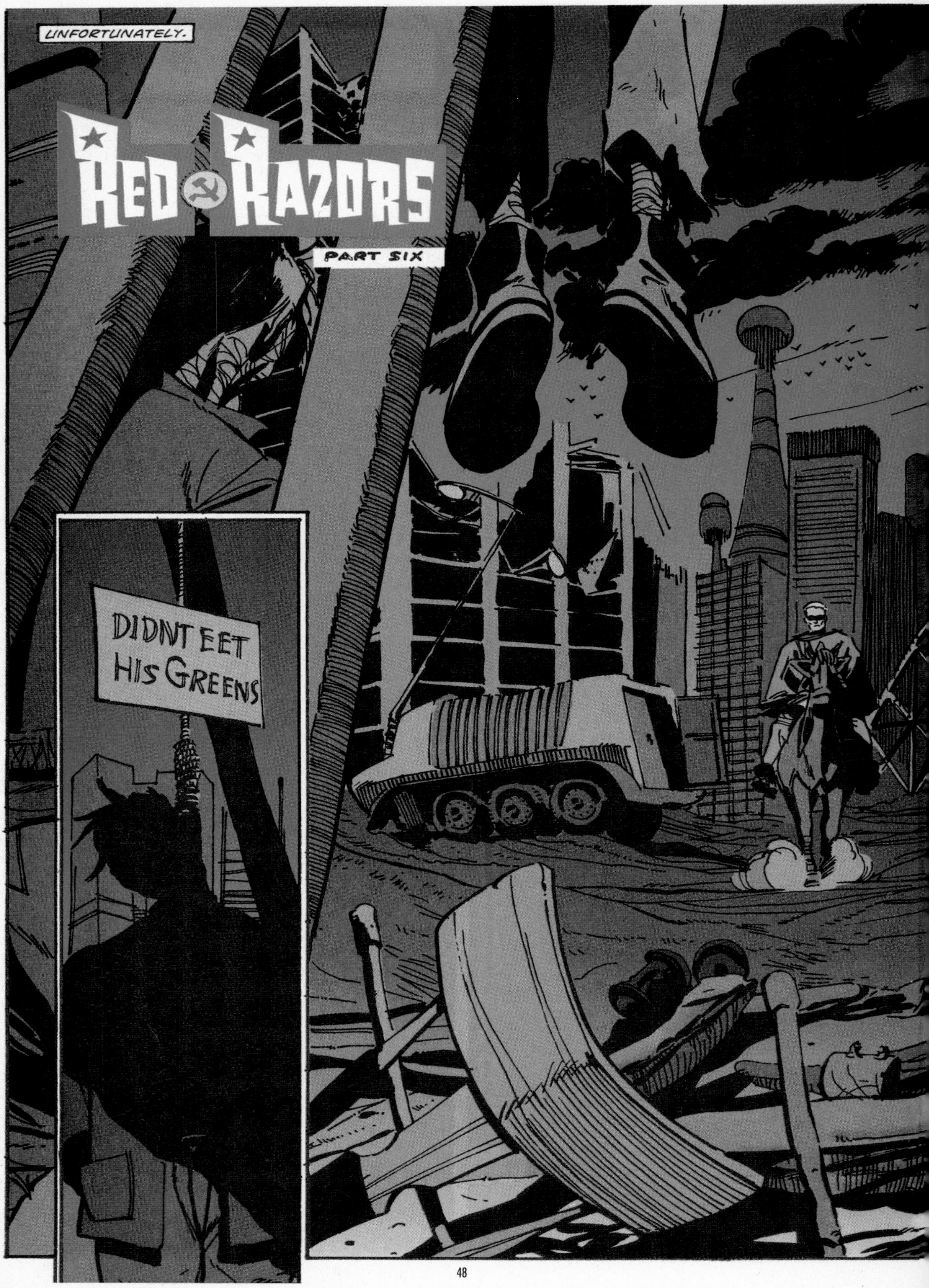
UNFORTUNATELY.
RED RAZORS
PART SIX
DIDNT EET HIS GREENS

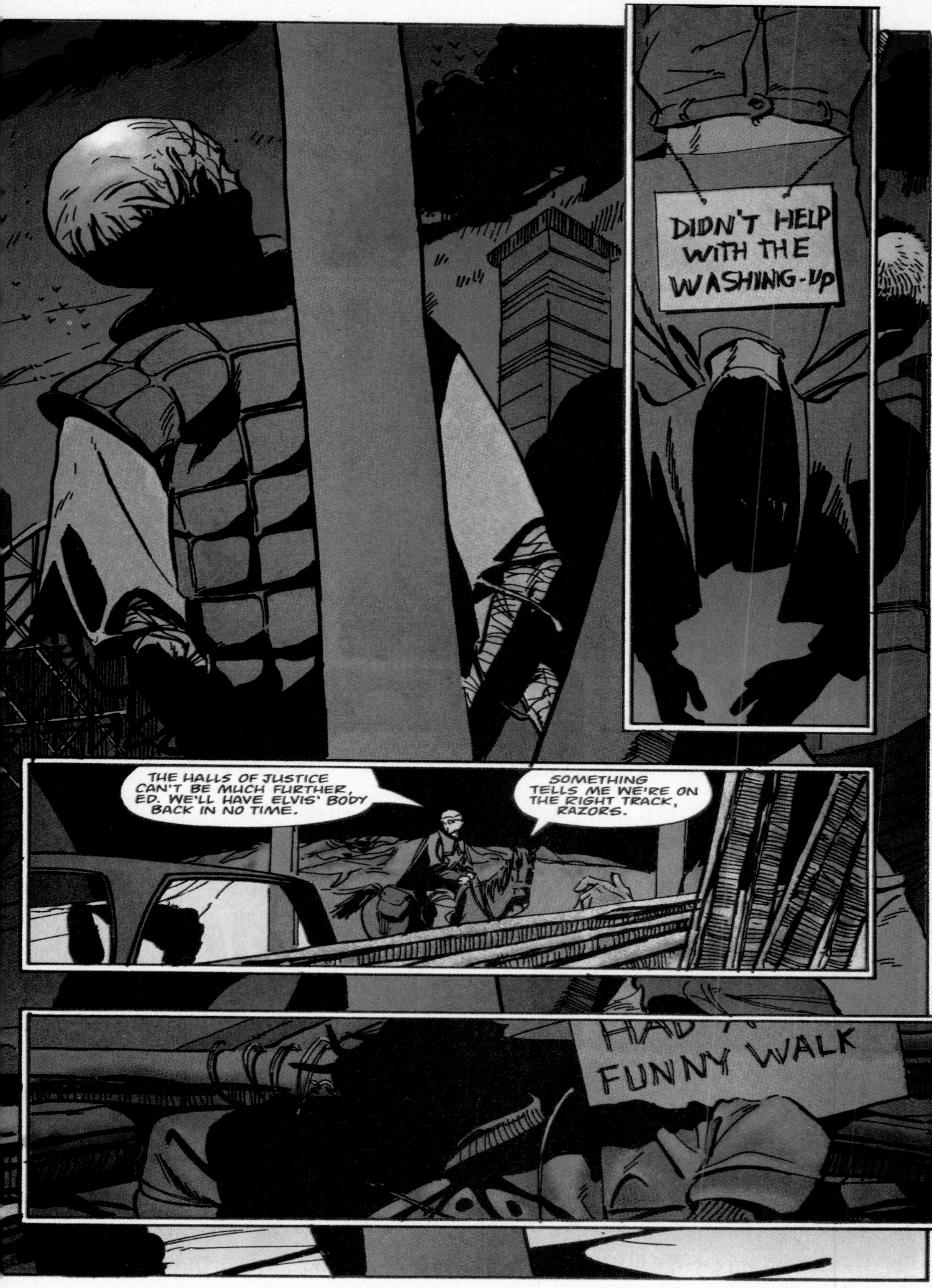
DIDN'T HELP WITH THE WASHING-UP
THE HALLS OF JUSTICE CAN'T BE MUCH FURTHER, ED. WE'LL HAVE ELVIS' BODY BACK IN NO TIME.
SOMETHING TELLS ME WE'RE ON THE RIGHT TRACK, RAZORS.
FUNNY WALK

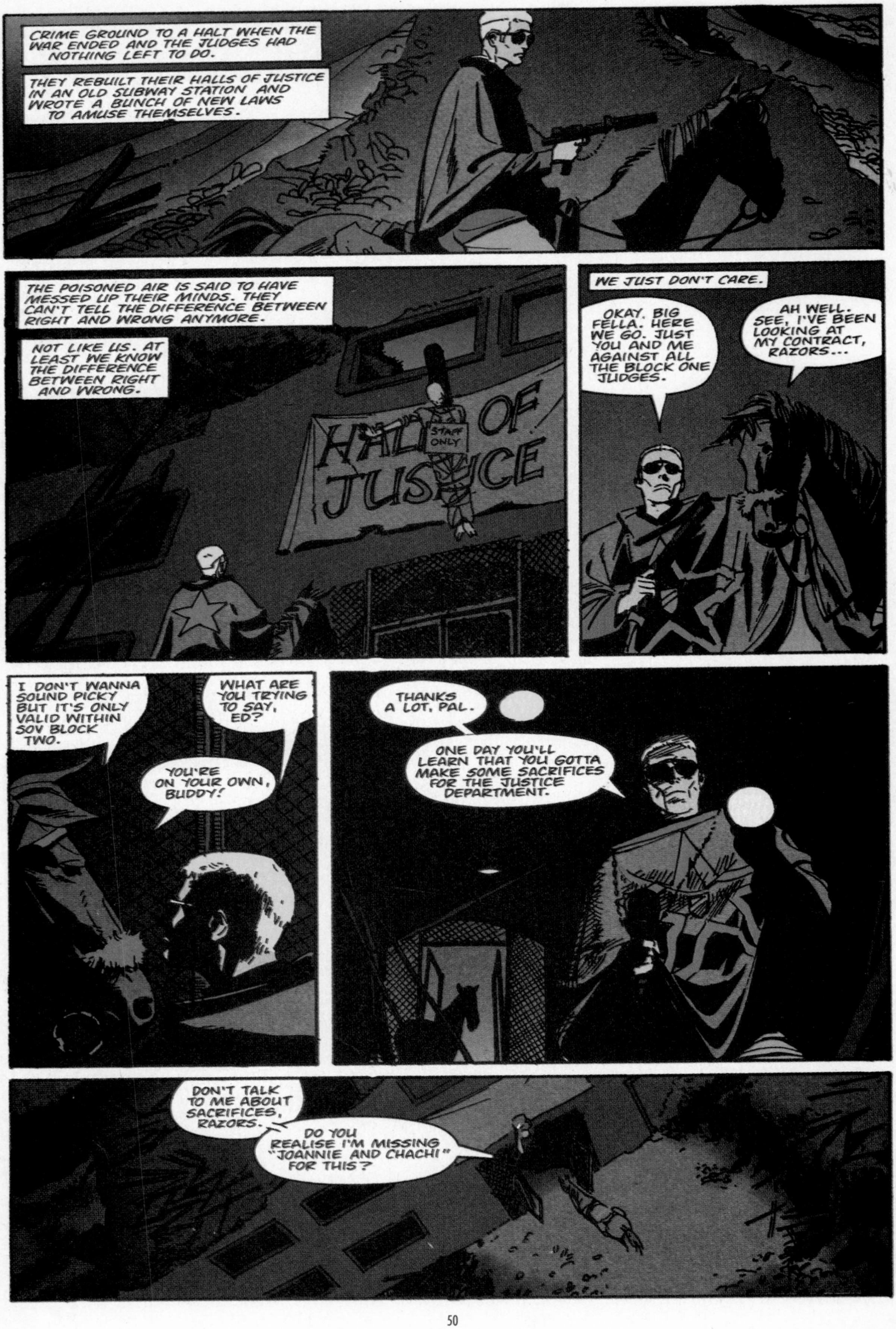
CRIME GROUND TO A HALT WHEN THE WAR ENDED AND THE JUDGES HAD NOTHING LEFT TO DO.
THEY REBUILT THEIR HALLS OF JUSTICE IN AN OLD SUBWAY STATION AND WROTE A BUNCH OF NEW LAWS TO AMUSE THEMSELVES.
THE POISONED AIR IS SAID TO HAVE MESSED UP THEIR MINDS. THEY CAN'T TELL THE DIFFERENCE BETWEEN RIGHT AND WRONG ANYMORE.
NOT LIKE US. AT LEAST WE KNOW THE DIFFERENCE BETWEEN RIGHT AND WRONG.
HALL OF JUSTICE
STAFF ONLY
WE JUST DON'T CARE.
OKAY. BIG FELLA. HERE WE GO. JUST YOU AND ME AGAINST ALL THE BLOCK ONE JUDGES.
AH WELL. SEE, I'VE BEEN LOOKING AT MY CONTRACT, RAZORS...
I DON'T WANNA SOUND PICKY BUT IT'S ONLY VALID WITHIN SOV BLOCK TWO.
WHAT ARE YOU TRYING TO SAY, ED?
YOU'RE ON YOUR OWN, BUDDY!
THANKS A LOT, PAL.
ONE DAY YOU'LL LEARN THAT YOU GOTTA MAKE SOME SACRIFICES FOR THE JUSTICE DEPARTMENT.
DON'T TALK TO ME ABOUT SACRIFICES, RAZORS.
DO YOU REALISE I'M MISSING "JOANNIE AND CHACHI" FOR THIS?

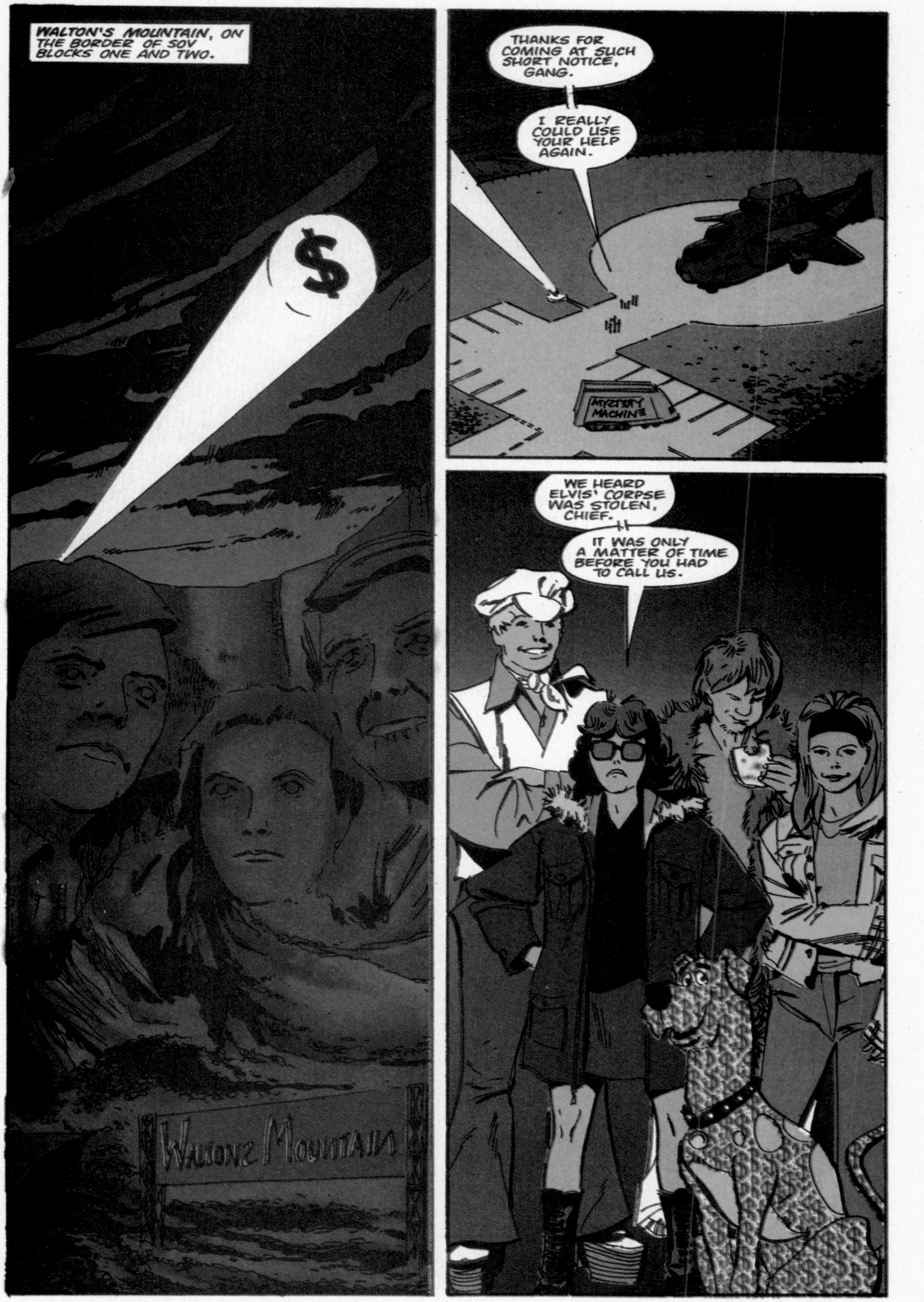
WALTON'S MOUNTAIN, ON THE BORDER OF SOV BLOCKS ONE AND TWO.
$
WALTONS MOUNTAIN
THANKS FOR COMING AT SUCH SHORT NOTICE, GANG.
I REALLY COULD USE YOUR HELP AGAIN.
MYSTERY MACHINE
WE HEARD ELVIS' CORPSE WAS STOLEN, CHIEF.
IT WAS ONLY A MATTER OF TIME BEFORE YOU HAD TO CALL US.

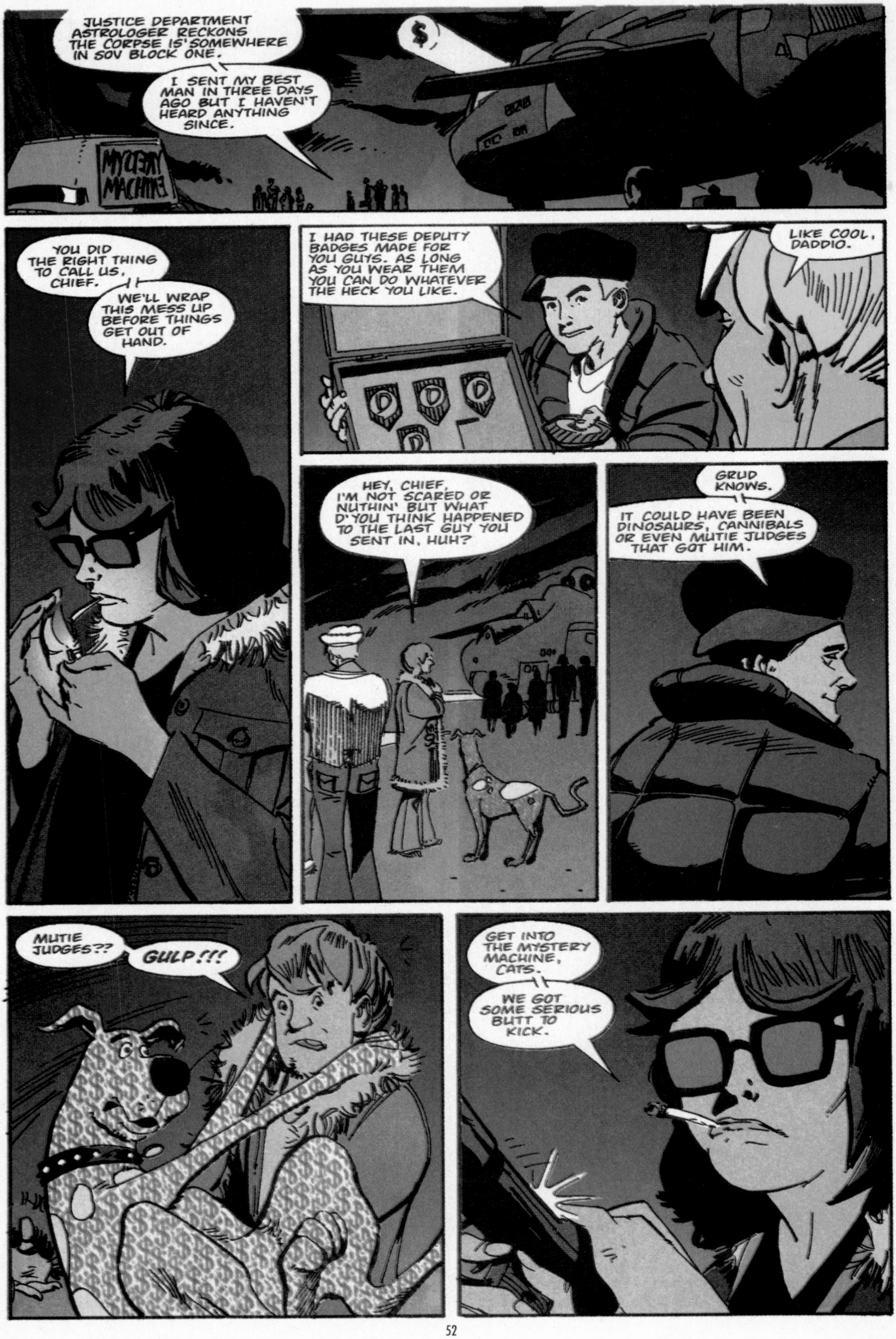
JUSTICE DEPARTMENT ASTROLOGER RECKONS THE CORPSE IS SOMEWHERE IN SOV BLOCK ONE.
I SENT MY BEST MAN IN THREE DAYS AGO BUT I HAVEN'T HEARD ANYTHING SINCE.
MYSTERY MACHINE
YOU DID THE RIGHT THING TO CALL US, CHIEF.
WE'LL WRAP THIS MESS UP BEFORE THINGS GET OUT OF HAND.
I HAD THESE DEPUTY BADGES MADE FOR YOU GUYS. AS LONG AS YOU WEAR THEM YOU CAN DO WHATEVER THE HECK YOU LIKE.
LIKE COOL, DADDIO.
HEY, CHIEF, I'M NOT SCARED OR NUTHIN' BUT WHAT D'YOU THINK HAPPENED TO THE LAST GUY YOU SENT IN, HUH?
GRUD KNOWS.
IT COULD HAVE BEEN DINOSAURS, CANNIBALS OR EVEN MUTIE JUDGES THAT GOT HIM.
MUTIE JUDGES??
GULP!!!
GET INTO THE MYSTERY MACHINE, CATS.
WE GOT SOME SERIOUS BUTT TO KICK.

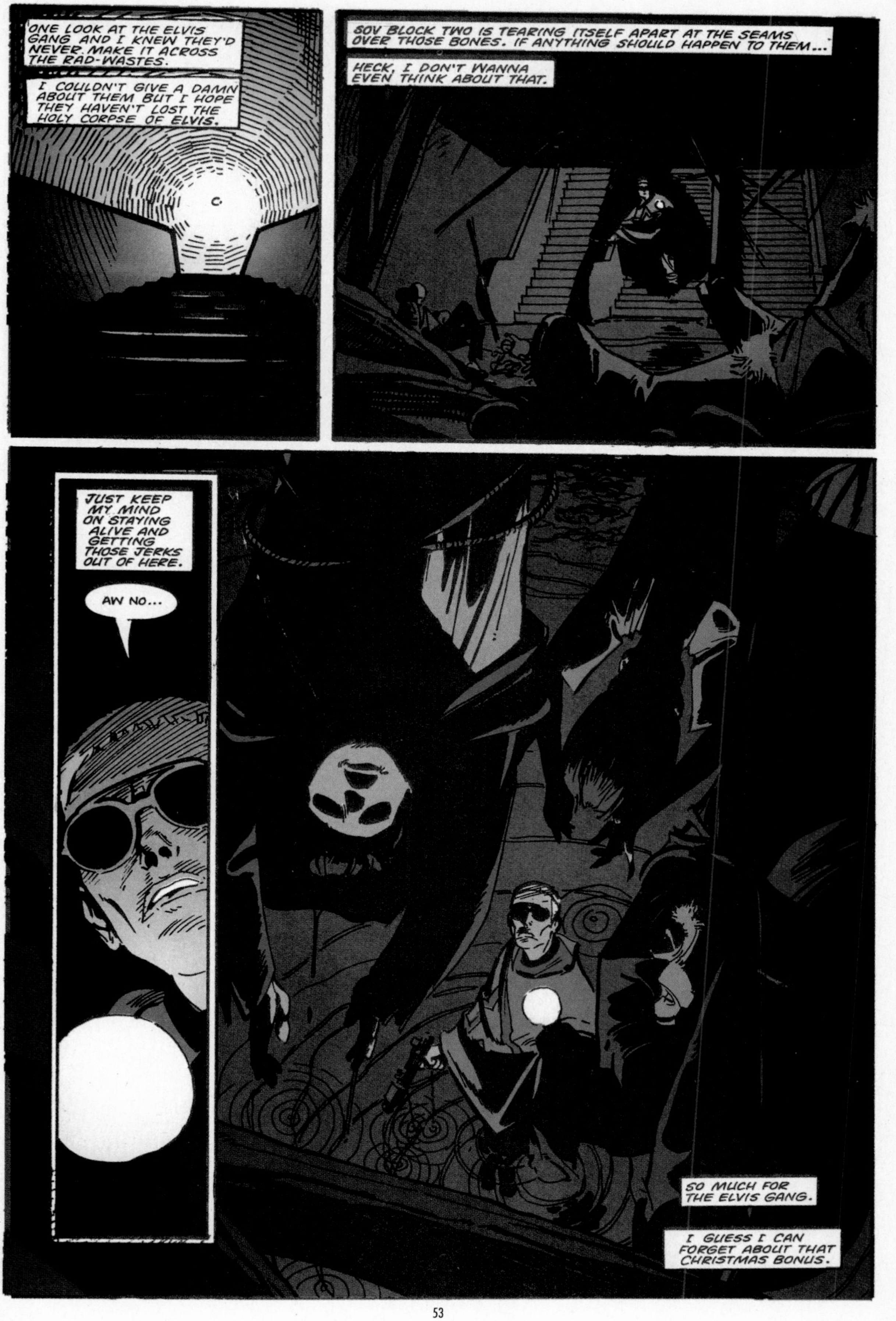
ONE LOOK AT THE ELVIS GANG AND I KNEW THEY'D NEVER MAKE IT ACROSS THE RAD-WASTES.
I COULDN'T GIVE A DAMN ABOUT THEM BUT I HOPE THEY HAVEN'T LOST THE HOLY CORPSE OF ELVIS.
SOV BLOCK TWO IS TEARING ITSELF APART AT THE SEAMS OVER THOSE BONES. IF ANYTHING SHOULD HAPPEN TO THEM...
HECK, I DON'T WANNA EVEN THINK ABOUT THAT.
JUST KEEP MY MIND ON STAYING ALIVE AND GETTING THOSE JERKS OUT OF HERE.
AW NO...
SO MUCH FOR THE ELVIS GANG.
I GUESS I CAN FORGET ABOUT THAT CHRISTMAS BONUS.

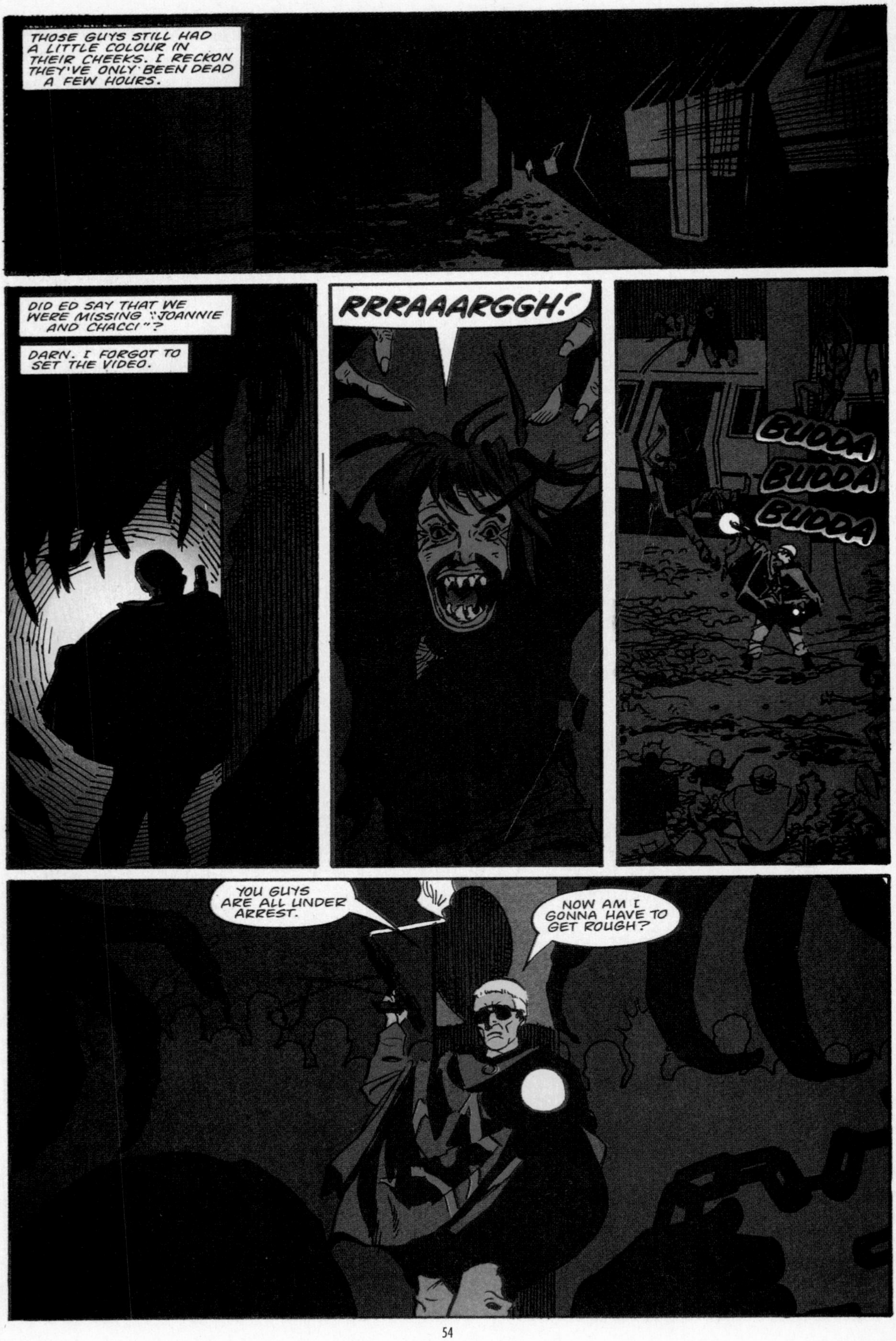
THOSE GUYS STILL HAD A LITTLE COLOUR IN THEIR CHEEKS. I RECKON THEY'VE ONLY BEEN DEAD A FEW HOURS.
DID ED SAY THAT WE WERE MISSING "JOANNIE AND CHACCI"?
DARN. I FORGOT TO SET THE VIDEO.
RRRAAARGGH!
BUDDA BUDDA BUDDA
YOU GUYS ARE ALL UNDER ARREST.
NOW AM I GONNA HAVE TO GET ROUGH?

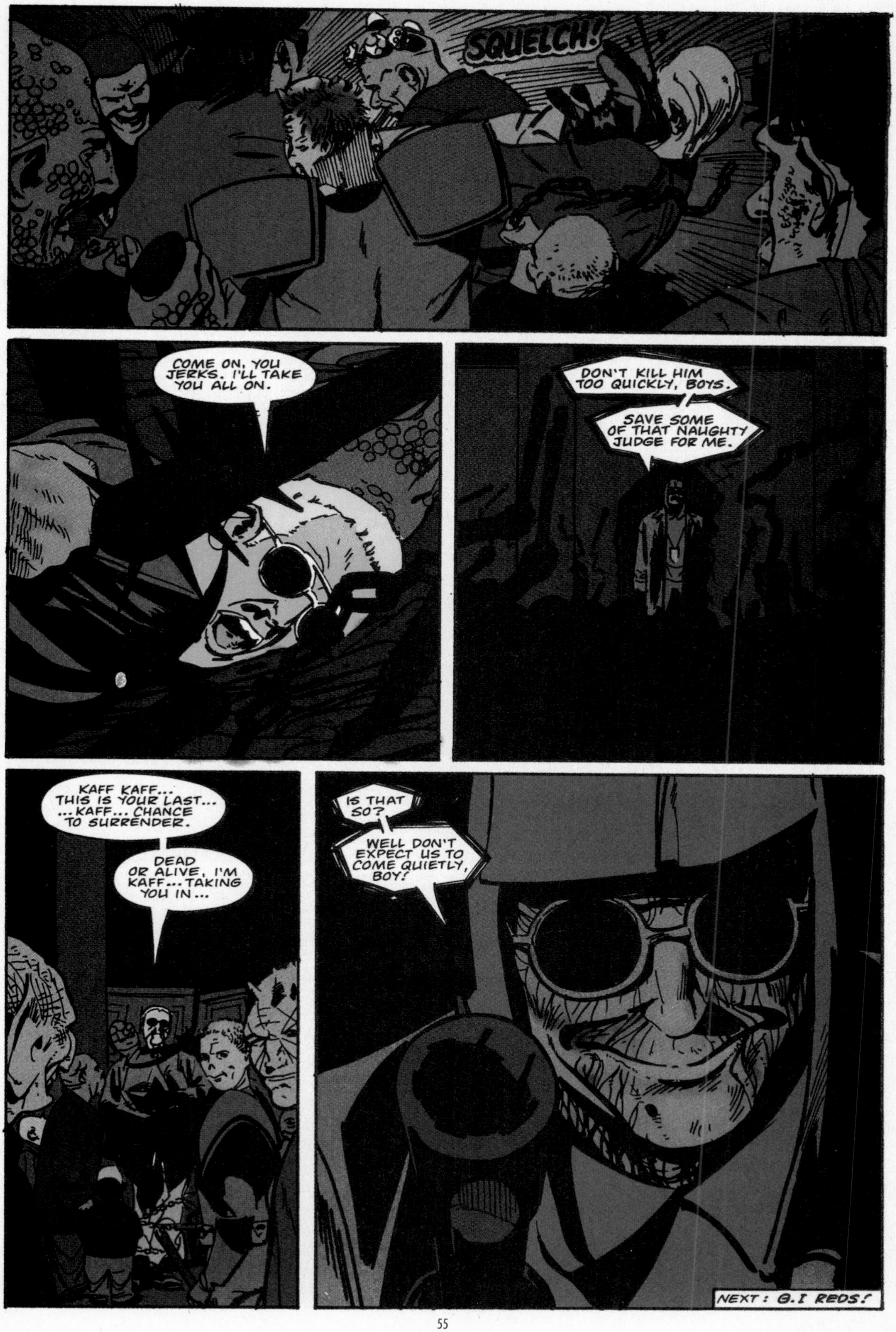

SQUELCH!
COME ON, YOU JERKS. I'LL TAKE YOU ALL ON.
DON'T KILL HIM TOO QUICKLY, BOYS.
SAVE SOME OF THAT NAUGHTY JUDGE FOR ME.
KAFF KAFF... THIS IS YOUR LAST... ...KAFF... CHANCE TO SURRENDER.
DEAD OR ALIVE, I'M KAFF... TAKING YOU IN...
IS THAT SO?
WELL DON'T EXPECT US TO COME QUIETLY, BOY!
NEXT: G.I REDS!

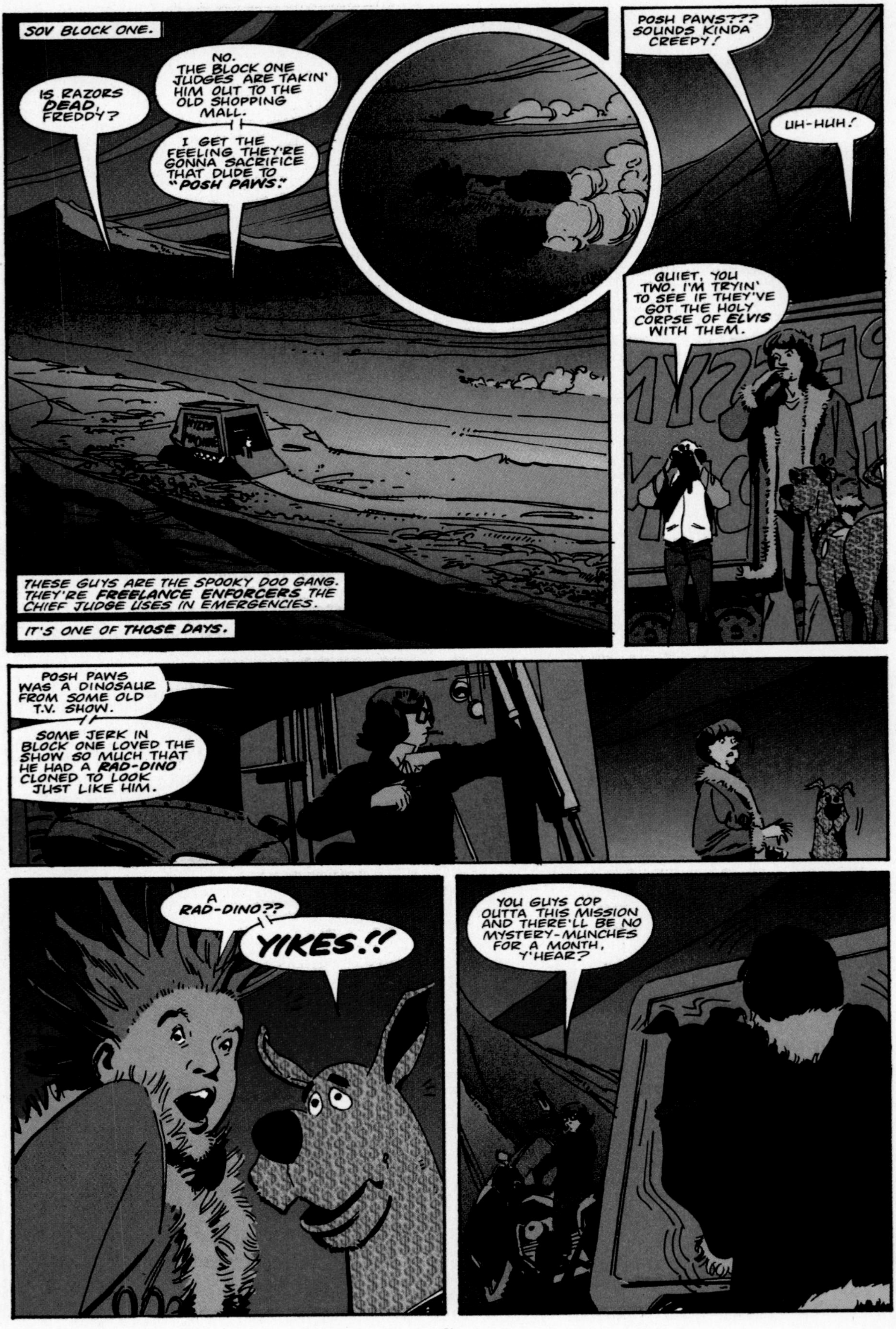
SOV BLOCK ONE.
IS RAZORS DEAD, FREDDY?
NO. THE BLOCK ONE JUDGES ARE TAKIN' HIM OUT TO THE OLD SHOPPING MALL.
I GET THE FEELING THEY'RE GONNA SACRIFICE THAT DUDE TO "POSH PAWS."
THESE GUYS ARE THE SPOOKY DOO GANG. THEY'RE FREELANCE ENFORCERS THE CHIEF JUDGE USES IN EMERGENCIES.
IT'S ONE OF THOSE DAYS.
POSH PAWS??? SOUNDS KINDA CREEPY!
UH-HUH!
QUIET, YOU TWO. I'M TRYIN' TO SEE IF THEY'VE GOT THE HOLY CORPSE OF ELVIS WITH THEM.
POSH PAWS WAS A DINOSAUR FROM SOME OLD T.V. SHOW.
SOME JERK IN BLOCK ONE LOVED THE SHOW SO MUCH THAT HE HAD A RAD-DINO CLONED TO LOOK JUST LIKE HIM.
A RAD-DINO??
YIKES.?!
YOU GUYS COP OUTTA THIS MISSION AND THERE'LL BE NO MYSTERY-MUNCHES FOR A MONTH, Y'HEAR?

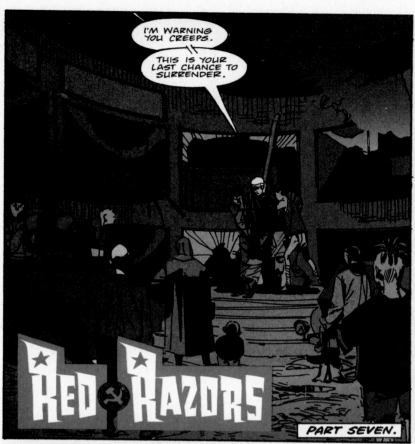

I'M WARNING YOU CREEPS.

THIS IS YOUR LAST CHANCE TO SURRENDER.

RED RAZORS

PART SEVEN.

BY THE POWER OF THIS SACRED "METAL MICKEY" ANNUAL I SENTENCE YOU TO DEATH FOR TRESPASSING ON OUR TURF.

I COMMAND THAT YOU BE EATEN ALIVE.

TAKE A RUNNING DROK, PAL.

THAT WASN'T VERY CLEVER, BOY...

JUDGE NUTMEG! JUDGE NUTMEG! HE'S COMING!

POSH PAWS IS COMING!

57

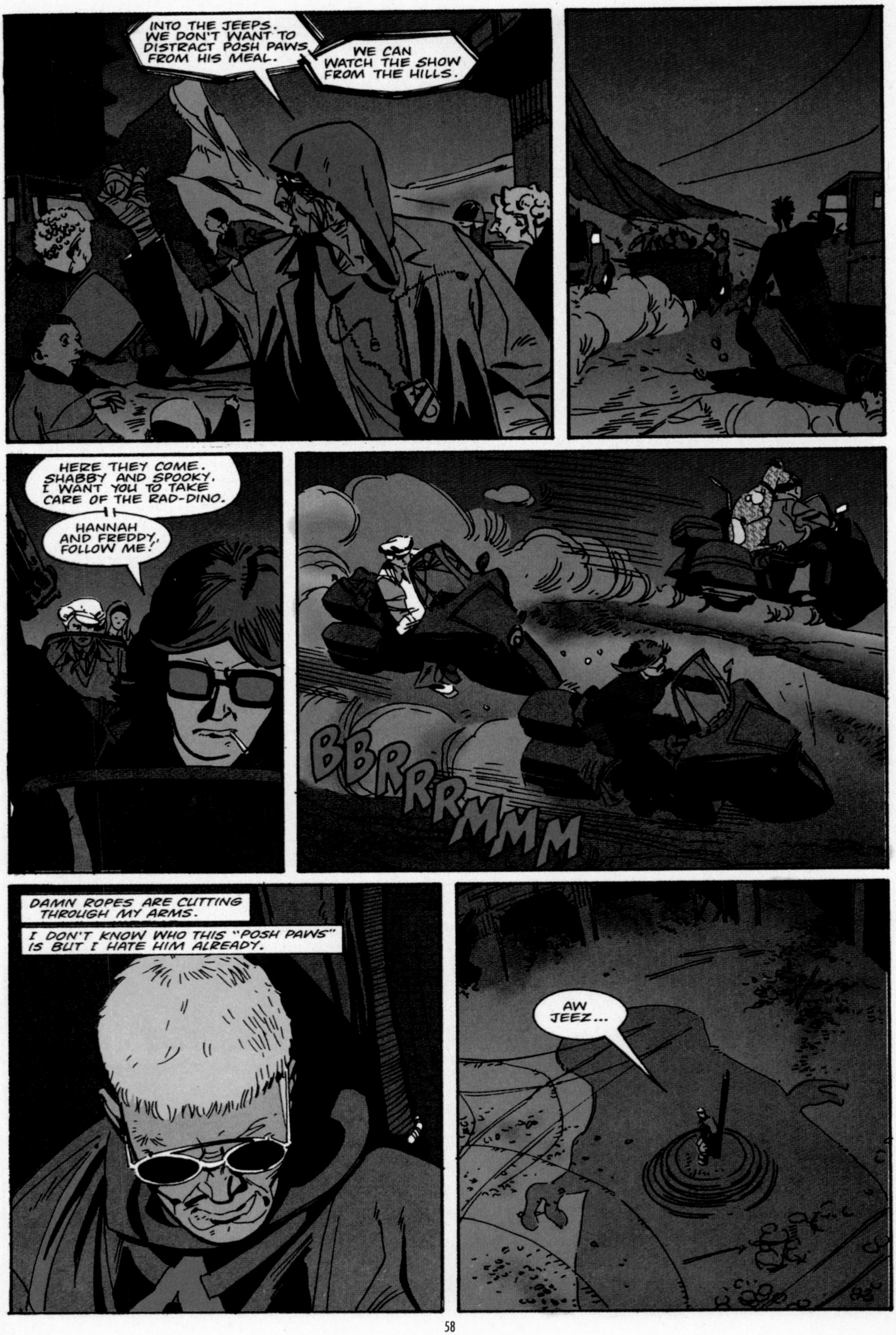
INTO THE JEEPS. WE DON'T WANT TO DISTRACT POSH PAWS FROM HIS MEAL.
WE CAN WATCH THE SHOW FROM THE HILLS.
HERE THEY COME. SHABBY AND SPOOKY, I WANT YOU TO TAKE CARE OF THE RAD-DINO.
HANNAH AND FREDDY, FOLLOW ME!
BBRRRMMMM
DAMN ROPES ARE CUTTING THROUGH MY ARMS.
I DON'T KNOW WHO THIS "POSH PAWS" IS BUT I HATE HIM ALREADY.
AW JEEZ...

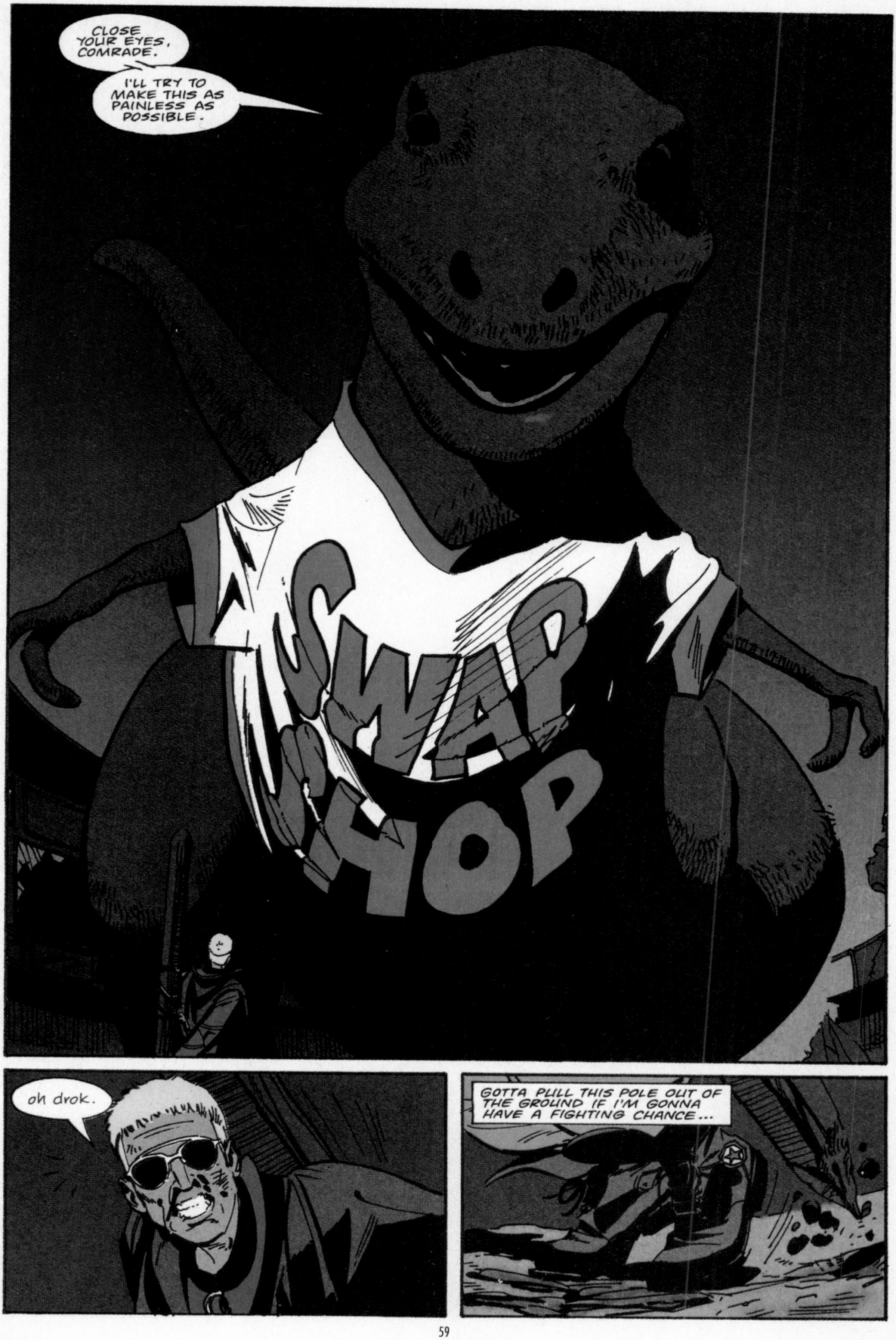

CLOSE YOUR EYES, COMRADE.
I'LL TRY TO MAKE THIS AS PAINLESS AS POSSIBLE.
oh drok.
GOTTA PULL THIS POLE OUT OF THE GROUND IF I'M GONNA HAVE A FIGHTING CHANCE...

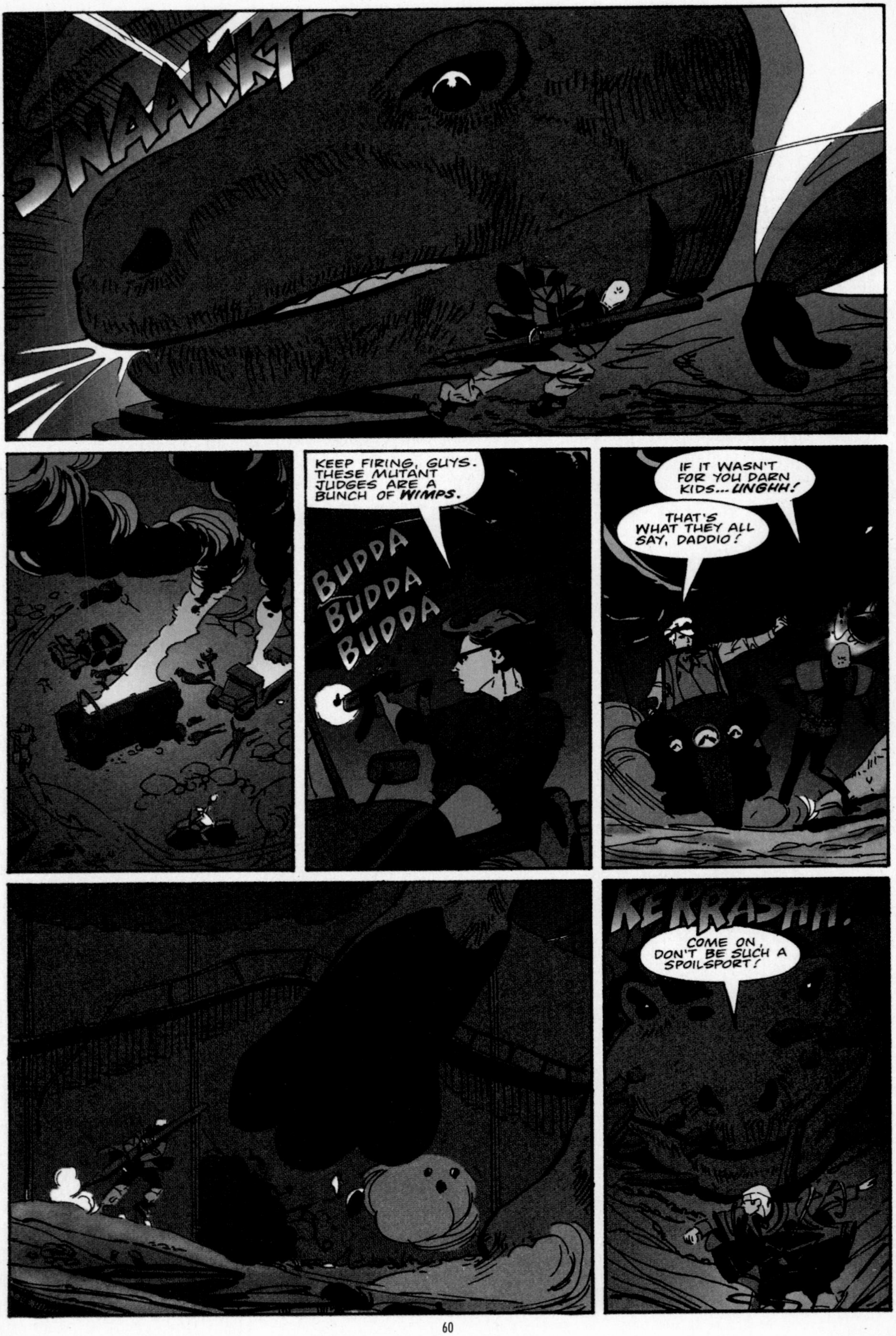

SNAAKKT
KEEP FIRING, GUYS. THESE MUTANT JUDGES ARE A BUNCH OF WIMPS.
BUDDA BUDDA BUDDA
IF IT WASN'T FOR YOU DARN KIDS... UNGHH!
THAT'S WHAT THEY ALL SAY, DADDIO!
KERRASHH!
COME ON, DON'T BE SUCH A SPOILSPORT!

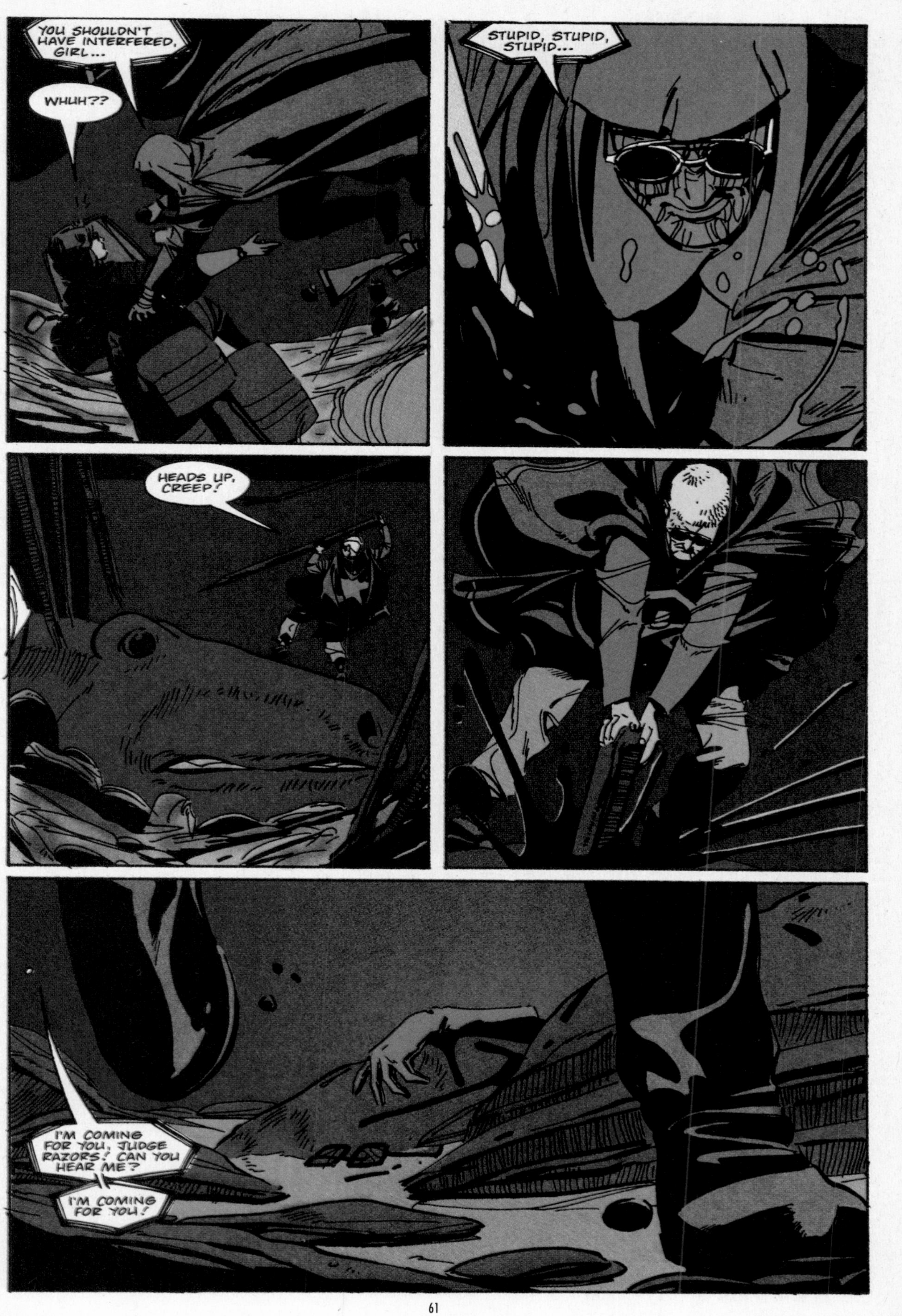

YOU SHOULDN'T HAVE INTERFERED, GIRL...
WHUH??
STUPID, STUPID, STUPID...
HEADS UP, CREEP!
I'M COMING FOR YOU, JUDGE RAZORS! CAN YOU HEAR ME?
I'M COMING FOR YOU!

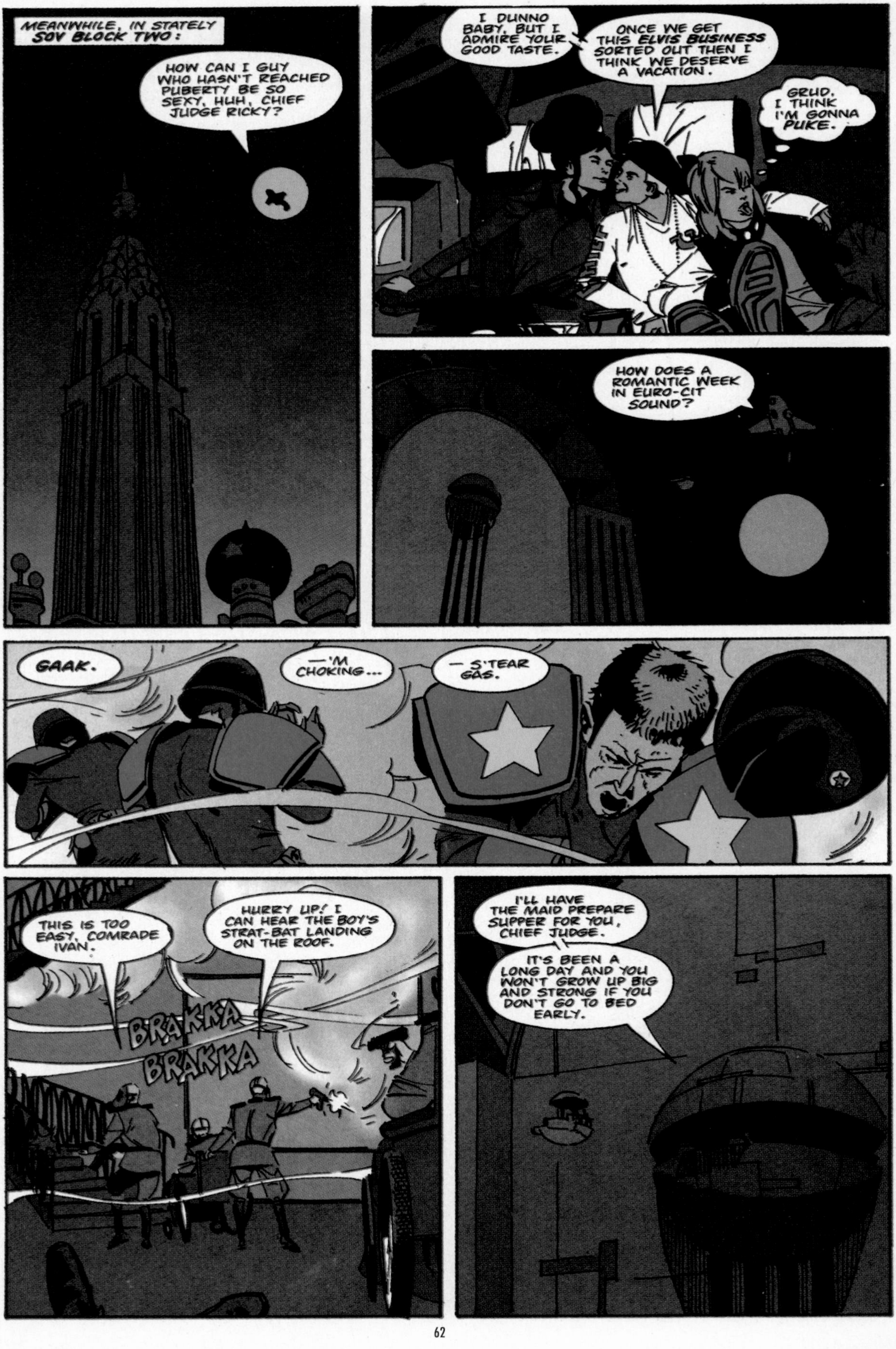

MEANWHILE, IN STATELY SOV BLOCK TWO:
HOW CAN I GUY WHO HASN'T REACHED PUBERTY BE SO SEXY, HUH, CHIEF JUDGE RICKY?
I DUNNO BABY, BUT I ADMIRE YOUR GOOD TASTE.
ONCE WE GET THIS ELVIS BUSINESS SORTED OUT THEN I THINK WE DESERVE A VACATION.
GRUD. I THINK I'M GONNA PUKE.
HOW DOES A ROMANTIC WEEK IN EURO-CIT SOUND?
GAAK.
—'M CHOKING...
— S'TEAR GAS.
THIS IS TOO EASY, COMRADE IVAN.
HURRY UP! I CAN HEAR THE BOY'S STRAT-BAT LANDING ON THE ROOF.
BRAKKA
BRAKKA
I'LL HAVE THE MAID PREPARE SUPPER FOR YOU, CHIEF JUDGE.
IT'S BEEN A LONG DAY AND YOU WON'T GROW UP BIG AND STRONG IF YOU DON'T GO TO BED EARLY.

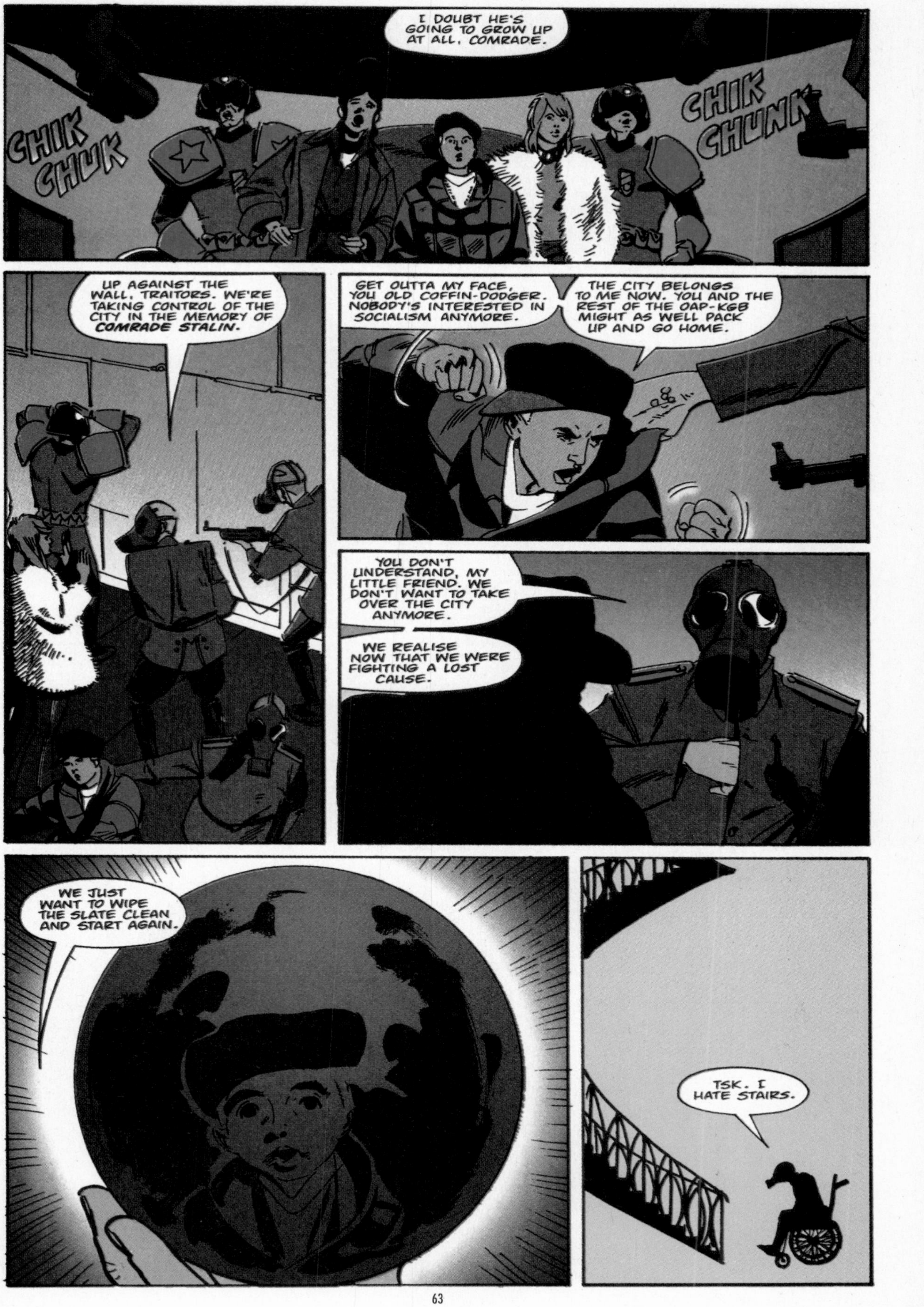
I DOUBT HE'S GOING TO GROW UP AT ALL, COMRADE.
CHIK CHUK
CHIK CHUNK
UP AGAINST THE WALL, TRAITORS. WE'RE TAKING CONTROL OF THE CITY IN THE MEMORY OF COMRADE STALIN.
GET OUTTA MY FACE, YOU OLD COFFIN-DODGER. NOBODY'S INTERESTED IN SOCIALISM ANYMORE.
THE CITY BELONGS TO ME NOW. YOU AND THE REST OF THE OAP-KGB MIGHT AS WELL PACK UP AND GO HOME.
YOU DON'T UNDERSTAND, MY LITTLE FRIEND. WE DON'T WANT TO TAKE OVER THE CITY ANYMORE.
WE REALISE NOW THAT WE WERE FIGHTING A LOST CAUSE.
WE JUST WANT TO WIPE THE SLATE CLEAN AND START AGAIN.
TSK. I HATE STAIRS.

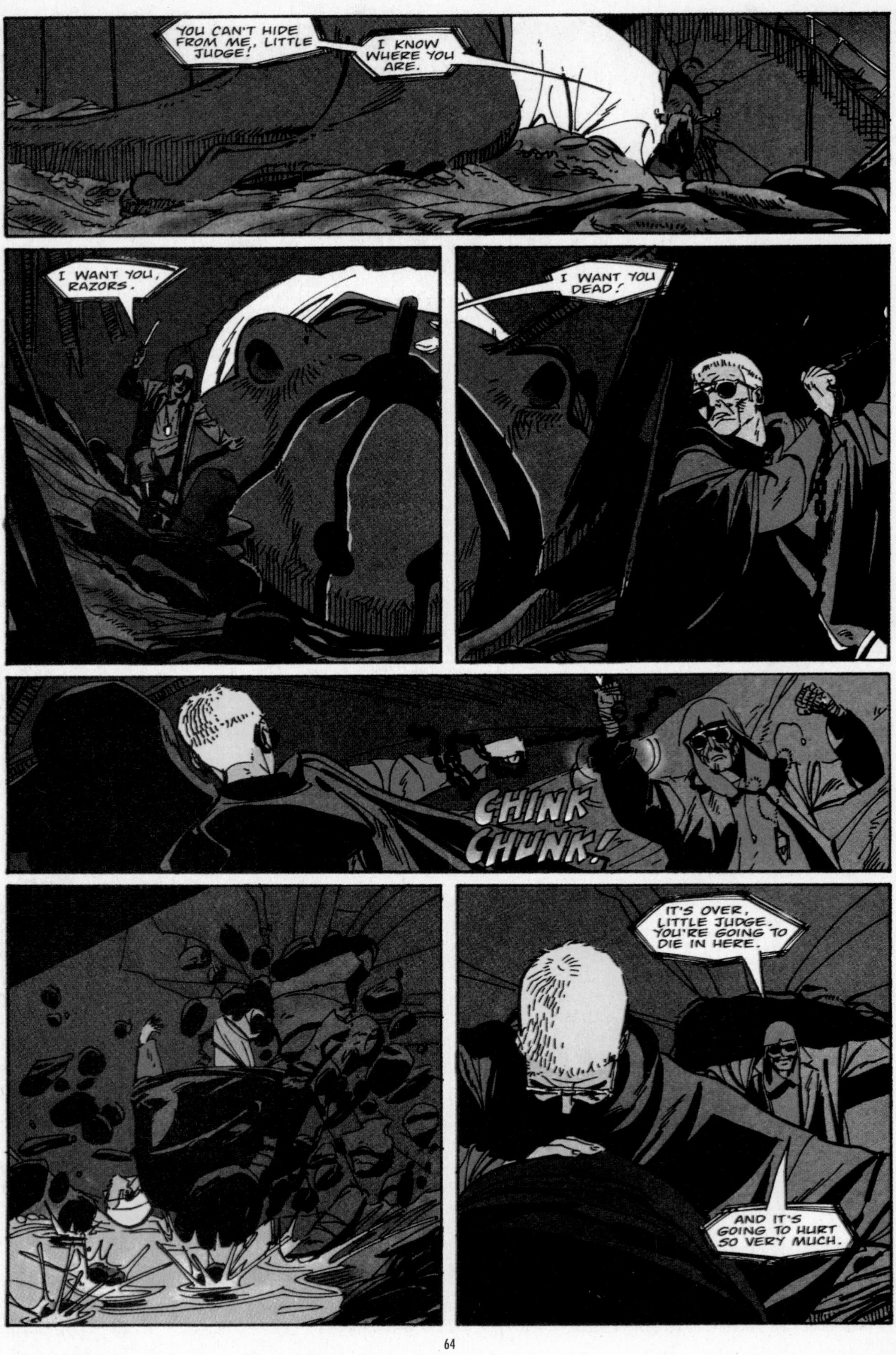

YOU CAN'T HIDE FROM ME, LITTLE JUDGE!
I KNOW WHERE YOU ARE.
I WANT YOU, RAZORS.
I WANT YOU DEAD!
CHINK CHUNK!
IT'S OVER, LITTLE JUDGE. YOU'RE GOING TO DIE IN HERE.
AND IT'S GOING TO HURT SO VERY MUCH.

MY LEGS FEEL LIKE LEAD. I CAN HARDLY KEEP MY BALANCE.

YOU'RE SLOWING DOWN, BOY...

...NOT MUCH LIFE LEFT IN YOU.

WHHUMFF!

SSSKKRIPPP!

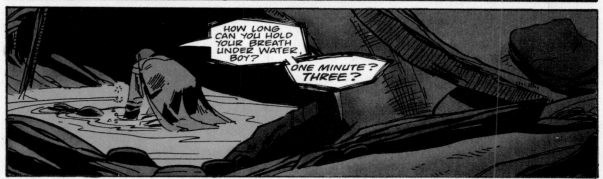

HOW LONG CAN YOU HOLD YOUR BREATH UNDER WATER, BOY?

ONE MINUTE? THREE?

MEANWHILE, OUTSIDE:

I HOPE IT DOESN'T RAIN. I FANCY A NICE GAME OF SWING-BALL WHEN WE GET BACK HOME.

65

NEXT: BABY GOT THE REDS!

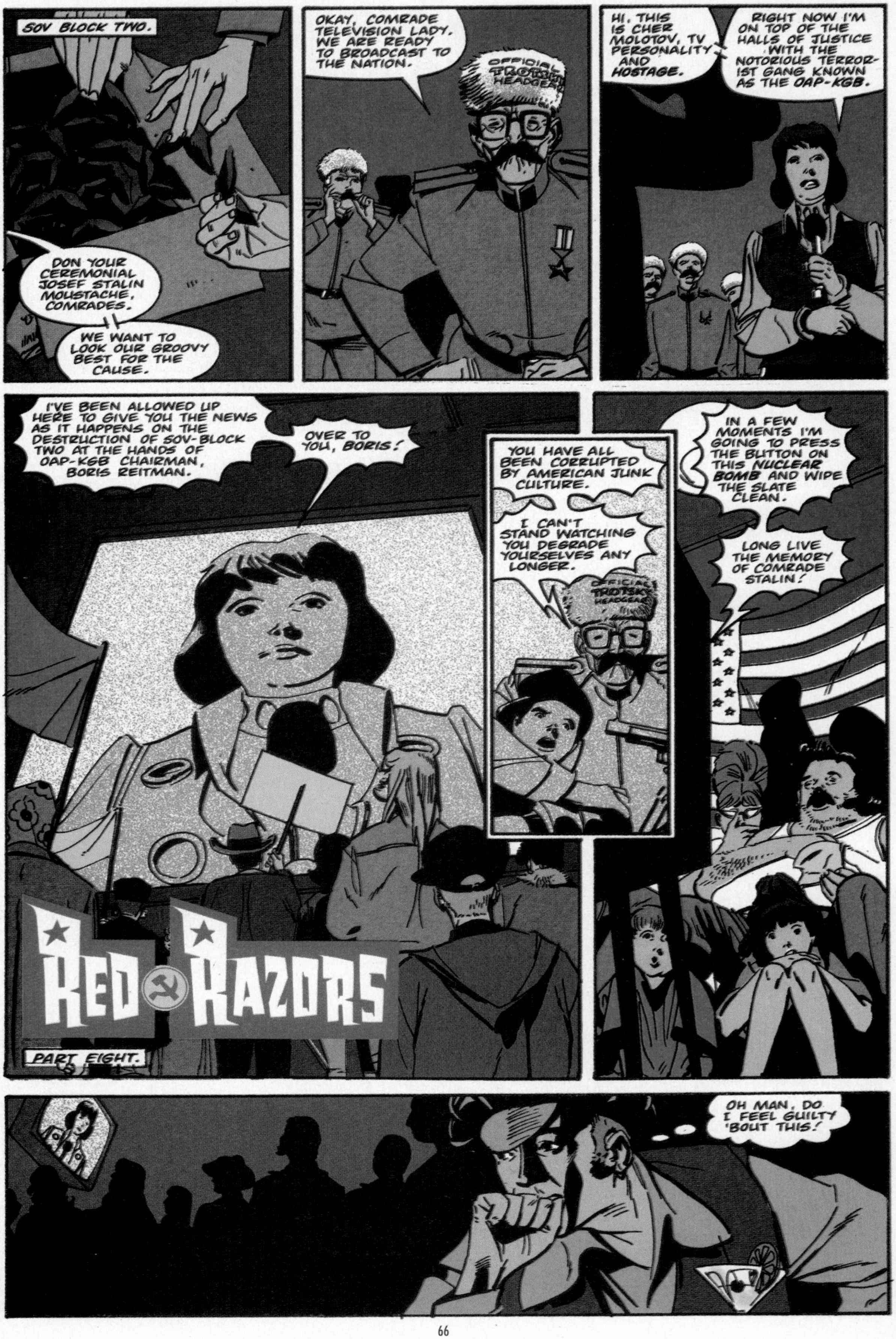
SOV BLOCK TWO.
DON YOUR CEREMONIAL JOSEF STALIN MOUSTACHE, COMRADES.
WE WANT TO LOOK OUR GROOVY BEST FOR THE CAUSE.
OKAY, COMRADE TELEVISION LADY. WE ARE READY TO BROADCAST TO THE NATION.
OFFICIAL TROTSKY HEADGEAR
HI. THIS IS CHER MOLOTOV, TV PERSONALITY AND HOSTAGE.
RIGHT NOW I'M ON TOP OF THE HALLS OF JUSTICE WITH THE NOTORIOUS TERRORIST GANG KNOWN AS THE OAP-KGB.
I'VE BEEN ALLOWED UP HERE TO GIVE YOU THE NEWS AS IT HAPPENS ON THE DESTRUCTION OF SOV-BLOCK TWO AT THE HANDS OF OAP-KGB CHAIRMAN, BORIS REITMAN.
OVER TO YOU, BORIS!
RED RAZORS
PART EIGHT.
YOU HAVE ALL BEEN CORRUPTED BY AMERICAN JUNK CULTURE.
I CAN'T STAND WATCHING YOU DEGRADE YOURSELVES ANY LONGER.
OFFICIAL TROTSKY HEADGEAR
IN A FEW MOMENTS I'M GOING TO PRESS THE BUTTON ON THIS NUCLEAR BOMB AND WIPE THE SLATE CLEAN.
LONG LIVE THE MEMORY OF COMRADE STALIN!
OH MAN, DO I FEEL GUILTY 'BOUT THIS!

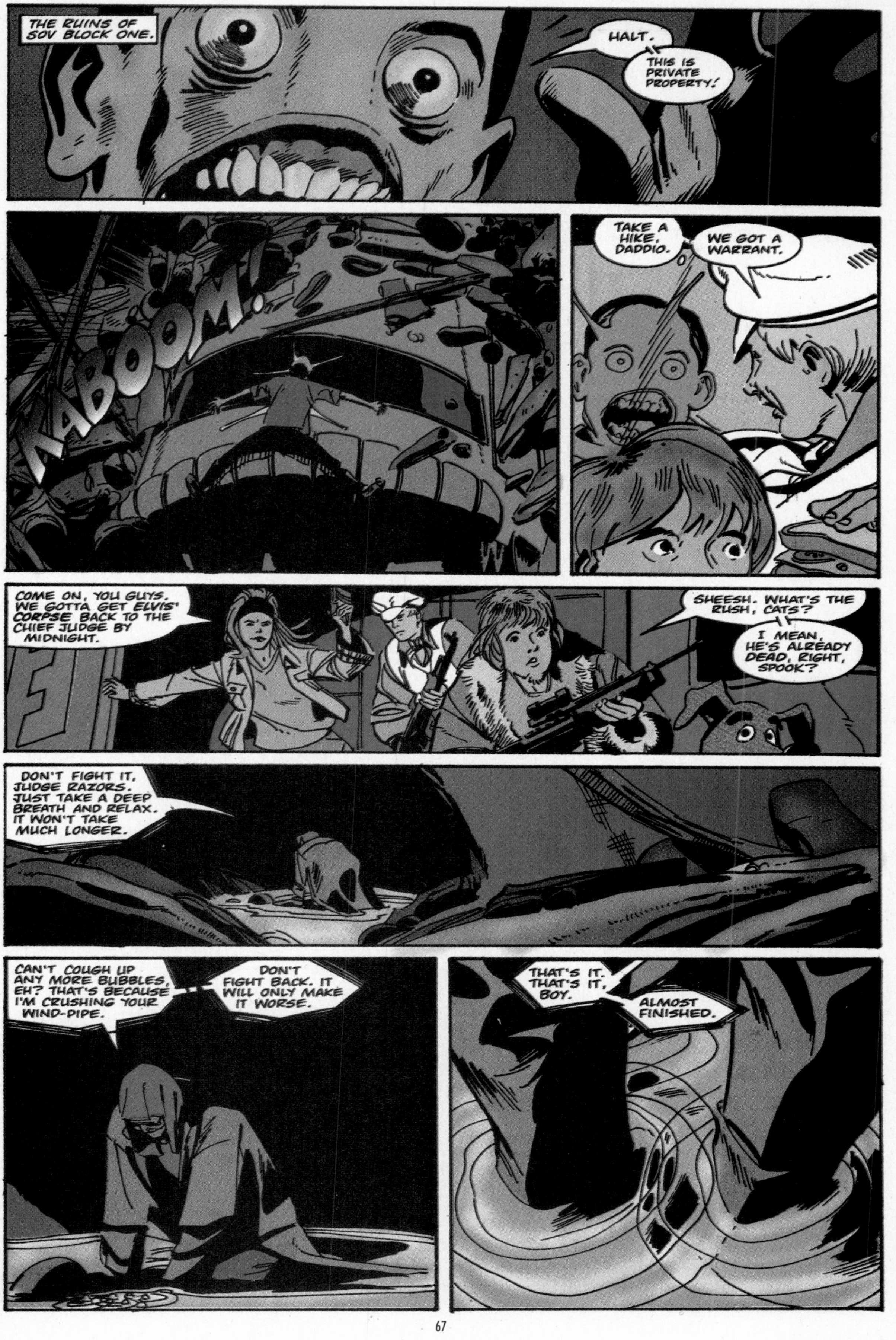
THE RUINS OF SOV BLOCK ONE.
HALT.
THIS IS PRIVATE PROPERTY!
KABOOM!
TAKE A HIKE, DADDIO.
WE GOT A WARRANT.
COME ON, YOU GUYS. WE GOTTA GET ELVIS' CORPSE BACK TO THE CHIEF JUDGE BY MIDNIGHT.
SHEESH. WHAT'S THE RUSH, CATS?
I MEAN, HE'S ALREADY DEAD, RIGHT, SPOOK?
DON'T FIGHT IT, JUDGE RAZORS. JUST TAKE A DEEP BREATH AND RELAX. IT WON'T TAKE MUCH LONGER.
CAN'T COUGH UP ANY MORE BUBBLES, EH? THAT'S BECAUSE I'M CRUSHING YOUR WIND-PIPE.
DON'T FIGHT BACK. IT WILL ONLY MAKE IT WORSE.
THAT'S IT. THAT'S IT, BOY.
ALMOST FINISHED.

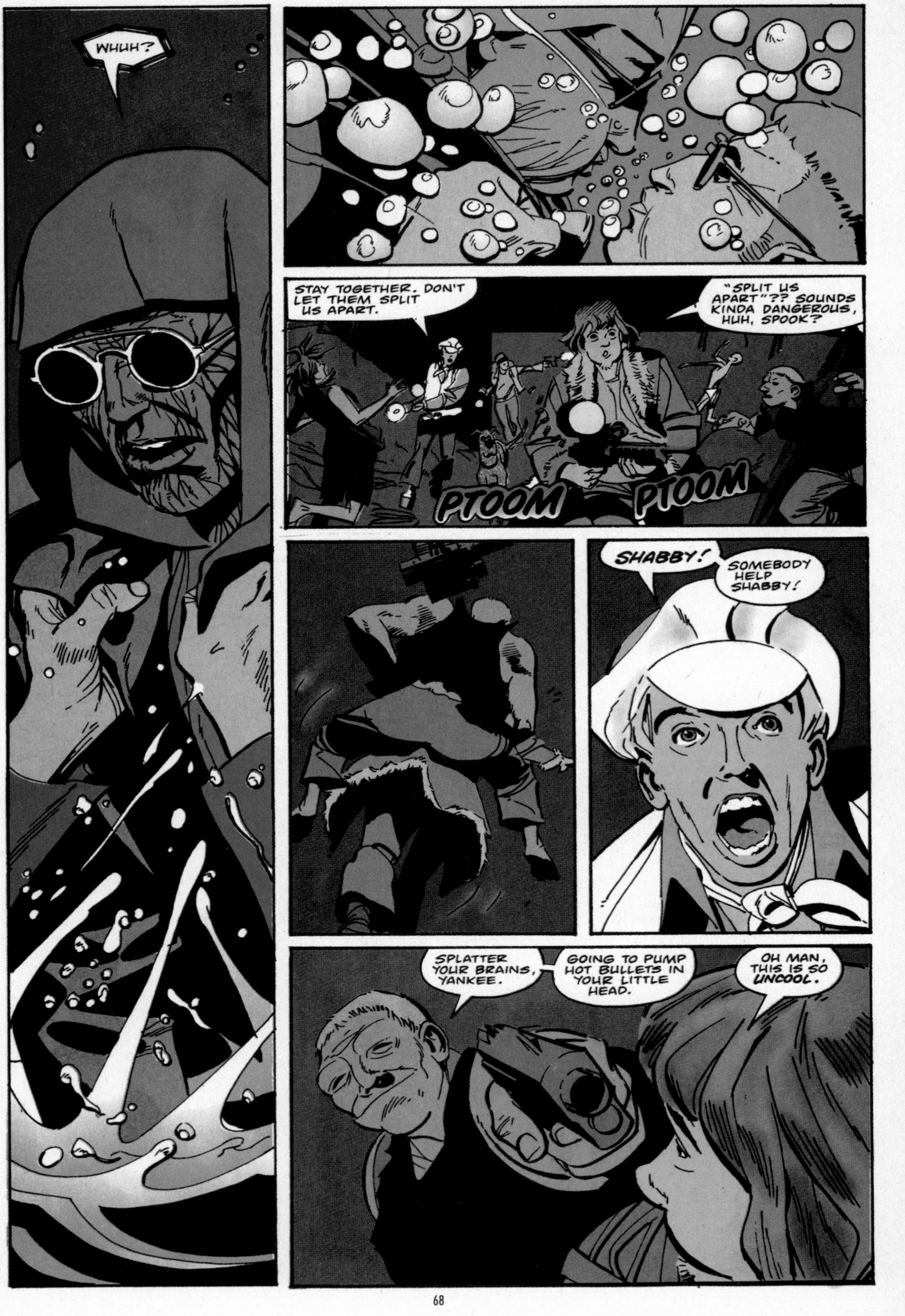
WHUH?
STAY TOGETHER. DON'T LET THEM SPLIT US APART.
"SPLIT US APART"?? SOUNDS KINDA DANGEROUS, HUH, SPOOK?
PTOOM
PTOOM
SHABBY!
SOMEBODY HELP SHABBY!
SPLATTER YOUR BRAINS, YANKEE.
GOING TO PUMP HOT BULLETS IN YOUR LITTLE HEAD.
OH MAN, THIS IS SO UNCOOL.

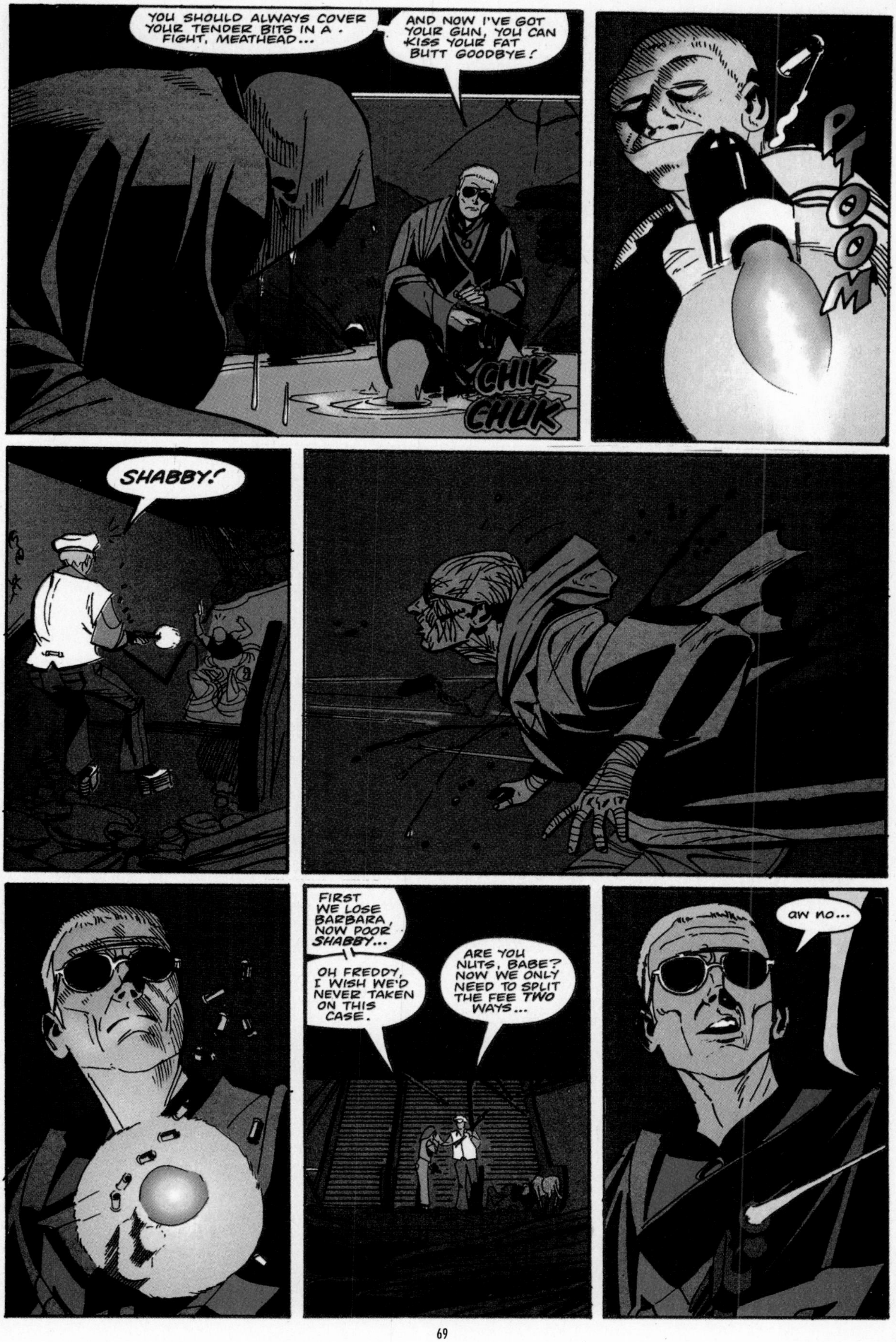
YOU SHOULD ALWAYS COVER YOUR TENDER BITS IN A FIGHT, MEATHEAD...
AND NOW I'VE GOT YOUR GUN, YOU CAN KISS YOUR FAT BUTT GOODBYE!
CHIK CHUK
PTOOM
SHABBY!
FIRST WE LOSE BARBARA, NOW POOR SHABBY...
OH FREDDY, I WISH WE'D NEVER TAKEN ON THIS CASE.
ARE YOU NUTS, BABE? NOW WE ONLY NEED TO SPLIT THE FEE TWO WAYS...
aw no...

I ... FELT THAT, YOU LITTLE WEASEL!

OVER HERE, HANNAH. SPOOKY'S FOUND SOMETHING!

GRUD IN GRACELAND! IT'S HIM!

LOOK, FREDDY... IT'S SAINT ELVIS!

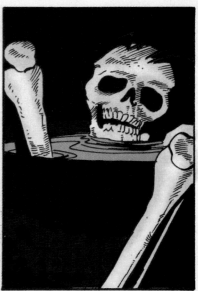

KRACKM

RELAX, JUDGE RAZORS.

YOU'RE GOING TO A NICER PLACE.

WHUMPFFF

YOU'RE STARTING TO SHIVER, LITTLE JUDGE. THAT MEANS WE'RE ALMOST FINISHED.

THAT MEANS THE FUN'S ALMOST OVER.

LOOK WHAT I FOUND, BOY JUDGE — A LAZ-SAW!

BEATS THAT NIGHT-STICK OF YOURS ANYDAY, EH?

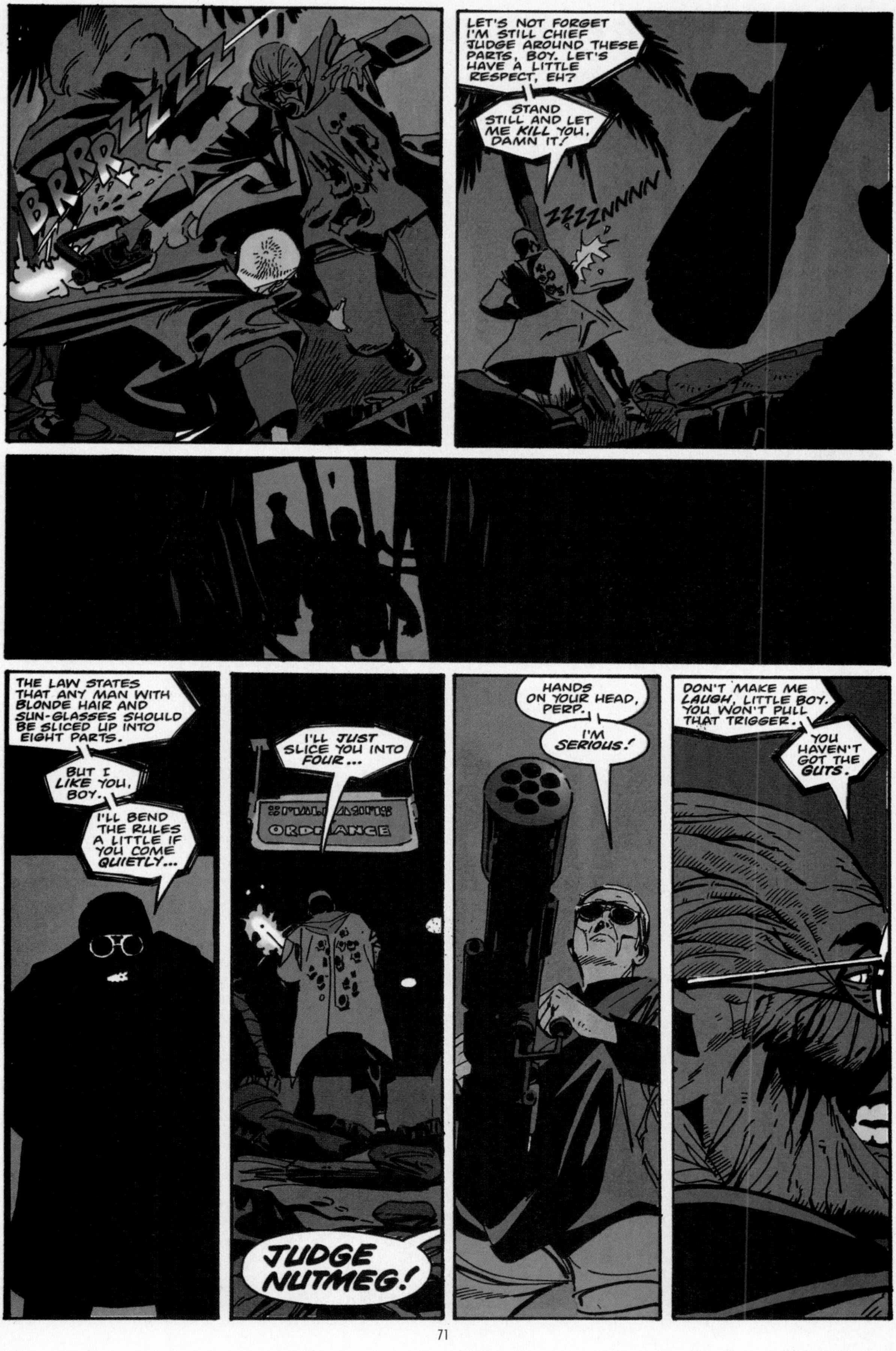
BRRRZZZZZ
LET'S NOT FORGET I'M STILL CHIEF JUDGE AROUND THESE PARTS, BOY. LET'S HAVE A LITTLE RESPECT, EH?
STAND STILL AND LET ME KILL YOU, DAMN IT!
ZZZZNNNN
THE LAW STATES THAT ANY MAN WITH BLONDE HAIR AND SUN-GLASSES SHOULD BE SLICED UP INTO EIGHT PARTS.
BUT I LIKE YOU, BOY.
I'LL BEND THE RULES A LITTLE IF YOU COME QUIETLY...
I'LL JUST SLICE YOU INTO FOUR...
ORDNANCE
JUDGE NUTMEG!
HANDS ON YOUR HEAD, PERP.
I'M SERIOUS!
DON'T MAKE ME LAUGH, LITTLE BOY. YOU WON'T PULL THAT TRIGGER.
YOU HAVEN'T GOT THE GUTS.

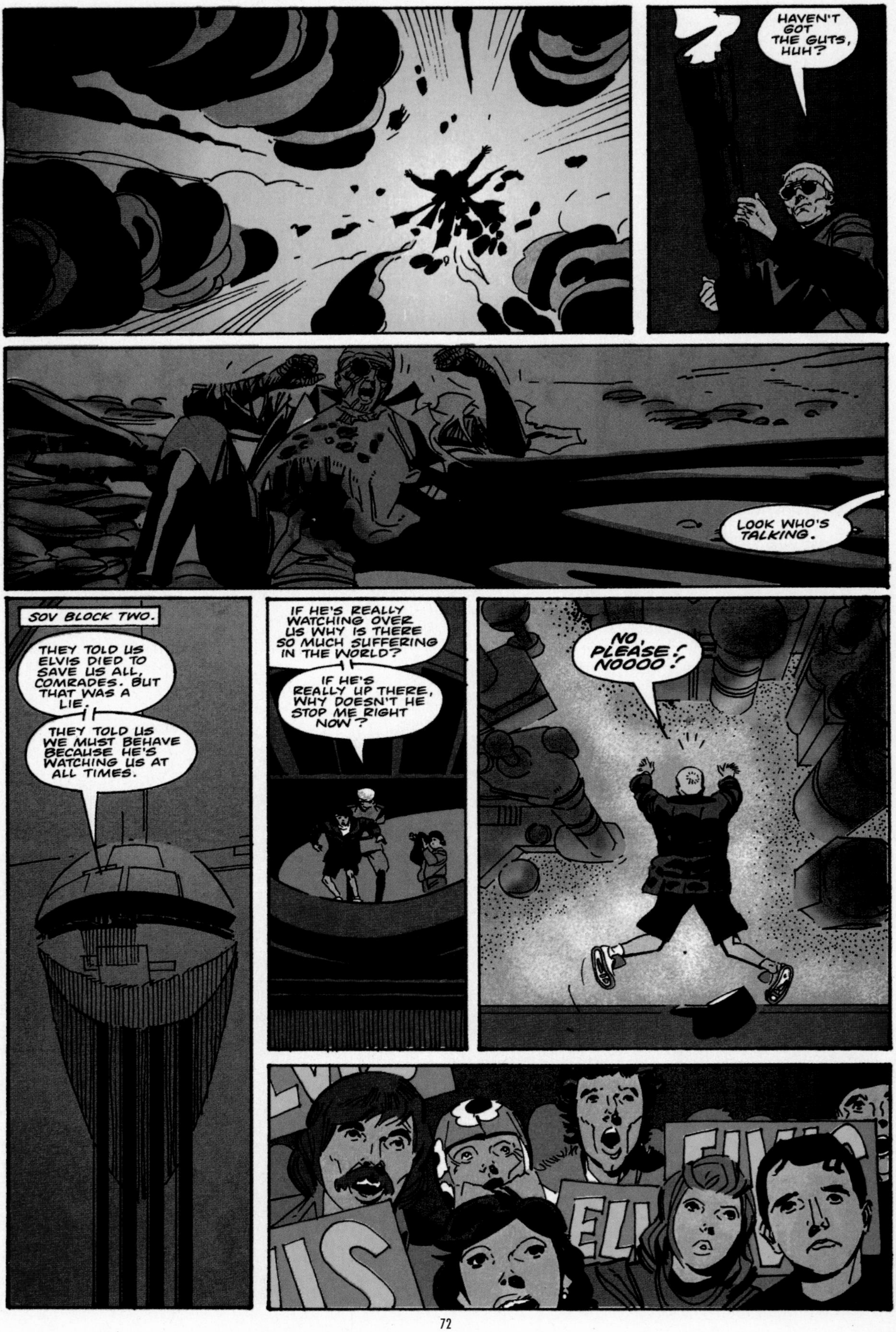
HAVEN'T GOT THE GUTS, HUH?
LOOK WHO'S TALKING.
SOV BLOCK TWO.
THEY TOLD US ELVIS DIED TO SAVE US ALL, COMRADES. BUT THAT WAS A LIE.
THEY TOLD US WE MUST BEHAVE BECAUSE HE'S WATCHING US AT ALL TIMES.
IF HE'S REALLY WATCHING OVER US WHY IS THERE SO MUCH SUFFERING IN THE WORLD?
IF HE'S REALLY UP THERE, WHY DOESN'T HE STOP ME RIGHT NOW?
NO, PLEASE! NOOOO!

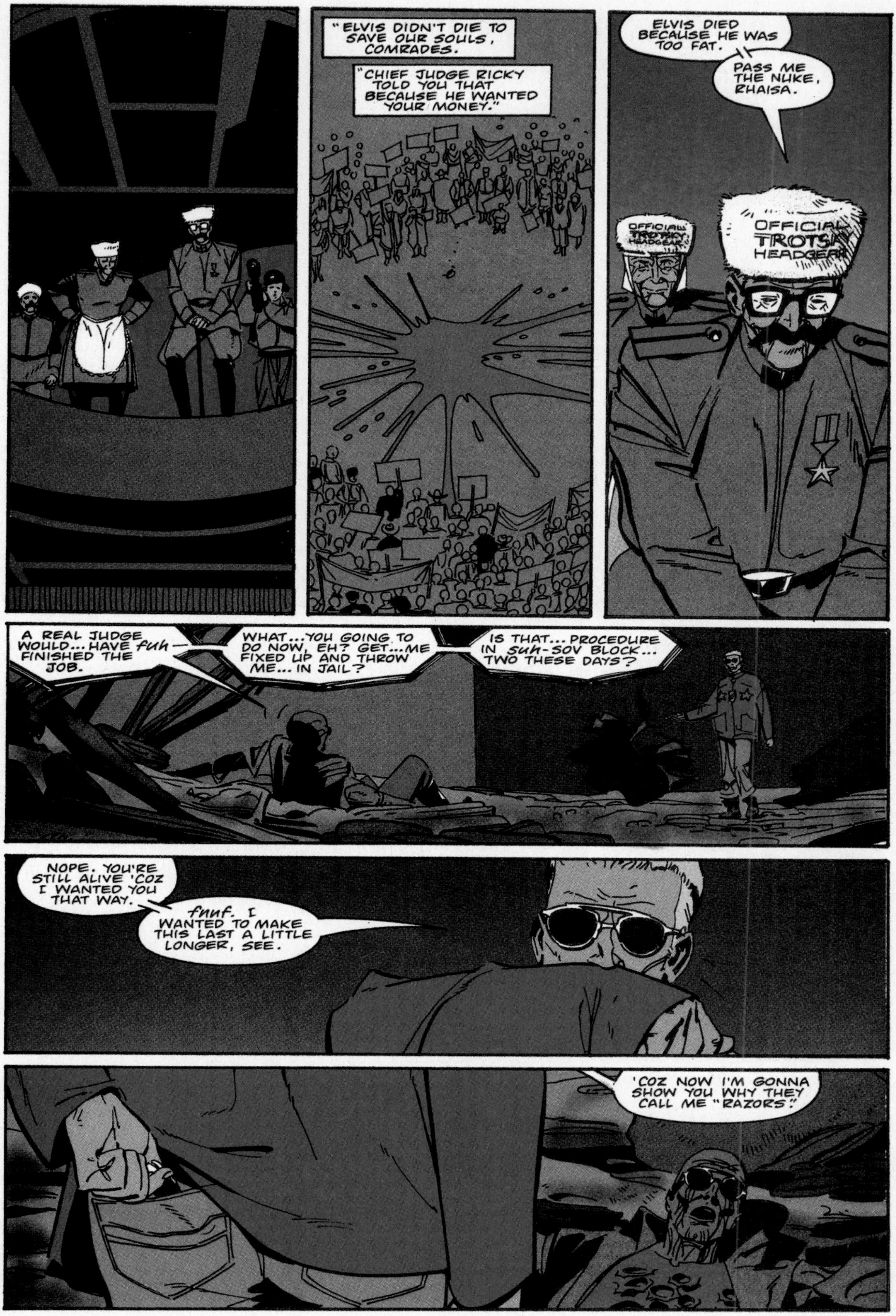
"ELVIS DIDN'T DIE TO SAVE OUR SOULS, COMRADES.
"CHIEF JUDGE RICKY TOLD YOU THAT BECAUSE HE WANTED YOUR MONEY."
ELVIS DIED BECAUSE HE WAS TOO FAT.
PASS ME THE NUKE, RHAISA.
OFFICIAL TROTSKY HEADGEAR
OFFICIAL TROTSKY HEADGEAR
A REAL JUDGE WOULD... HAVE *fuh*— FINISHED THE JOB.
WHAT... YOU GOING TO DO NOW, EH? GET... ME FIXED UP AND THROW ME... IN JAIL?
IS THAT... PROCEDURE IN *suh*-SOV BLOCK... TWO THESE DAYS?
NOPE. YOU'RE STILL ALIVE 'COZ I WANTED YOU THAT WAY.
fnuf. I WANTED TO MAKE THIS LAST A LITTLE LONGER, SEE.
'COZ NOW I'M GONNA SHOW YOU WHY THEY CALL ME "RAZORS".

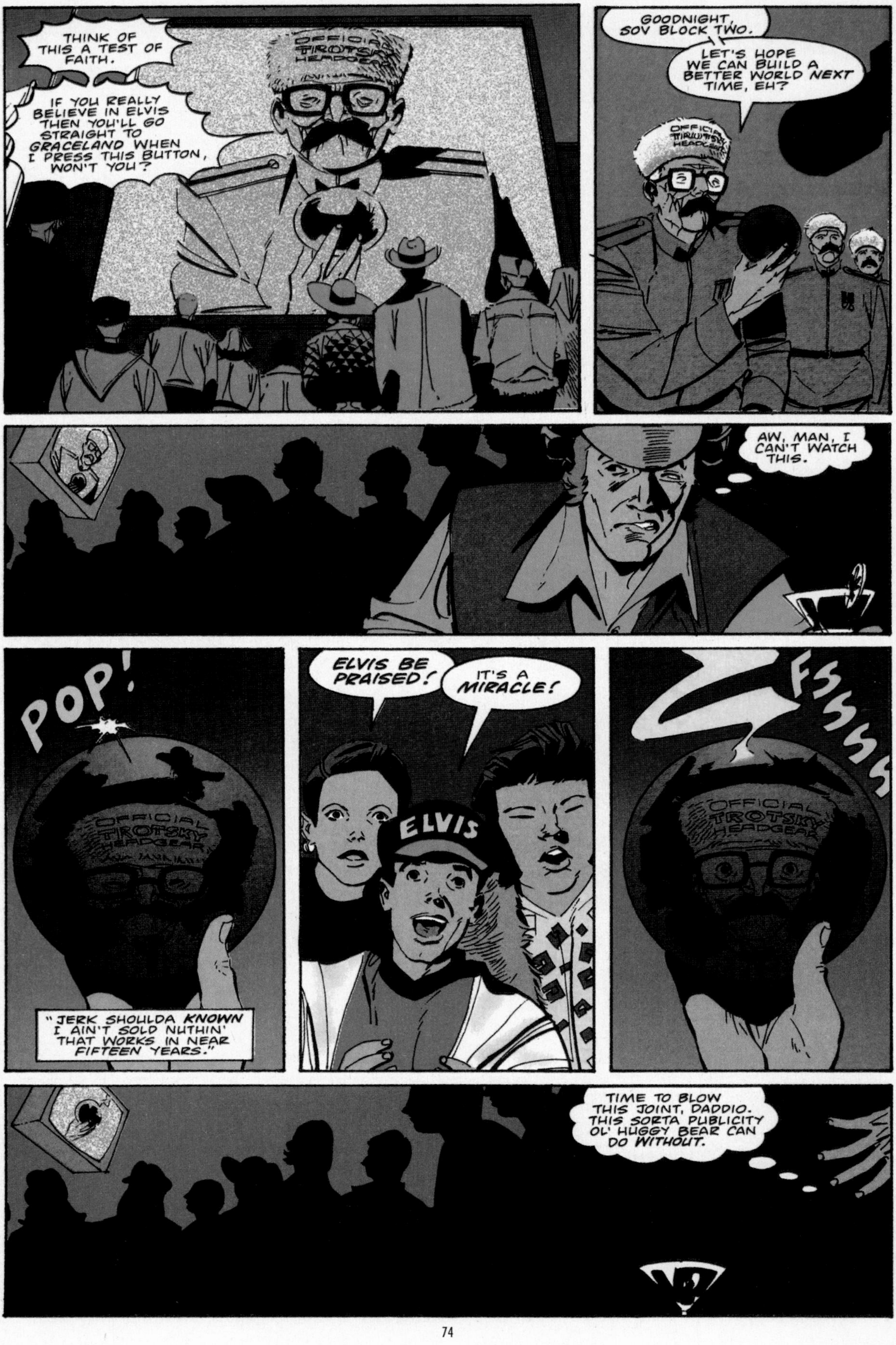
THINK OF THIS A TEST OF FAITH.
IF YOU REALLY BELIEVE IN ELVIS THEN YOU'LL GO STRAIGHT TO GRACELAND WHEN I PRESS THIS BUTTON, WON'T YOU?
OFFICIAL TROTSKY HEADGEAR
GOODNIGHT, SOV BLOCK TWO.
LET'S HOPE WE CAN BUILD A BETTER WORLD NEXT TIME, EH?
AW, MAN, I CAN'T WATCH THIS.
POP!
OFFICIAL TROTSKY HEADGEAR
"JERK SHOULDA KNOWN I AIN'T SOLD NUTHIN' THAT WORKS IN NEAR FIFTEEN YEARS."
ELVIS BE PRAISED!
IT'S A MIRACLE!
ELVIS
FSSSSS
OFFICIAL TROTSKY HEADGEAR
TIME TO BLOW THIS JOINT, DADDIO. THIS SORTA PUBLICITY OL' HUGGY BEAR CAN DO WITHOUT.

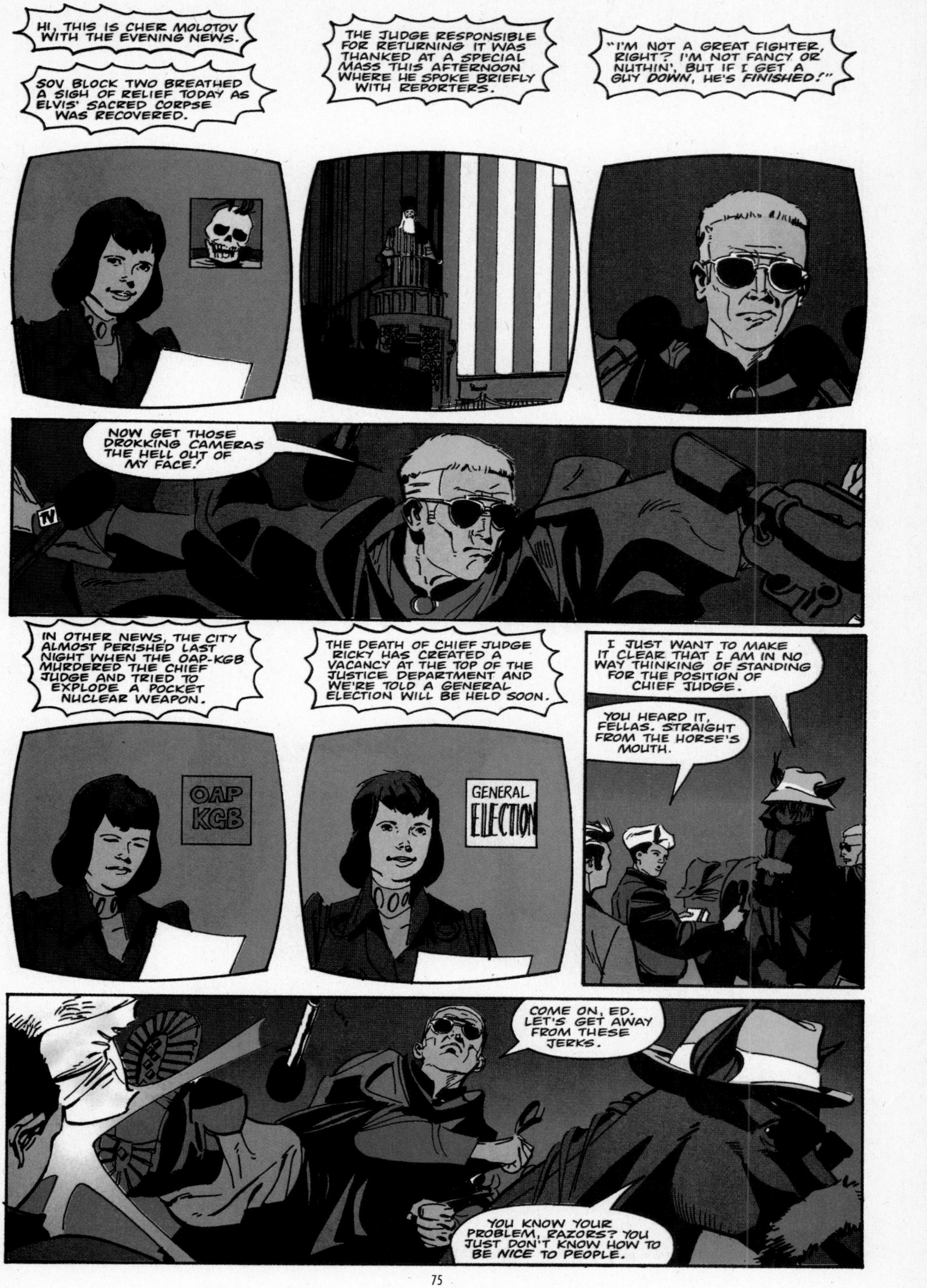
HI, THIS IS CHER MOLOTOV WITH THE EVENING NEWS.
SOV BLOCK TWO BREATHED A SIGH OF RELIEF TODAY AS ELVIS' SACRED CORPSE WAS RECOVERED.
THE JUDGE RESPONSIBLE FOR RETURNING IT WAS THANKED AT A SPECIAL MASS THIS AFTERNOON WHERE HE SPOKE BRIEFLY WITH REPORTERS.
"I'M NOT A GREAT FIGHTER, RIGHT? I'M NOT FANCY OR NUTHIN', BUT IF I GET A GUY DOWN, HE'S FINISHED!"
NOW GET THOSE DROKKING CAMERAS THE HELL OUT OF MY FACE.'
TV
IN OTHER NEWS, THE CITY ALMOST PERISHED LAST NIGHT WHEN THE OAP-KGB MURDERED THE CHIEF JUDGE AND TRIED TO EXPLODE A POCKET NUCLEAR WEAPON.
OAP KGB
THE DEATH OF CHIEF JUDGE RICKY HAS CREATED A VACANCY AT THE TOP OF THE JUSTICE DEPARTMENT AND WE'RE TOLD A GENERAL ELECTION WILL BE HELD SOON.
GENERAL ELECTION
I JUST WANT TO MAKE IT CLEAR THAT I AM IN NO WAY THINKING OF STANDING FOR THE POSITION OF CHIEF JUDGE.
YOU HEARD IT, FELLAS. STRAIGHT FROM THE HORSE'S MOUTH.
COME ON, ED. LET'S GET AWAY FROM THESE JERKS.
YOU KNOW YOUR PROBLEM, RAZORS? YOU JUST DON'T KNOW HOW TO BE NICE TO PEOPLE.

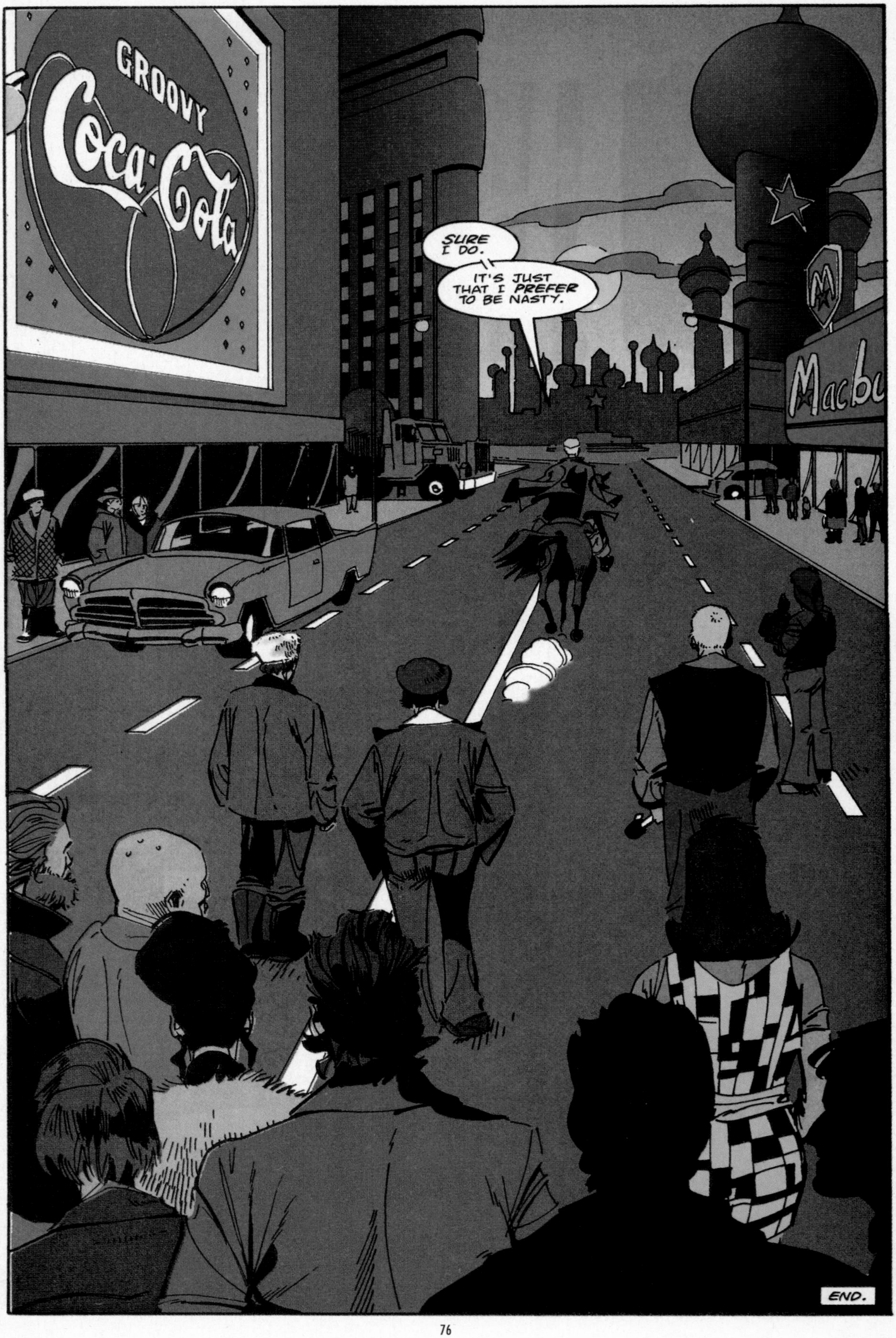
GROOVY
Coca-Cola
SURE I DO.
IT'S JUST THAT I PREFER TO BE NASTY.
Macbu
END.

THE HUNT FOR RED RAZORS

Script: Mark Millar

Art: Nigel Dobbyn

Letters: Annie Parkhouse

Originally published in *2000 AD* Progs 908–917

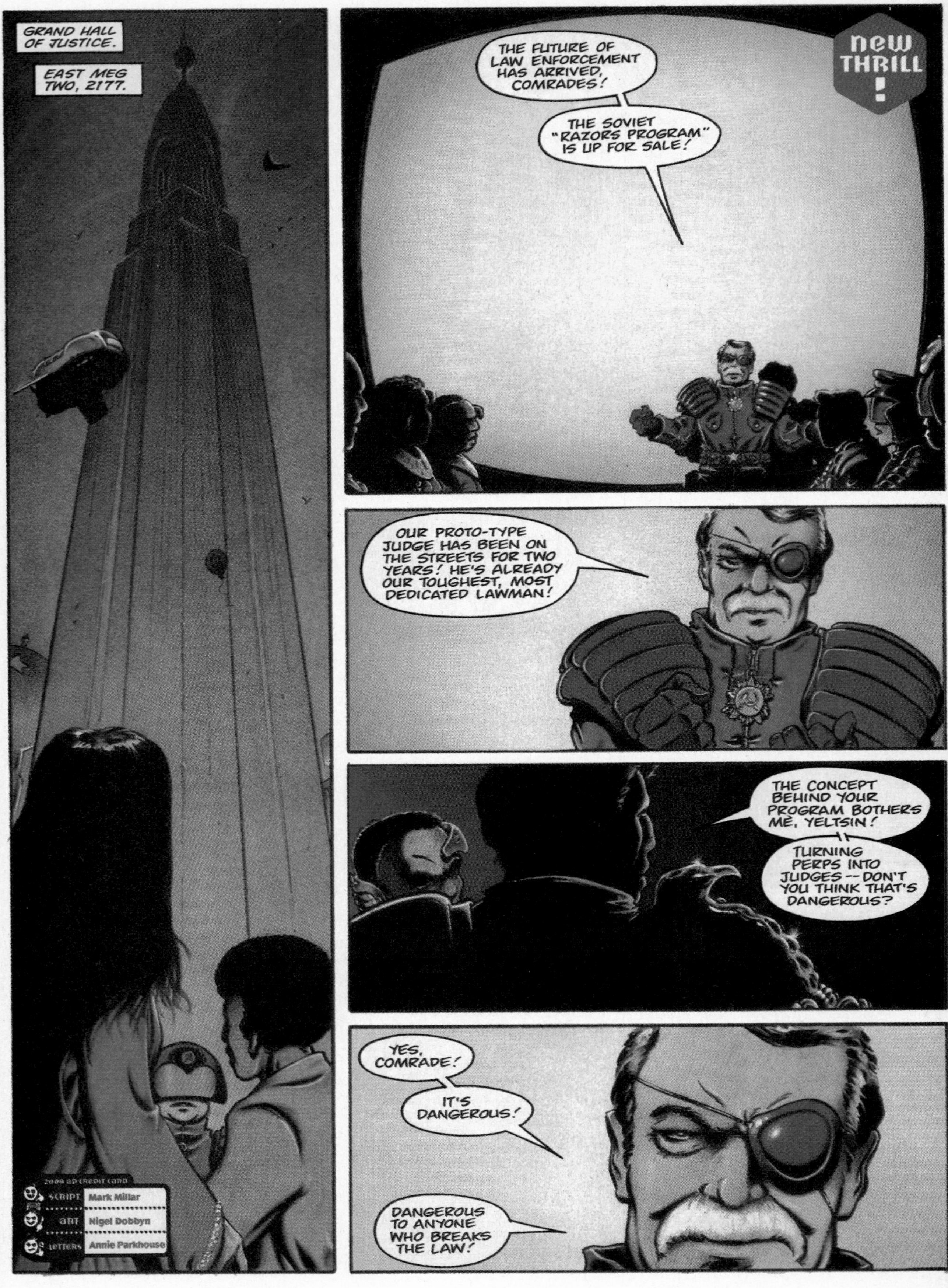
GRAND HALL OF JUSTICE.
EAST MEG TWO, 2177.
2000 AD CREDIT CARD
SCRIPT Mark Millar
ART Nigel Dobbyn
LETTERS Annie Parkhouse
NEW THRILL!
THE FUTURE OF LAW ENFORCEMENT HAS ARRIVED, COMRADES!
THE SOVIET "RAZORS PROGRAM" IS UP FOR SALE!
OUR PROTO-TYPE JUDGE HAS BEEN ON THE STREETS FOR TWO YEARS! HE'S ALREADY OUR TOUGHEST, MOST DEDICATED LAWMAN!
THE CONCEPT BEHIND YOUR PROGRAM BOTHERS ME, YELTSIN!
TURNING PERPS INTO JUDGES -- DON'T YOU THINK THAT'S DANGEROUS?
YES, COMRADE!
IT'S DANGEROUS!
DANGEROUS TO ANYONE WHO BREAKS THE LAW!

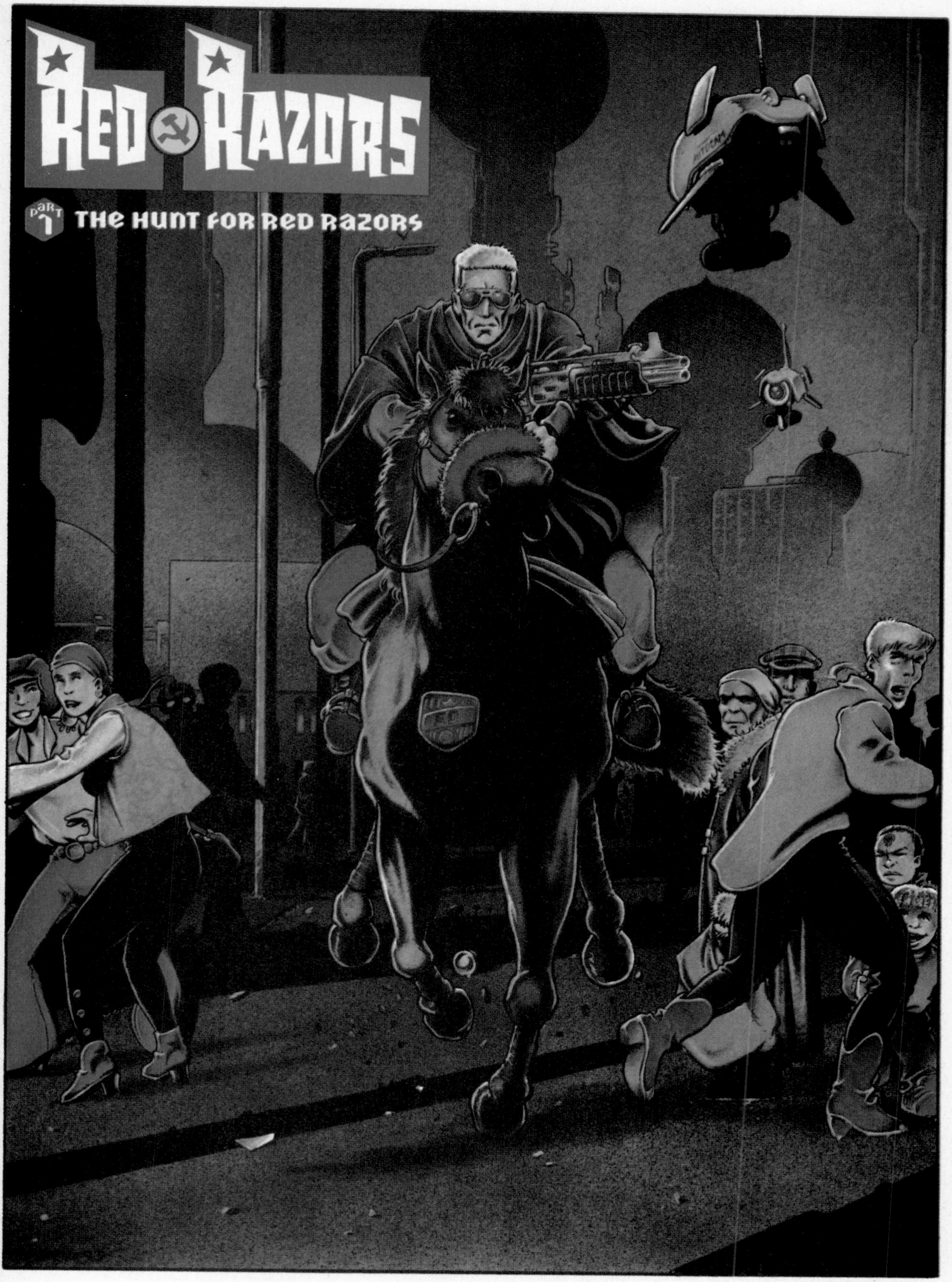
RED RAZORS
PART 1 THE HUNT FOR RED RAZORS

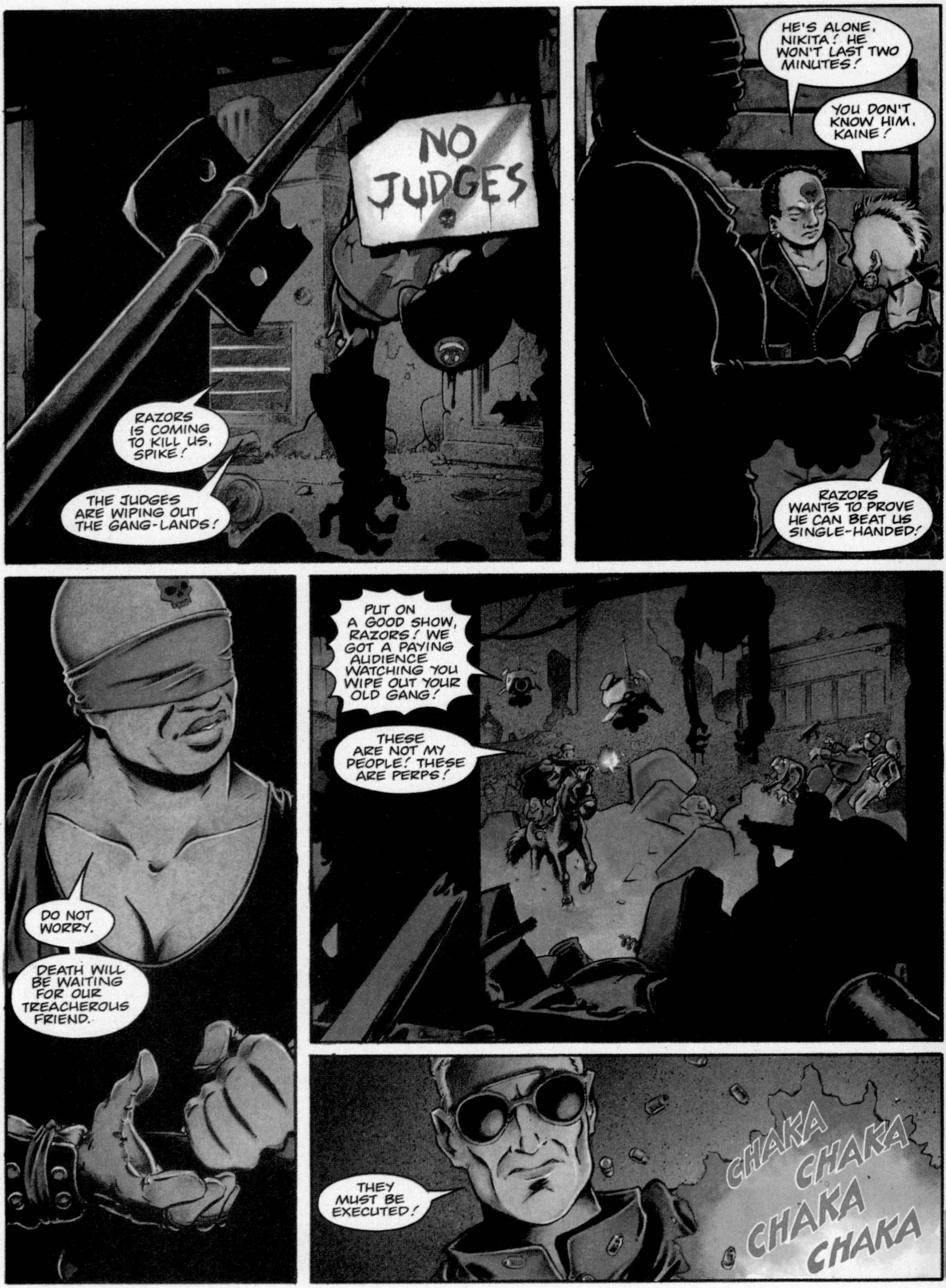
NO JUDGES
RAZORS IS COMING TO KILL US, SPIKE!
THE JUDGES ARE WIPING OUT THE GANG-LANDS!
HE'S ALONE, NIKITA! HE WON'T LAST TWO MINUTES!
YOU DON'T KNOW HIM, KAINE!
RAZORS WANTS TO PROVE HE CAN BEAT US SINGLE-HANDED!
DO NOT WORRY.
DEATH WILL BE WAITING FOR OUR TREACHEROUS FRIEND.
PUT ON A GOOD SHOW, RAZORS! WE GOT A PAYING AUDIENCE WATCHING YOU WIPE OUT YOUR OLD GANG!
THESE ARE NOT MY PEOPLE! THESE ARE PERPS!
THEY MUST BE EXECUTED!
CHAKA CHAKA CHAKA CHAKA

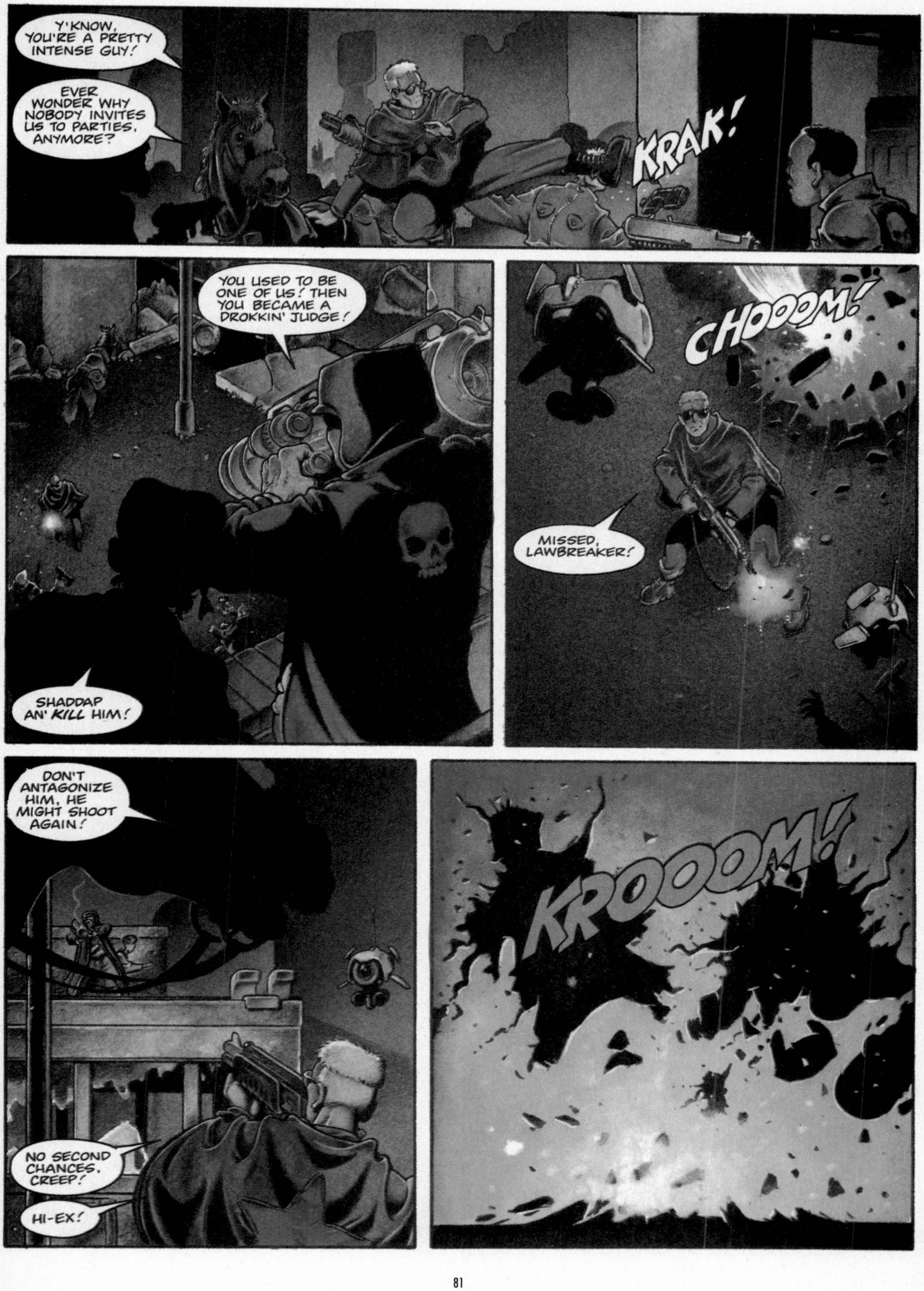

Y'KNOW, YOU'RE A PRETTY INTENSE GUY!
EVER WONDER WHY NOBODY INVITES US TO PARTIES, ANYMORE?
KRAK!
YOU USED TO BE ONE OF US! THEN YOU BECAME A DROKKIN' JUDGE!
SHADDAP AN' KILL HIM!
CHOOOM!
MISSED, LAWBREAKER!
DON'T ANTAGONIZE HIM, HE MIGHT SHOOT AGAIN!
NO SECOND CHANCES, CREEP!
HI-EX!
KROOOM!

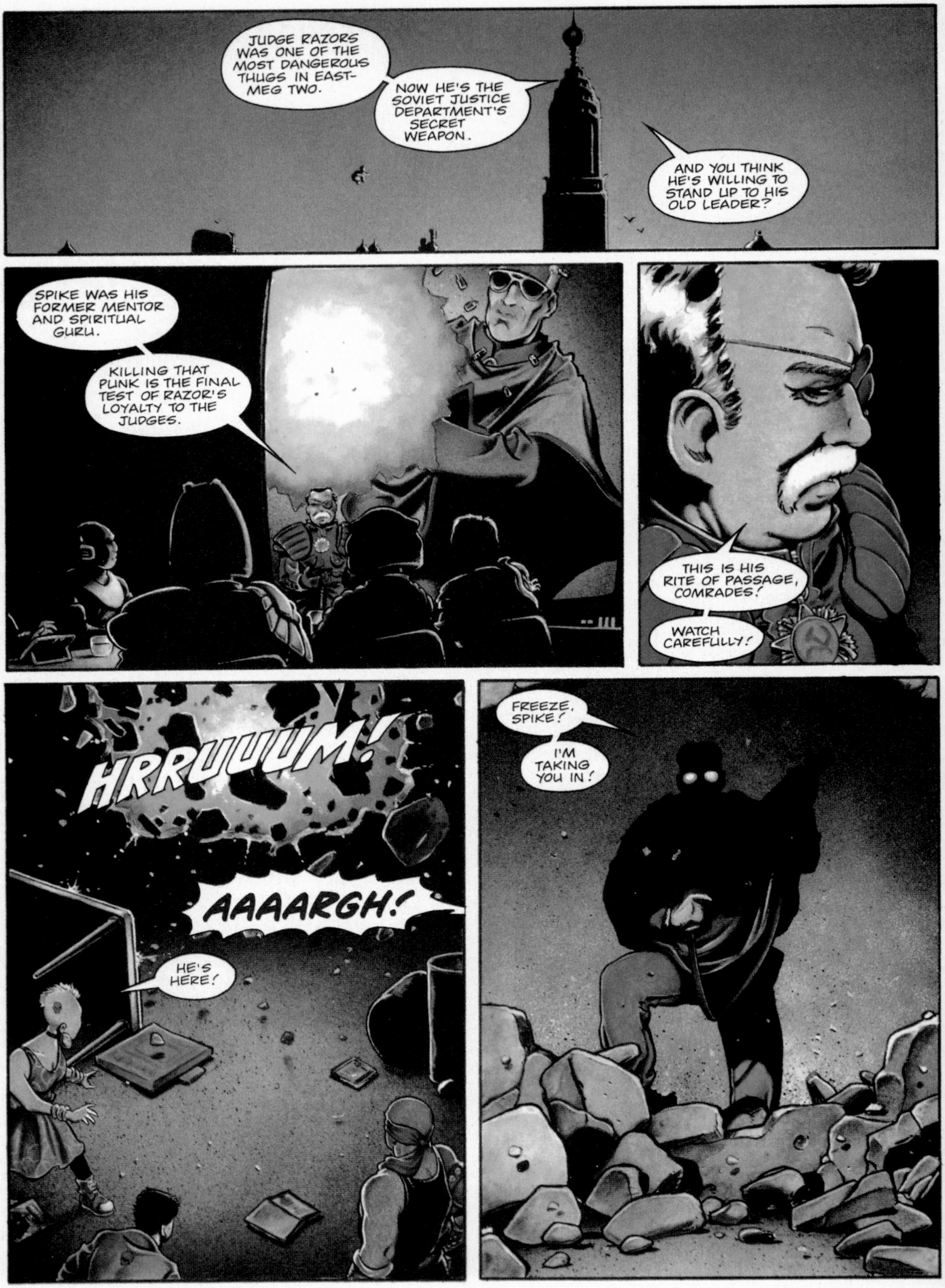
JUDGE RAZORS WAS ONE OF THE MOST DANGEROUS THUGS IN EAST-MEG TWO.
NOW HE'S THE SOVIET JUSTICE DEPARTMENT'S SECRET WEAPON.
AND YOU THINK HE'S WILLING TO STAND UP TO HIS OLD LEADER?
SPIKE WAS HIS FORMER MENTOR AND SPIRITUAL GURU.
KILLING THAT PUNK IS THE FINAL TEST OF RAZOR'S LOYALTY TO THE JUDGES.
THIS IS HIS RITE OF PASSAGE, COMRADES!
WATCH CAREFULLY!
HRRUUUUM!
AAAARGH!
HE'S HERE!
FREEZE, SPIKE!
I'M TAKING YOU IN!

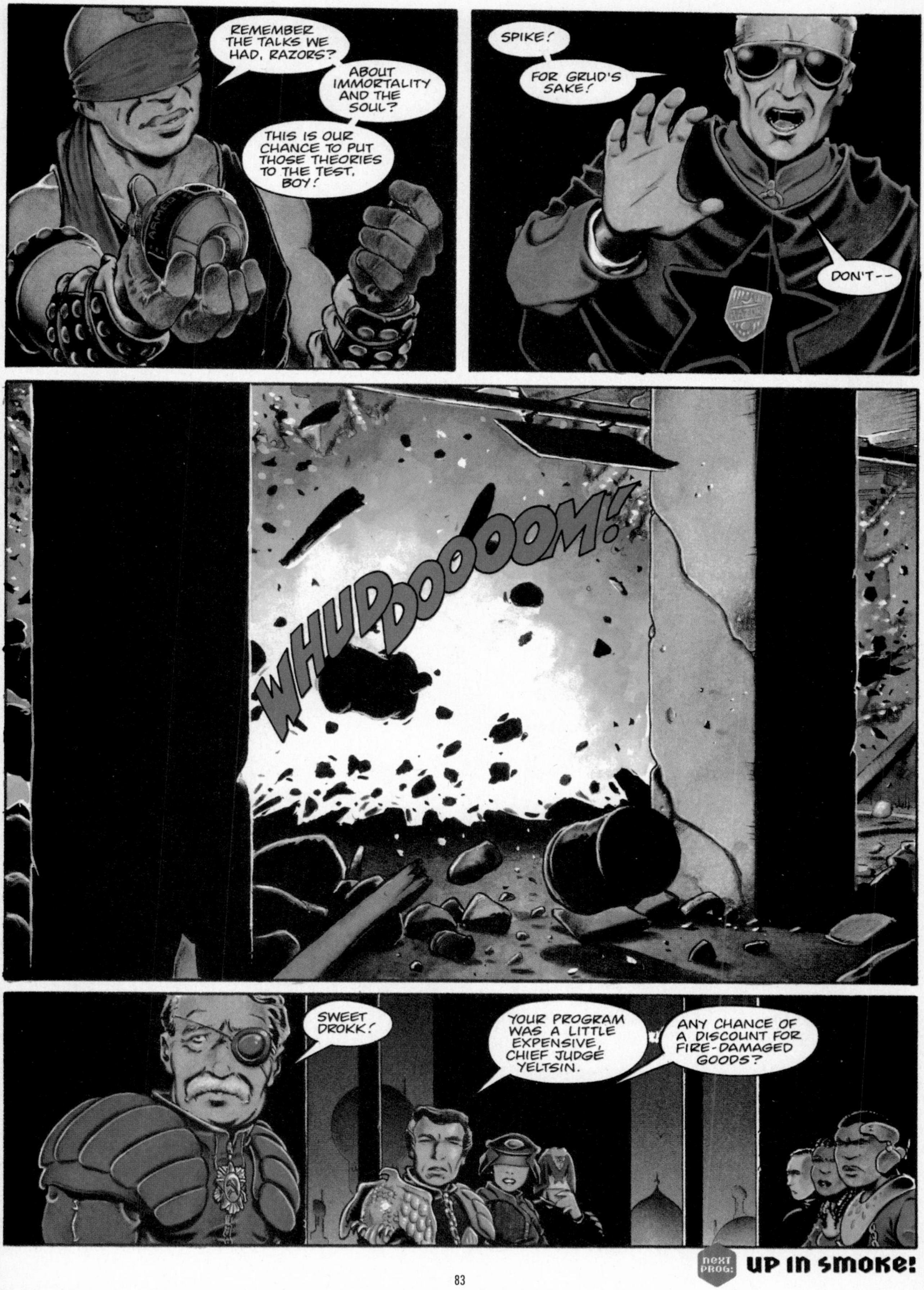
REMEMBER THE TALKS WE HAD, RAZORS?
ABOUT IMMORTALITY AND THE SOUL?
THIS IS OUR CHANCE TO PUT THOSE THEORIES TO THE TEST, BOY!
SPIKE!
FOR GRUD'S SAKE!
DON'T--
WHUDDOOOOM!
SWEET DROKK!
YOUR PROGRAM WAS A LITTLE EXPENSIVE, CHIEF JUDGE YELTSIN.
ANY CHANCE OF A DISCOUNT FOR FIRE-DAMAGED GOODS?

NEXT PROG: UP IN SMOKE!

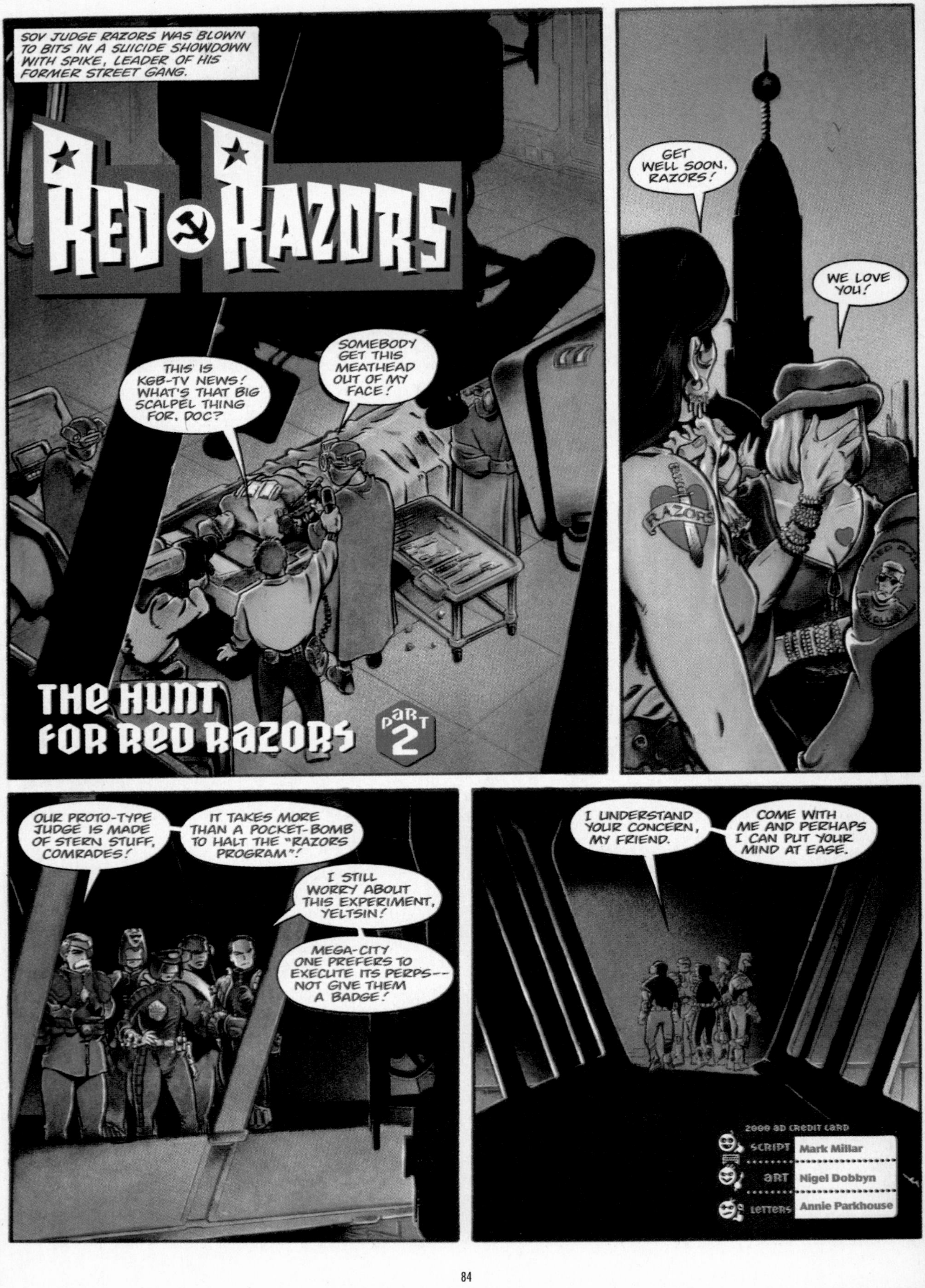
SOV JUDGE RAZORS WAS BLOWN TO BITS IN A SUICIDE SHOWDOWN WITH SPIKE, LEADER OF HIS FORMER STREET GANG.
RED RAZORS
THIS IS KGB-TV NEWS! WHAT'S THAT BIG SCALPEL THING FOR, DOC?
SOMEBODY GET THIS MEATHEAD OUT OF MY FACE!
THE HUNT FOR RED RAZORS
PART 2
GET WELL SOON, RAZORS!
WE LOVE YOU!
RAZORS
OUR PROTO-TYPE JUDGE IS MADE OF STERN STUFF, COMRADES!
IT TAKES MORE THAN A POCKET-BOMB TO HALT THE "RAZORS PROGRAM"!
I STILL WORRY ABOUT THIS EXPERIMENT, YELTSIN!
MEGA-CITY ONE PREFERS TO EXECUTE ITS PERPS-- NOT GIVE THEM A BADGE!
I UNDERSTAND YOUR CONCERN, MY FRIEND.
COME WITH ME AND PERHAPS I CAN PUT YOUR MIND AT EASE.
2000 AD CREDIT CARD
SCRIPT Mark Millar
ART Nigel Dobbyn
LETTERS Annie Parkhouse

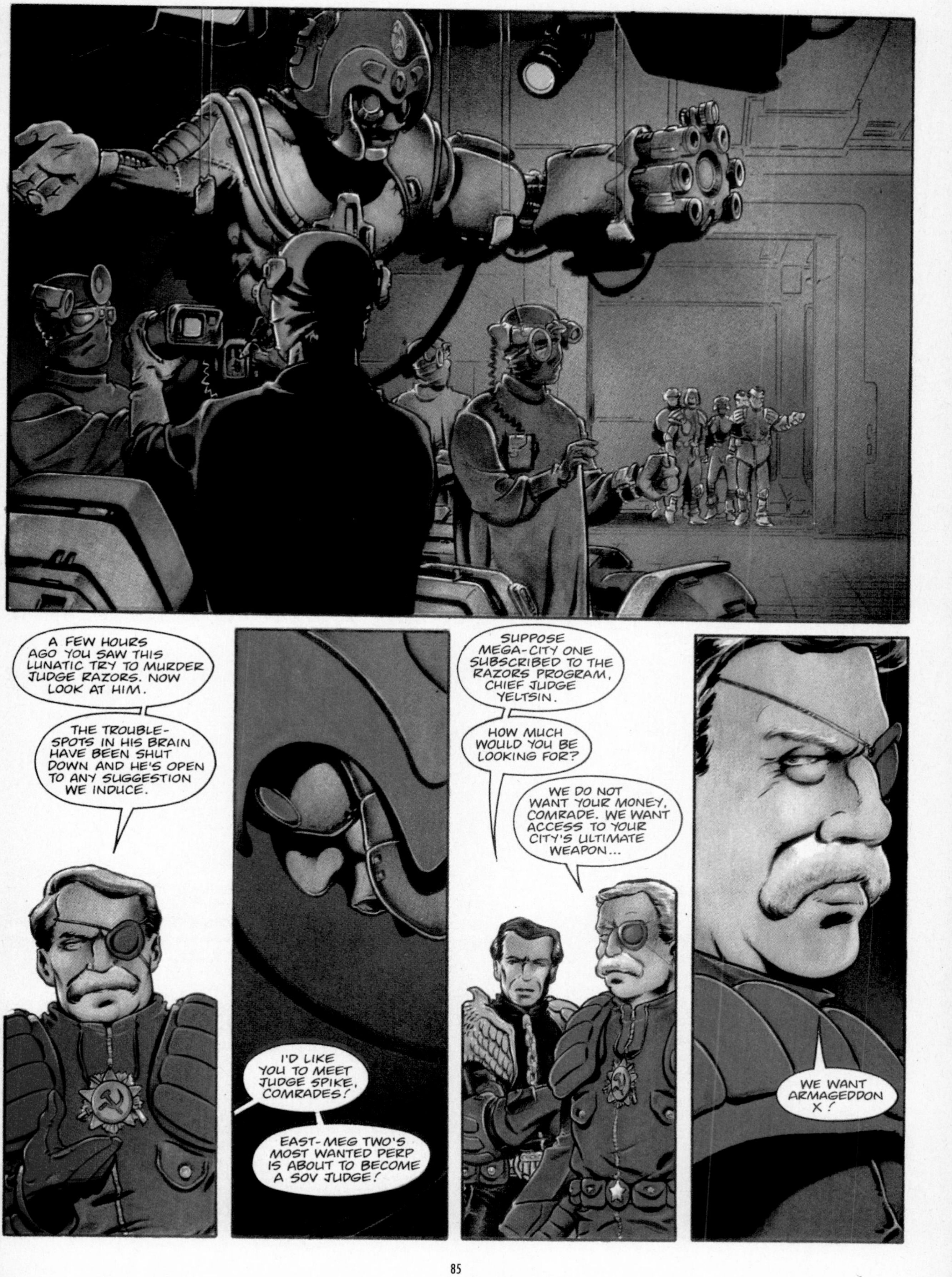
A FEW HOURS AGO YOU SAW THIS LUNATIC TRY TO MURDER JUDGE RAZORS. NOW LOOK AT HIM.
THE TROUBLE-SPOTS IN HIS BRAIN HAVE BEEN SHUT DOWN AND HE'S OPEN TO ANY SUGGESTION WE INDUCE.
I'D LIKE YOU TO MEET JUDGE SPIKE, COMRADES!
EAST-MEG TWO'S MOST WANTED PERP IS ABOUT TO BECOME A SOV JUDGE!
SUPPOSE MEGA-CITY ONE SUBSCRIBED TO THE RAZORS PROGRAM, CHIEF JUDGE YELTSIN.
HOW MUCH WOULD YOU BE LOOKING FOR?
WE DO NOT WANT YOUR MONEY, COMRADE. WE WANT ACCESS TO YOUR CITY'S ULTIMATE WEAPON...
WE WANT ARMAGEDDON X!

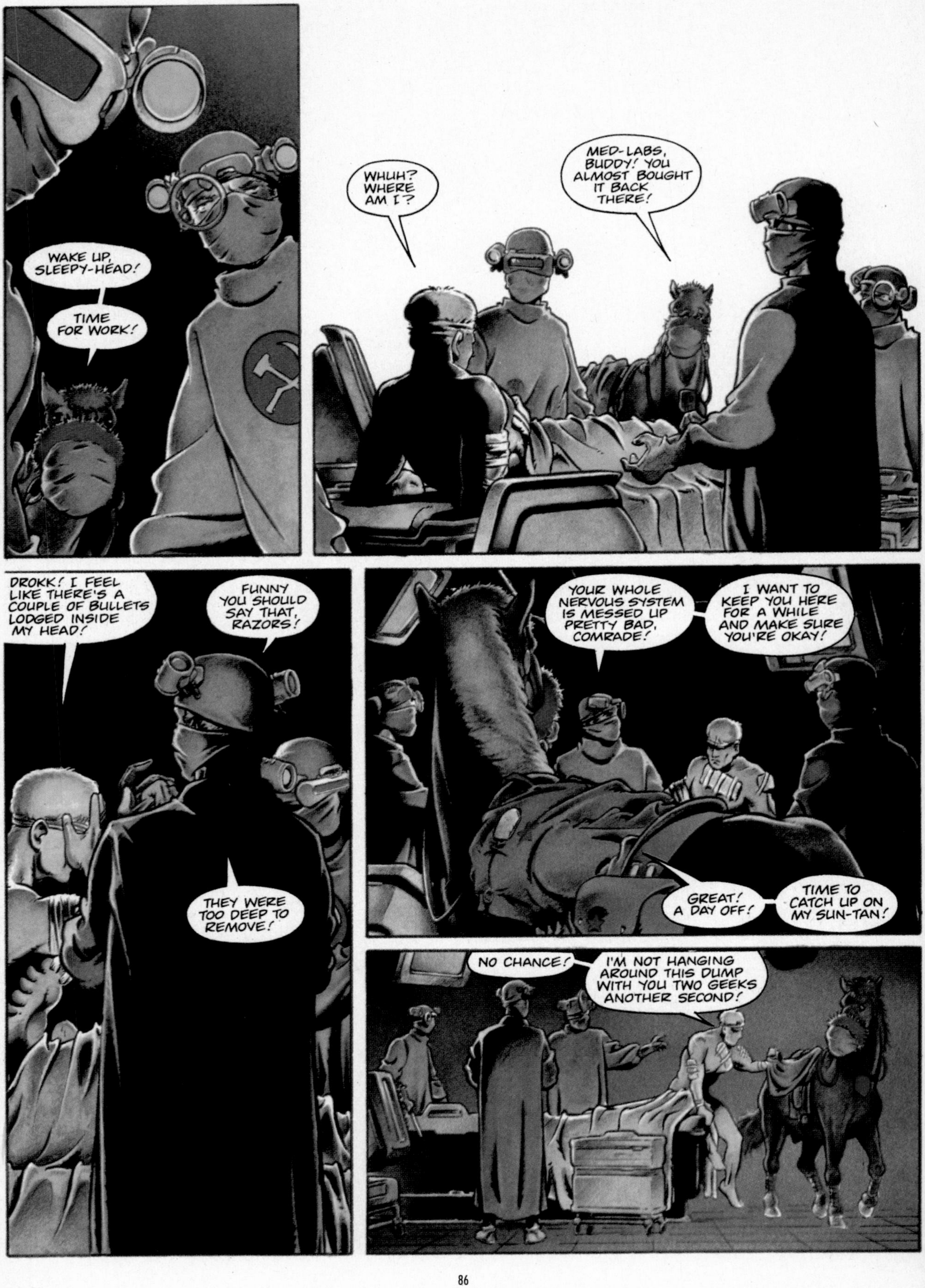
WAKE UP, SLEEPY-HEAD!
TIME FOR WORK!
WHUH? WHERE AM I?
MED-LABS, BUDDY! YOU ALMOST BOUGHT IT BACK THERE!
DROKK! I FEEL LIKE THERE'S A COUPLE OF BULLETS LODGED INSIDE MY HEAD!
FUNNY YOU SHOULD SAY THAT, RAZORS!
THEY WERE TOO DEEP TO REMOVE!
YOUR WHOLE NERVOUS SYSTEM IS MESSED UP PRETTY BAD, COMRADE!
I WANT TO KEEP YOU HERE FOR A WHILE AND MAKE SURE YOU'RE OKAY!
GREAT! A DAY OFF!
TIME TO CATCH UP ON MY SUN-TAN!
NO CHANCE!
I'M NOT HANGING AROUND THIS DUMP WITH YOU TWO GEEKS ANOTHER SECOND!

COME ON, ED!

LET'S HUSTLE!

GET BACK HERE, RAZORS! THAT'S AN ORDER!

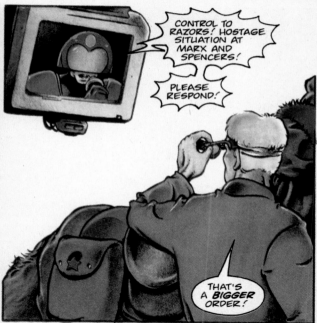

CONTROL TO RAZORS! HOSTAGE SITUATION AT MARX AND SPENCERS!

PLEASE RESPOND!

THAT'S A *BIGGER* ORDER!

CATCH YOU LATER, BOYS!

HEY! CAN SOMEBODY TAPE "WELCOME BACK KOTTER" WHILE WE'RE GONE?

I FORGOT TO TELL HIM ABOUT SPIKE!

MAYBE IT'S FOR THE BEST.

WHEN HE FINDS OUT WE PIECED THAT MANIAC BACK TOGETHER THE MUNCE IS *REALLY* GOING TO HIT THE FAN!

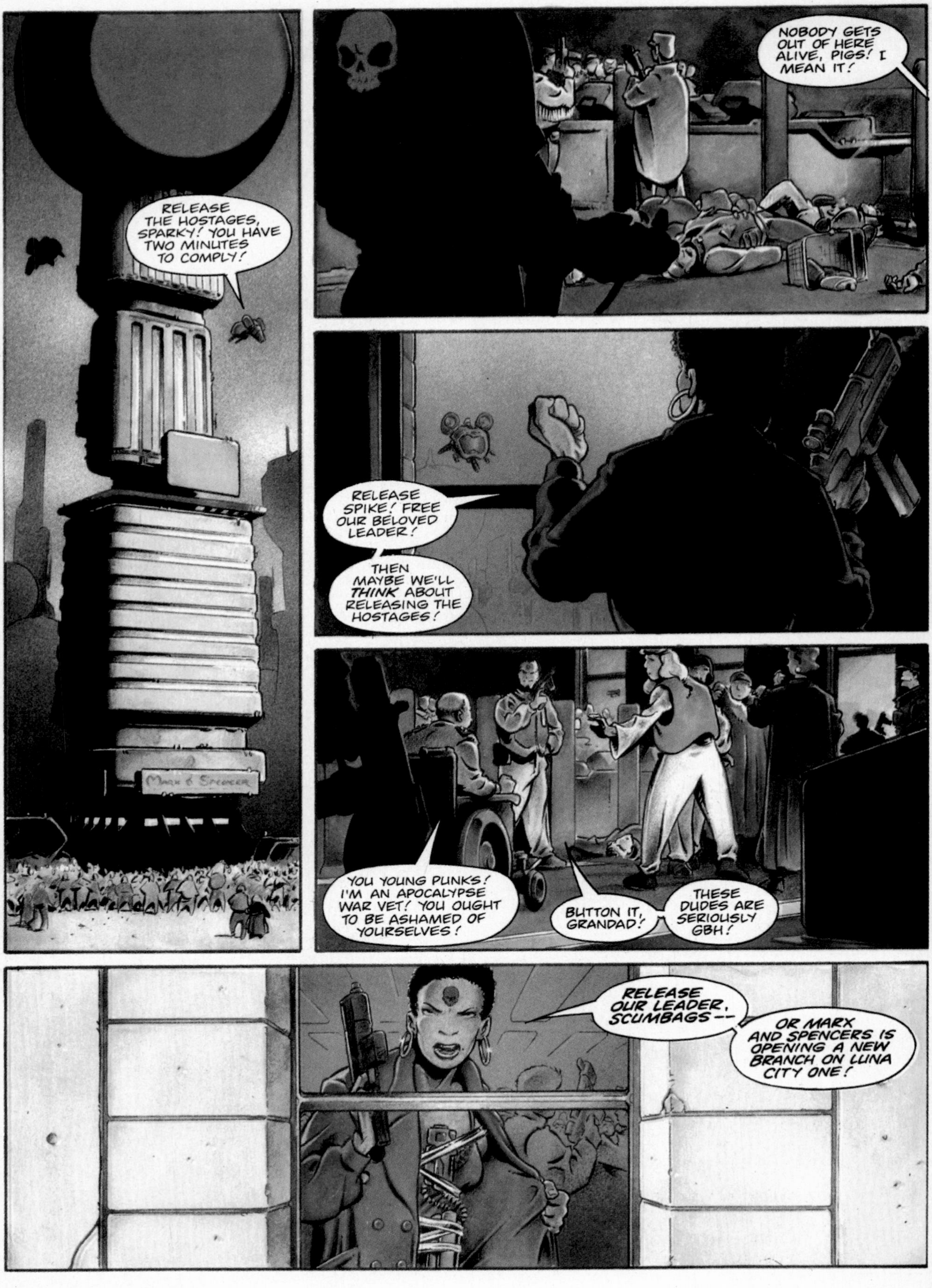
RELEASE THE HOSTAGES, SPARKY! YOU HAVE TWO MINUTES TO COMPLY!
MARX & SPENCER
NOBODY GETS OUT OF HERE ALIVE, PIGS! I MEAN IT!
RELEASE SPIKE! FREE OUR BELOVED LEADER!
THEN MAYBE WE'LL THINK ABOUT RELEASING THE HOSTAGES!
YOU YOUNG PUNKS! I'M AN APOCALYPSE WAR VET! YOU OUGHT TO BE ASHAMED OF YOURSELVES!
BUTTON IT, GRANDAD!
THESE DUDES ARE SERIOUSLY GBH!
RELEASE OUR LEADER, SCUMBAGS--
OR MARX AND SPENCERS IS OPENING A NEW BRANCH ON LUNA CITY ONE!

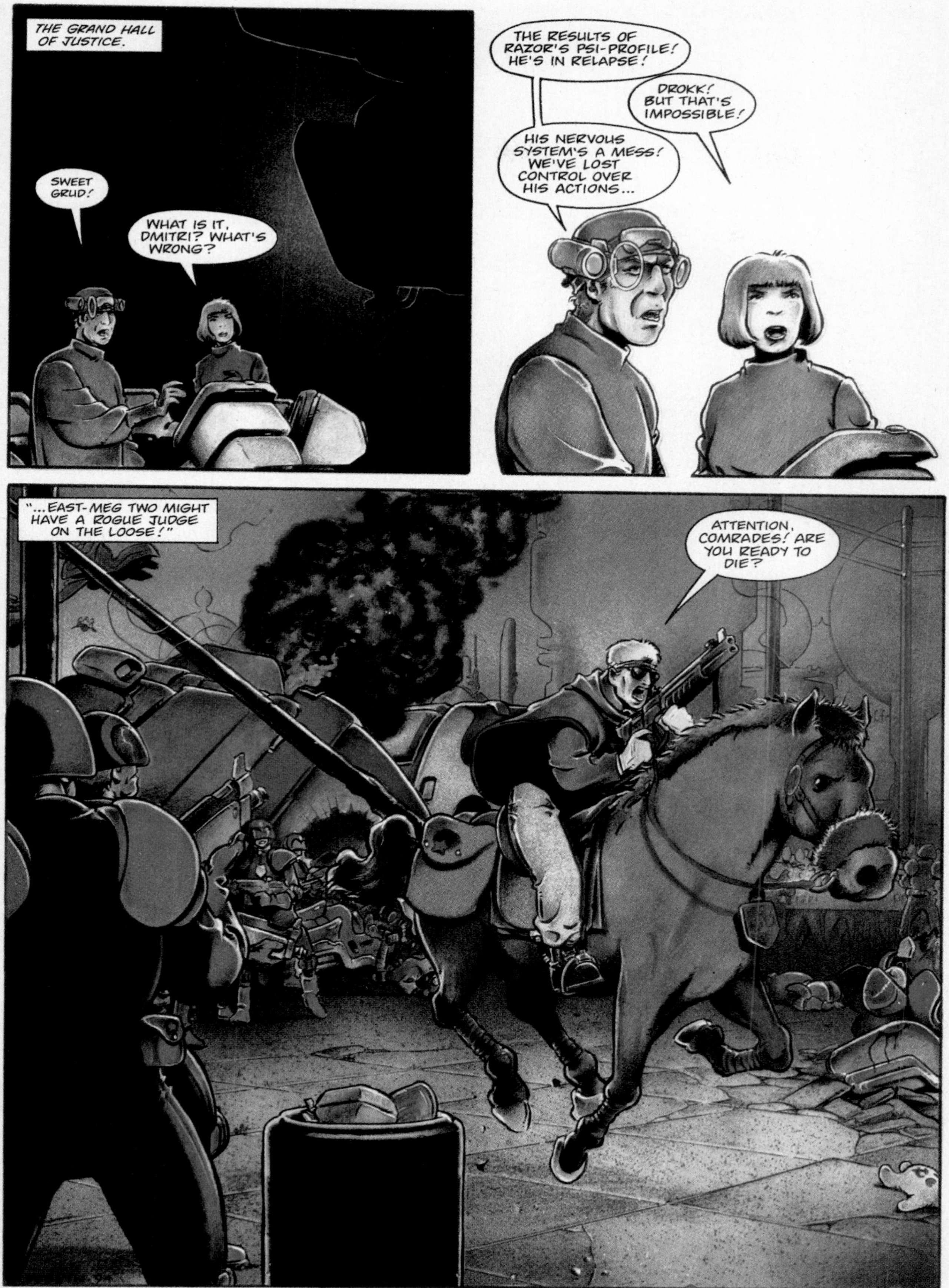
THE GRAND HALL OF JUSTICE.
SWEET GRUD!
WHAT IS IT, DMITRI? WHAT'S WRONG?
THE RESULTS OF RAZOR'S PSI-PROFILE! HE'S IN RELAPSE!
DROKK! BUT THAT'S IMPOSSIBLE!
HIS NERVOUS SYSTEM'S A MESS! WE'VE LOST CONTROL OVER HIS ACTIONS...
"...EAST-MEG TWO MIGHT HAVE A ROGUE JUDGE ON THE LOOSE!"
ATTENTION, COMRADES! ARE YOU READY TO DIE?

NEXT PROG: MISTER BAD GUY!

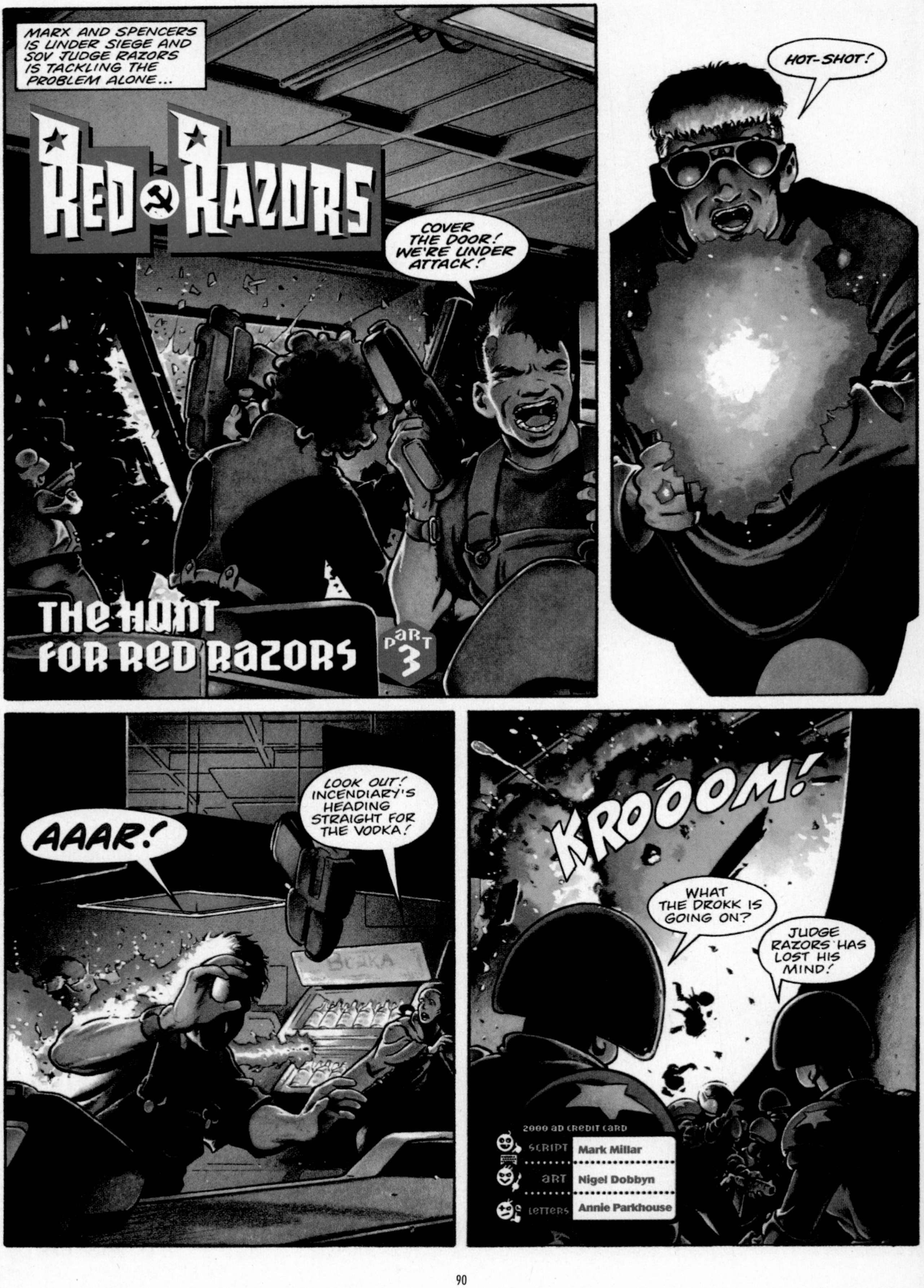
MARX AND SPENCERS IS UNDER SIEGE AND SOV JUDGE RAZORS IS TACKLING THE PROBLEM ALONE...
RED RAZORS
COVER THE DOOR! WE'RE UNDER ATTACK!
THE HUNT FOR RED RAZORS
PART 3
HOT-SHOT!
AAAR!
LOOK OUT! INCENDIARY'S HEADING STRAIGHT FOR THE VODKA!
KROOOM!
WHAT THE DROKK IS GOING ON?
JUDGE RAZORS HAS LOST HIS MIND!
2000 AD CREDIT CARD
SCRIPT Mark Millar
ART Nigel Dobbyn
LETTERS Annie Parkhouse

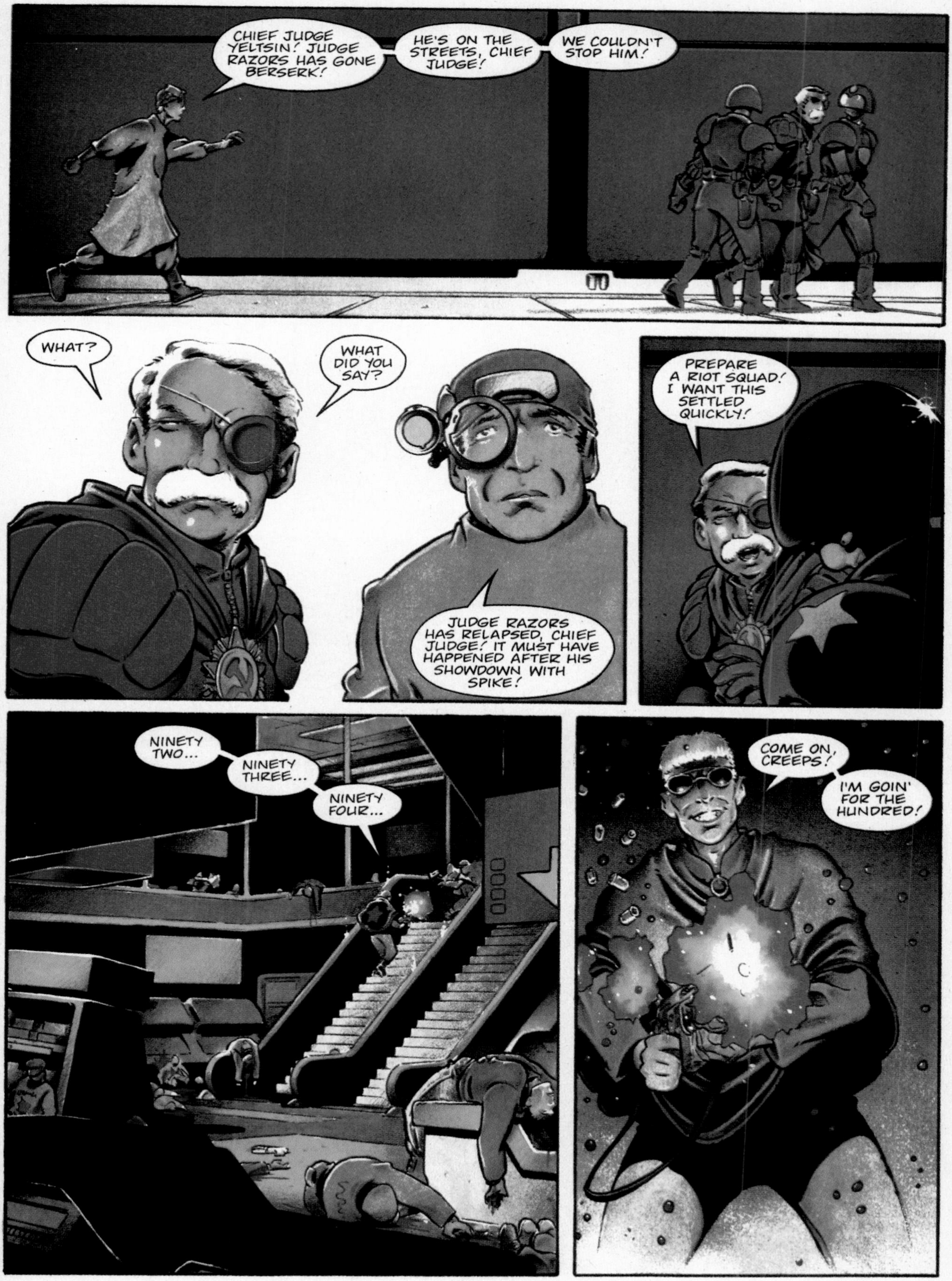
CHIEF JUDGE YELTSIN! JUDGE RAZORS HAS GONE BERSERK!
HE'S ON THE STREETS, CHIEF JUDGE!
WE COULDN'T STOP HIM!
WHAT?
WHAT DID YOU SAY?
JUDGE RAZORS HAS RELAPSED, CHIEF JUDGE! IT MUST HAVE HAPPENED AFTER HIS SHOWDOWN WITH SPIKE!
PREPARE A RIOT SQUAD! I WANT THIS SETTLED QUICKLY!
NINETY TWO...
NINETY THREE...
NINETY FOUR...
COME ON, CREEPS!
I'M GOIN' FOR THE HUNDRED!

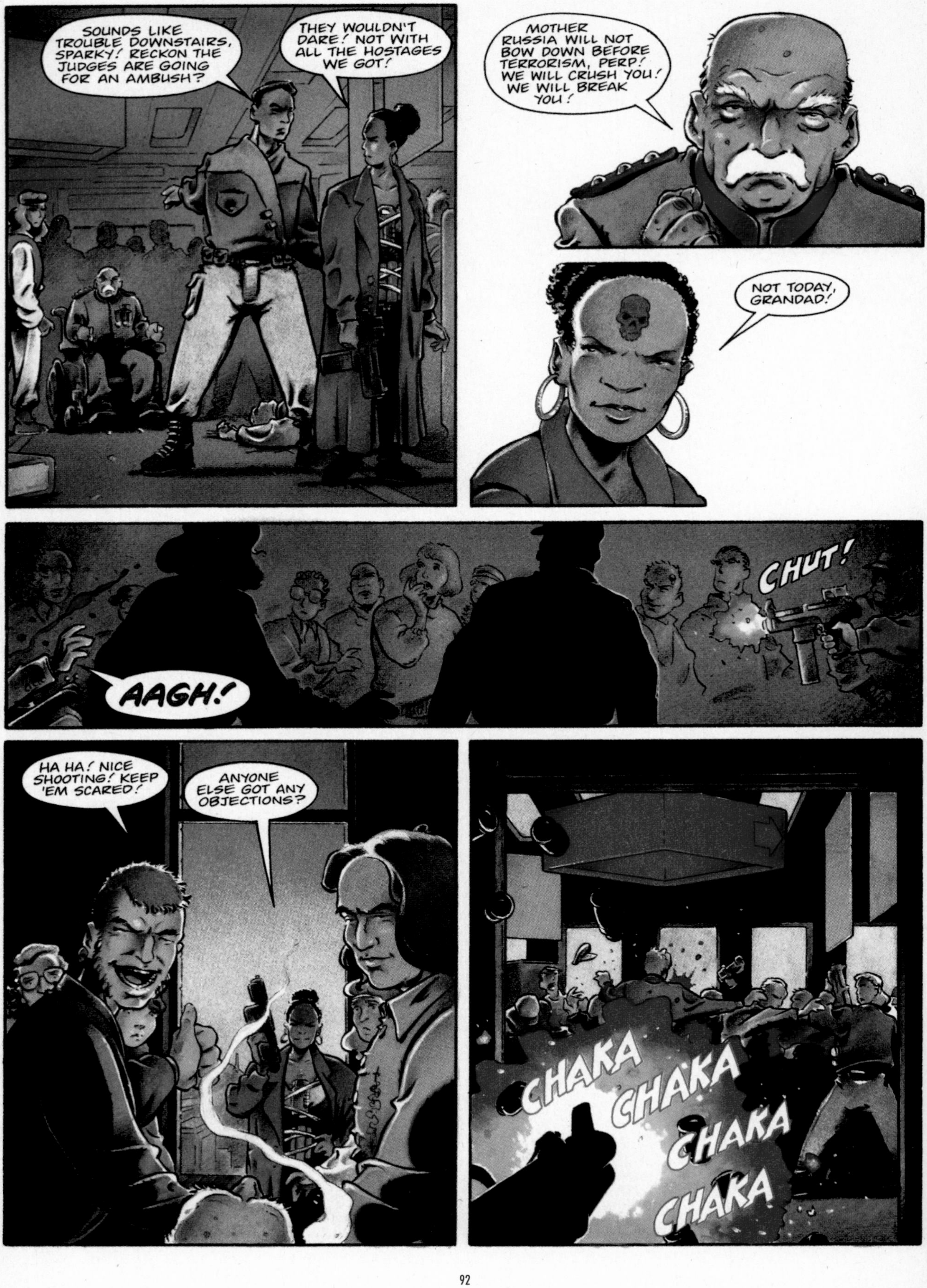
SOUNDS LIKE TROUBLE DOWNSTAIRS, SPARKY! RECKON THE JUDGES ARE GOING FOR AN AMBUSH?
THEY WOULDN'T DARE! NOT WITH ALL THE HOSTAGES WE GOT!
MOTHER RUSSIA WILL NOT BOW DOWN BEFORE TERRORISM, PERP! WE WILL CRUSH YOU! WE WILL BREAK YOU!
NOT TODAY, GRANDAD!
CHUT!
AAGH!
HA HA! NICE SHOOTING! KEEP 'EM SCARED!
ANYONE ELSE GOT ANY OBJECTIONS?
CHAKA
CHAKA
CHAKA
CHAKA

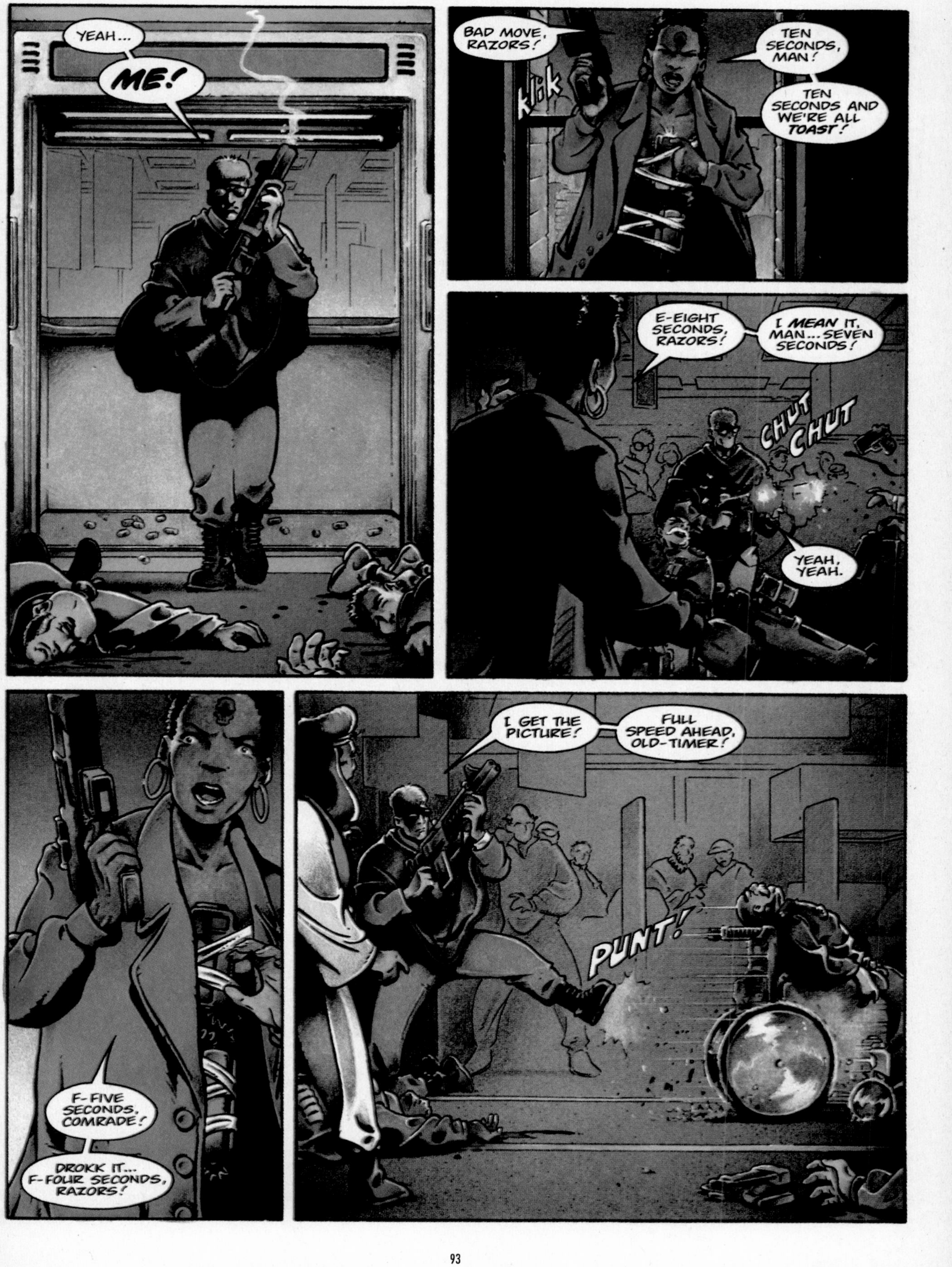
YEAH...
ME!
BAD MOVE, RAZORS!
KLIK
TEN SECONDS, MAN!
TEN SECONDS AND WE'RE ALL TOAST!
E-EIGHT SECONDS, RAZORS!
I MEAN IT, MAN... SEVEN SECONDS!
CHUT CHUT
YEAH, YEAH.
F-FIVE SECONDS, COMRADE!
DROKK IT... F-FOUR SECONDS, RAZORS!
I GET THE PICTURE!
FULL SPEED AHEAD, OLD-TIMER!
PUNT!

THREE
SECONDS--
OOF!

WHrrrrrrr

BON
VOYAGE,
BITCH!

TWO
SECONDS...

ONE...

KROOOM!

JUDGE
RAZORS...
THANK
GRUD!

THAT
MANIAC!

I DIDN'T
THINK WE WERE
GOING TO GET
OUT ALIVE!

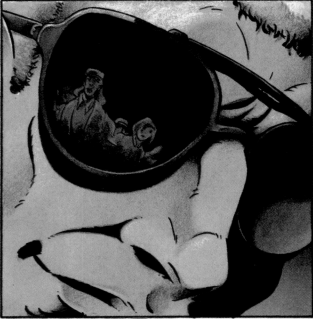

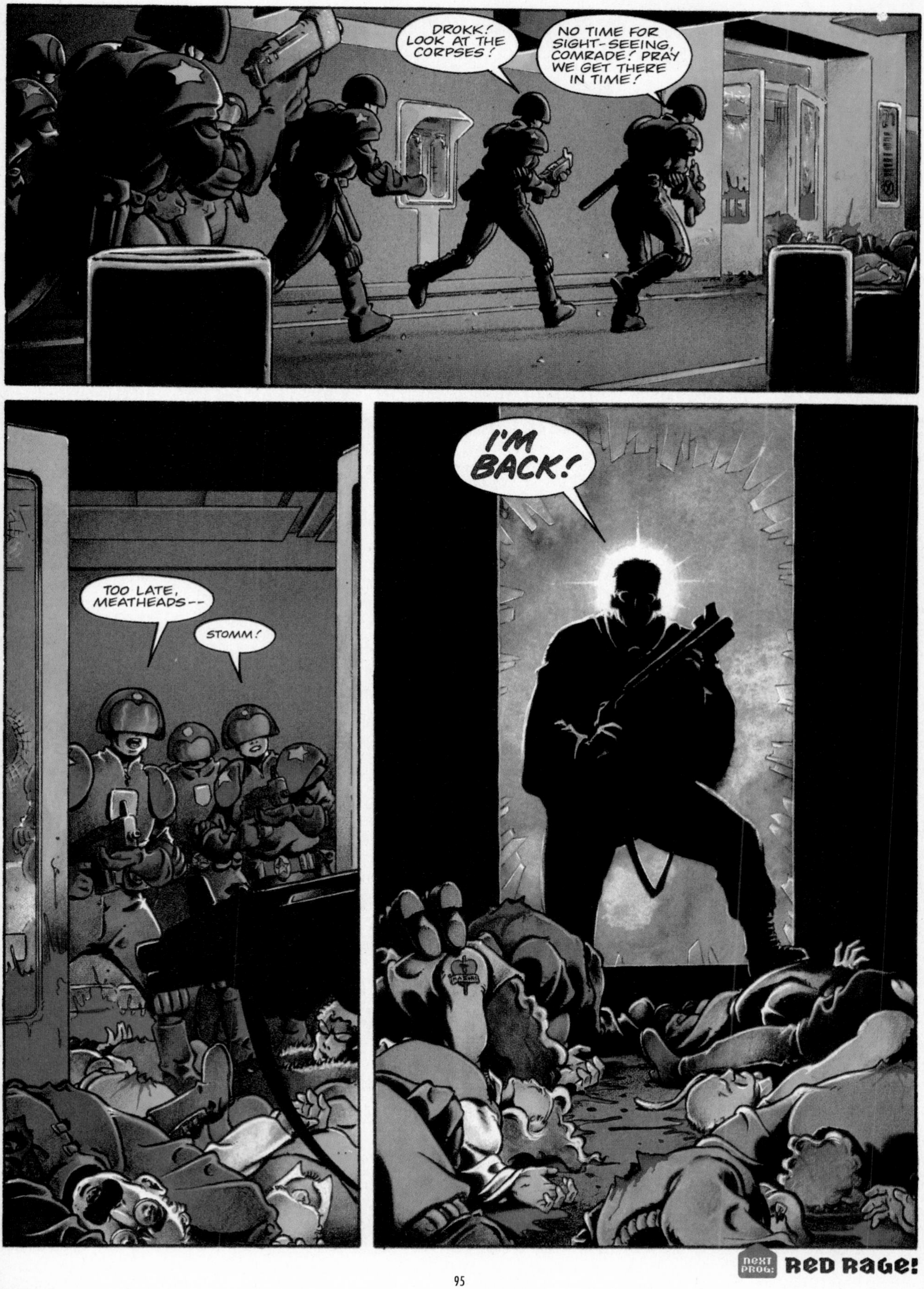
DROKK! LOOK AT THE CORPSES!
NO TIME FOR SIGHT-SEEING, COMRADE! PRAY WE GET THERE IN TIME!
TOO LATE, MEATHEADS--
STOMM!
I'M BACK!
NEXT PROG: RED RAGE!

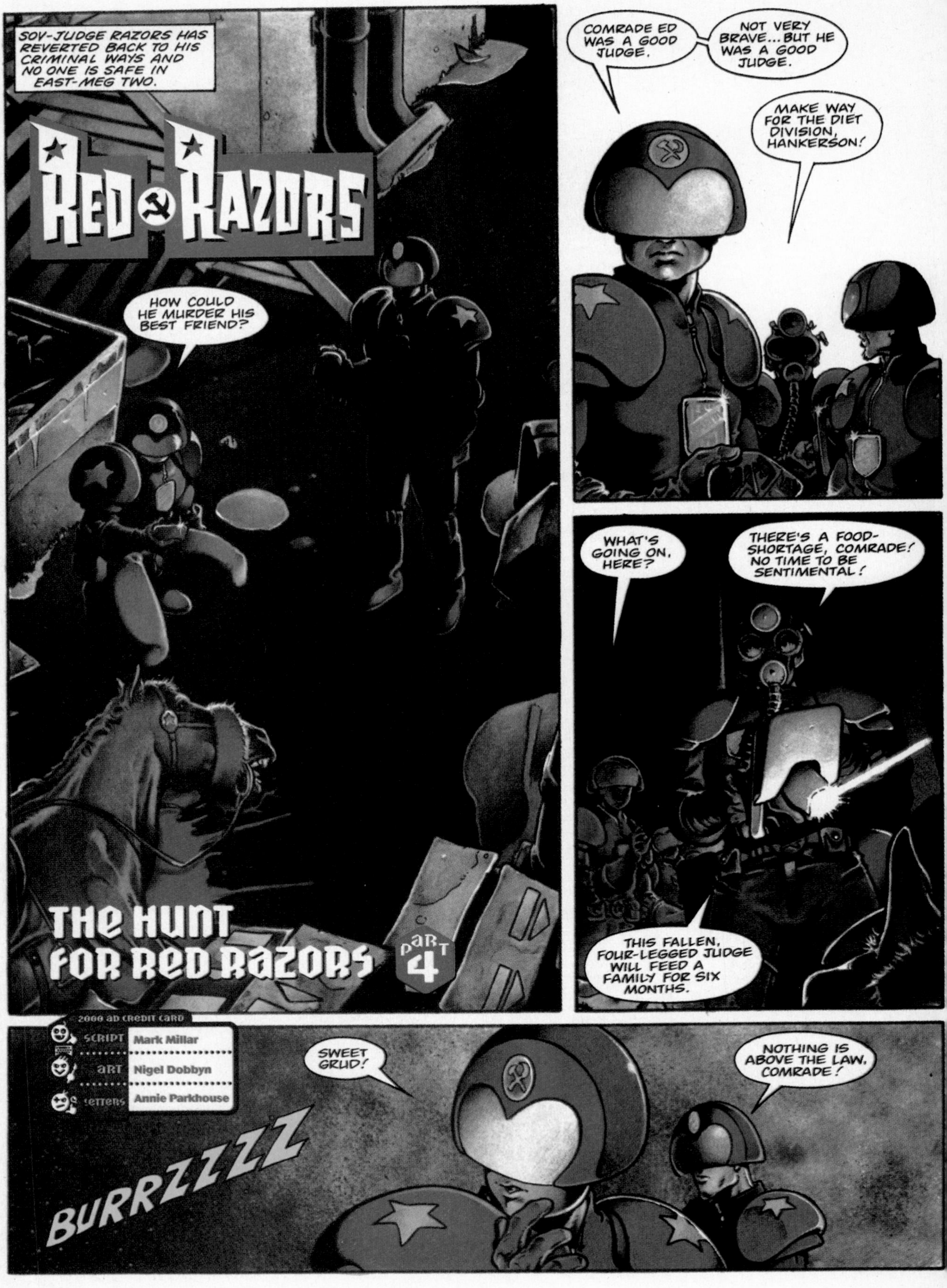
SOV-JUDGE RAZORS HAS REVERTED BACK TO HIS CRIMINAL WAYS AND NO ONE IS SAFE IN EAST-MEG TWO.
RED RAZORS
HOW COULD HE MURDER HIS BEST FRIEND?
THE HUNT FOR RED RAZORS
PART 4
COMRADE ED WAS A GOOD JUDGE.
NOT VERY BRAVE... BUT HE WAS A GOOD JUDGE.
MAKE WAY FOR THE DIET DIVISION, HANKERSON!
WHAT'S GOING ON, HERE?
THERE'S A FOOD-SHORTAGE, COMRADE! NO TIME TO BE SENTIMENTAL!
THIS FALLEN, FOUR-LEGGED JUDGE WILL FEED A FAMILY FOR SIX MONTHS.
2000 AD CREDIT CARD
SCRIPT Mark Millar
ART Nigel Dobbyn
LETTERS Annie Parkhouse
SWEET GRUD!
NOTHING IS ABOVE THE LAW, COMRADE!
BURRZZZZ

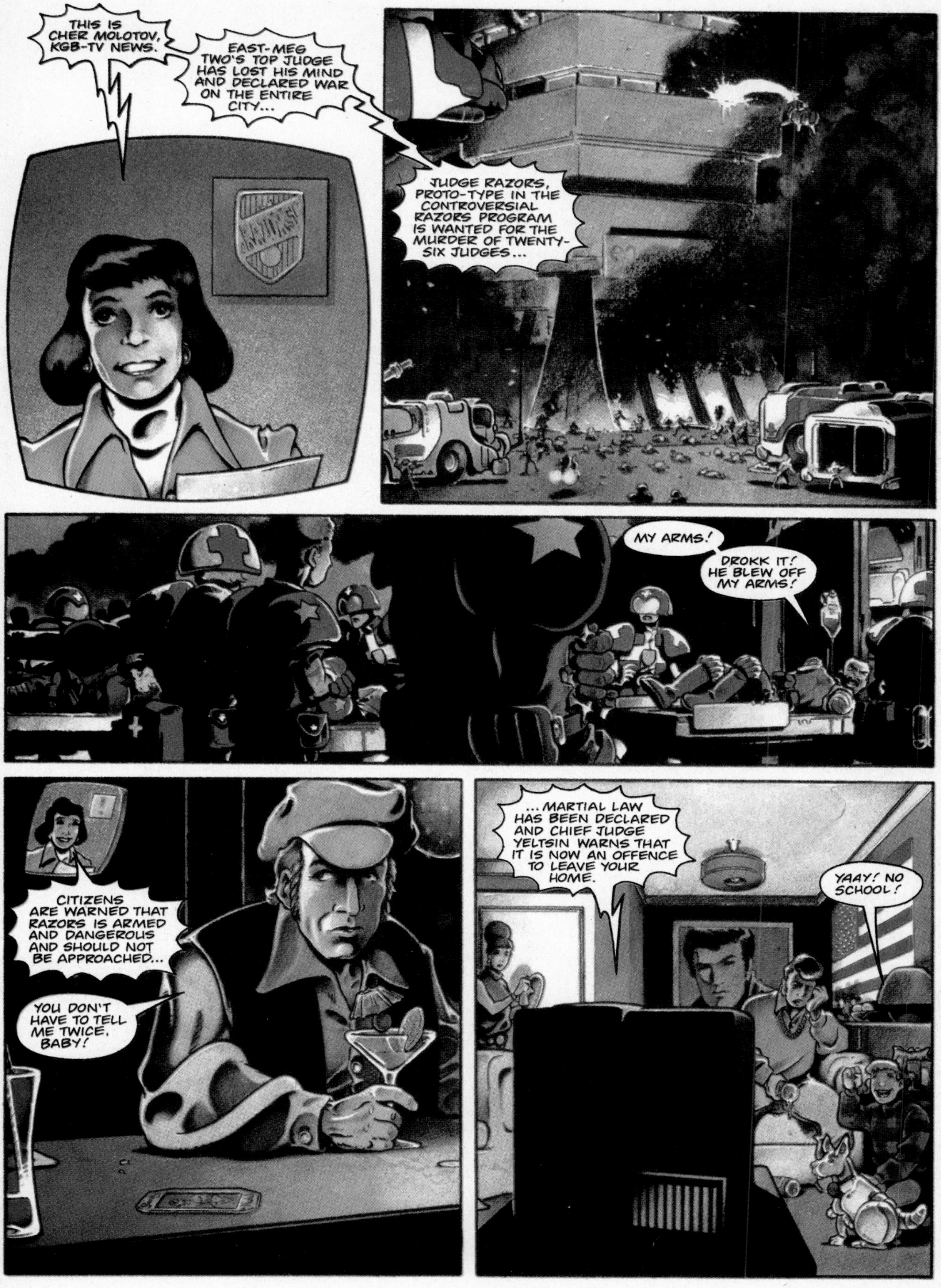
THIS IS CHER MOLOTOV, KGB-TV NEWS.
EAST-MEG TWO'S TOP JUDGE HAS LOST HIS MIND AND DECLARED WAR ON THE ENTIRE CITY...
JUDGE RAZORS, PROTO-TYPE IN THE CONTROVERSIAL RAZORS PROGRAM IS WANTED FOR THE MURDER OF TWENTY-SIX JUDGES...
MY ARMS!
DROKK IT! HE BLEW OFF MY ARMS!
CITIZENS ARE WARNED THAT RAZORS IS ARMED AND DANGEROUS AND SHOULD NOT BE APPROACHED...
YOU DON'T HAVE TO TELL ME TWICE, BABY!
...MARTIAL LAW HAS BEEN DECLARED AND CHIEF JUDGE YELTSIN WARNS THAT IT IS NOW AN OFFENCE TO LEAVE YOUR HOME.
YAAY! NO SCHOOL!

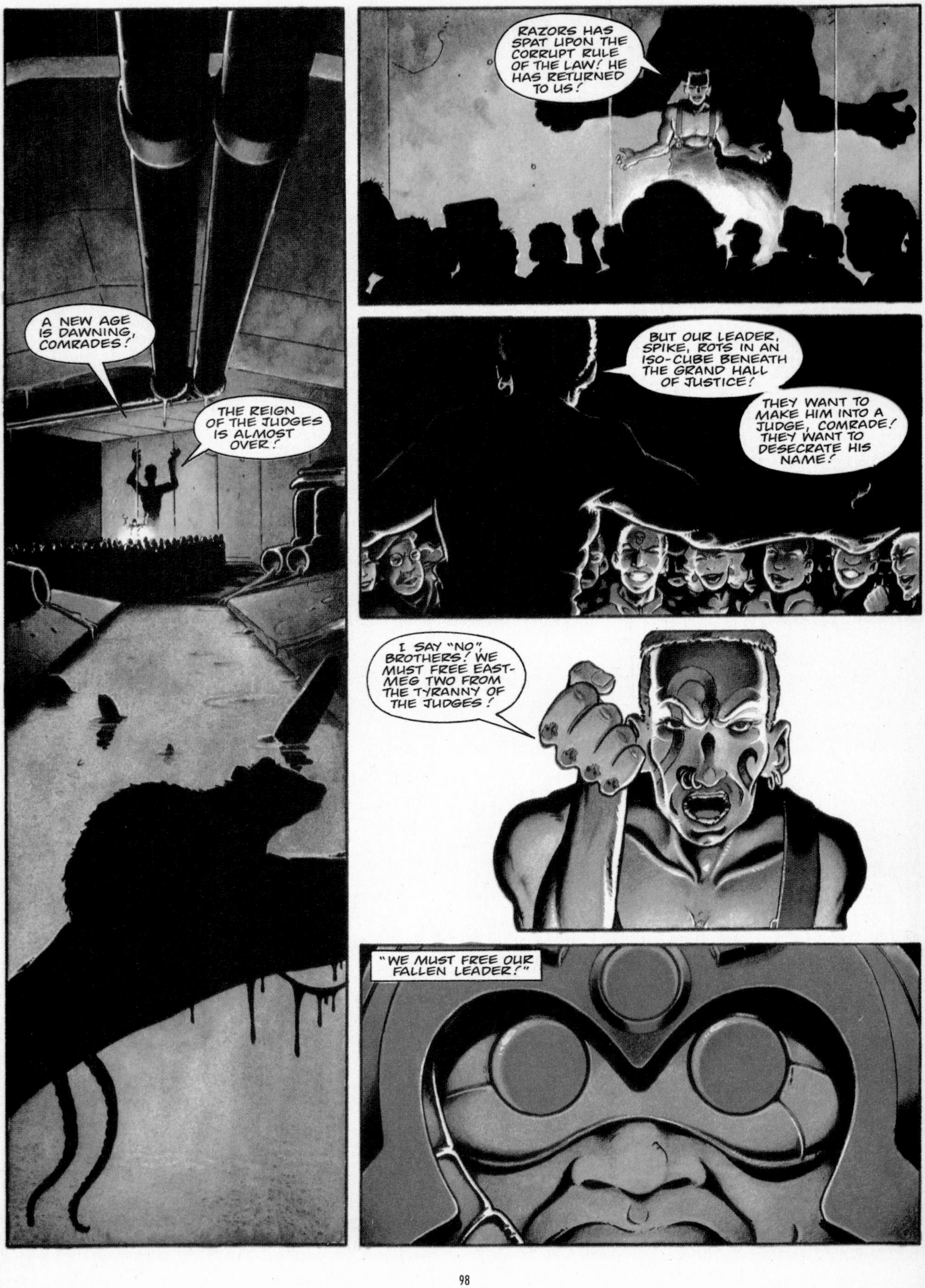
A NEW AGE IS DAWNING, COMRADES!
THE REIGN OF THE JUDGES IS ALMOST OVER!
RAZORS HAS SPAT UPON THE CORRUPT RULE OF THE LAW! HE HAS RETURNED TO US!
BUT OUR LEADER, SPIKE, ROTS IN AN ISO-CUBE BENEATH THE GRAND HALL OF JUSTICE!
THEY WANT TO MAKE HIM INTO A JUDGE, COMRADE! THEY WANT TO DESECRATE HIS NAME!
I SAY "NO", BROTHERS! WE MUST FREE EAST-MEG TWO FROM THE TYRANNY OF THE JUDGES!
"WE MUST FREE OUR FALLEN LEADER!"

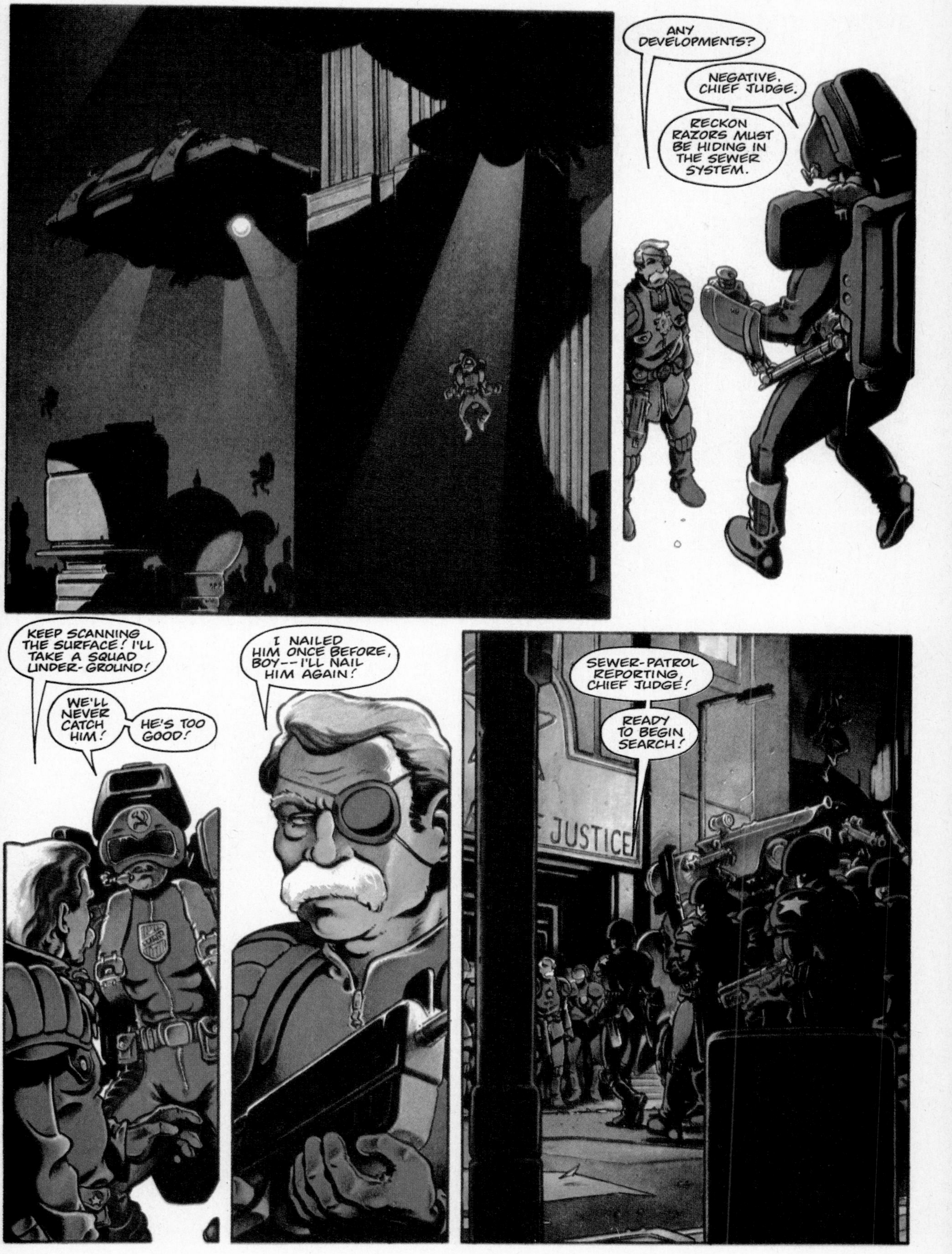

ANY DEVELOPMENTS?
NEGATIVE. CHIEF JUDGE.
RECKON RAZORS MUST BE HIDING IN THE SEWER SYSTEM.
KEEP SCANNING THE SURFACE! I'LL TAKE A SQUAD UNDER-GROUND!
WE'LL NEVER CATCH HIM!
HE'S TOO GOOD!
I NAILED HIM ONCE BEFORE, BOY--I'LL NAIL HIM AGAIN!
SEWER-PATROL REPORTING, CHIEF JUDGE!
READY TO BEGIN SEARCH!
JUSTICE

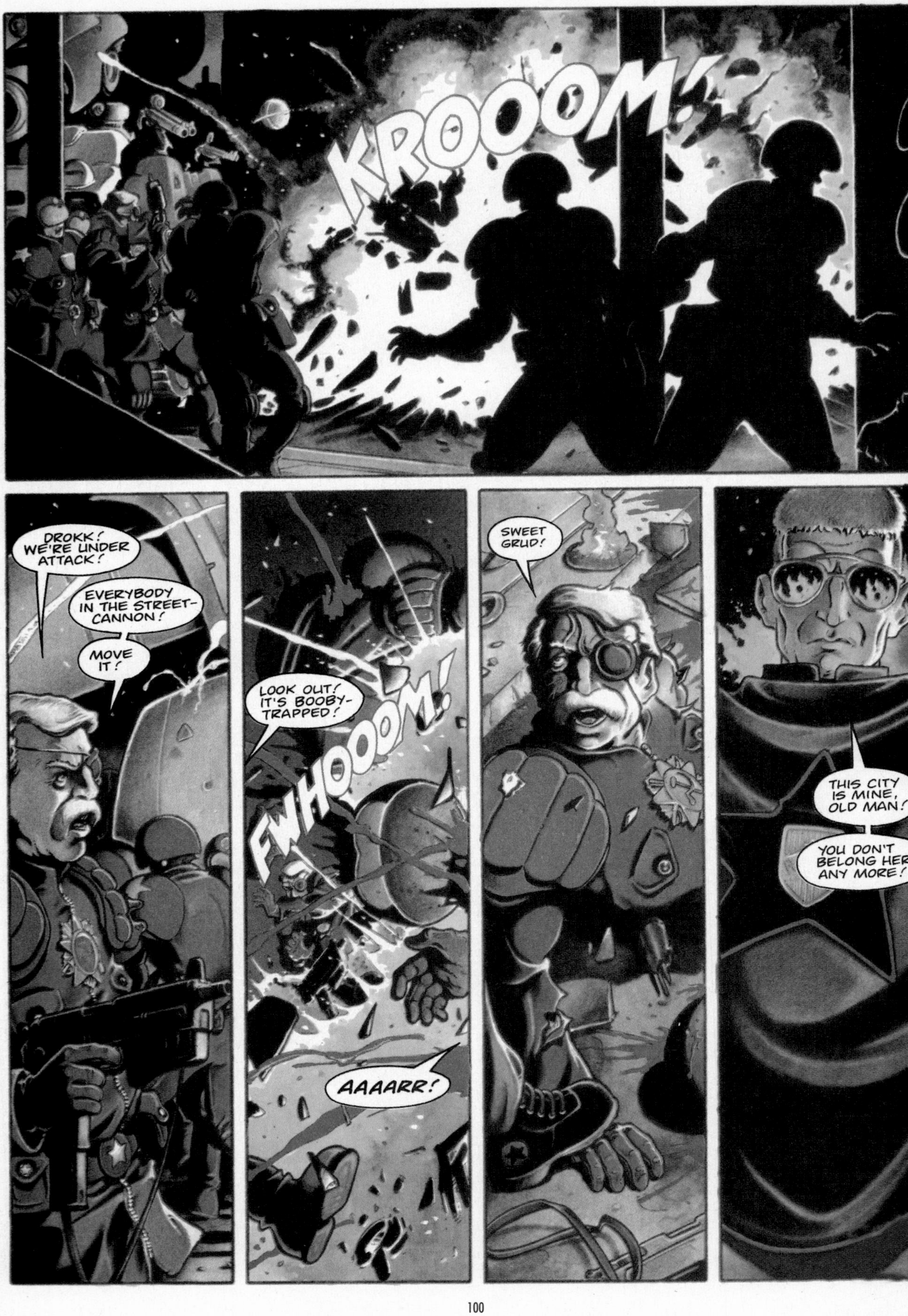
KROOOM!
DROKK! WE'RE UNDER ATTACK!
EVERYBODY IN THE STREET-CANNON!
MOVE IT!
LOOK OUT! IT'S BOOBY-TRAPPED!
FWHOOOM!
AAAARR!
SWEET GRUD!
THIS CITY IS MINE, OLD MAN!
YOU DON'T BELONG HERE ANY MORE!

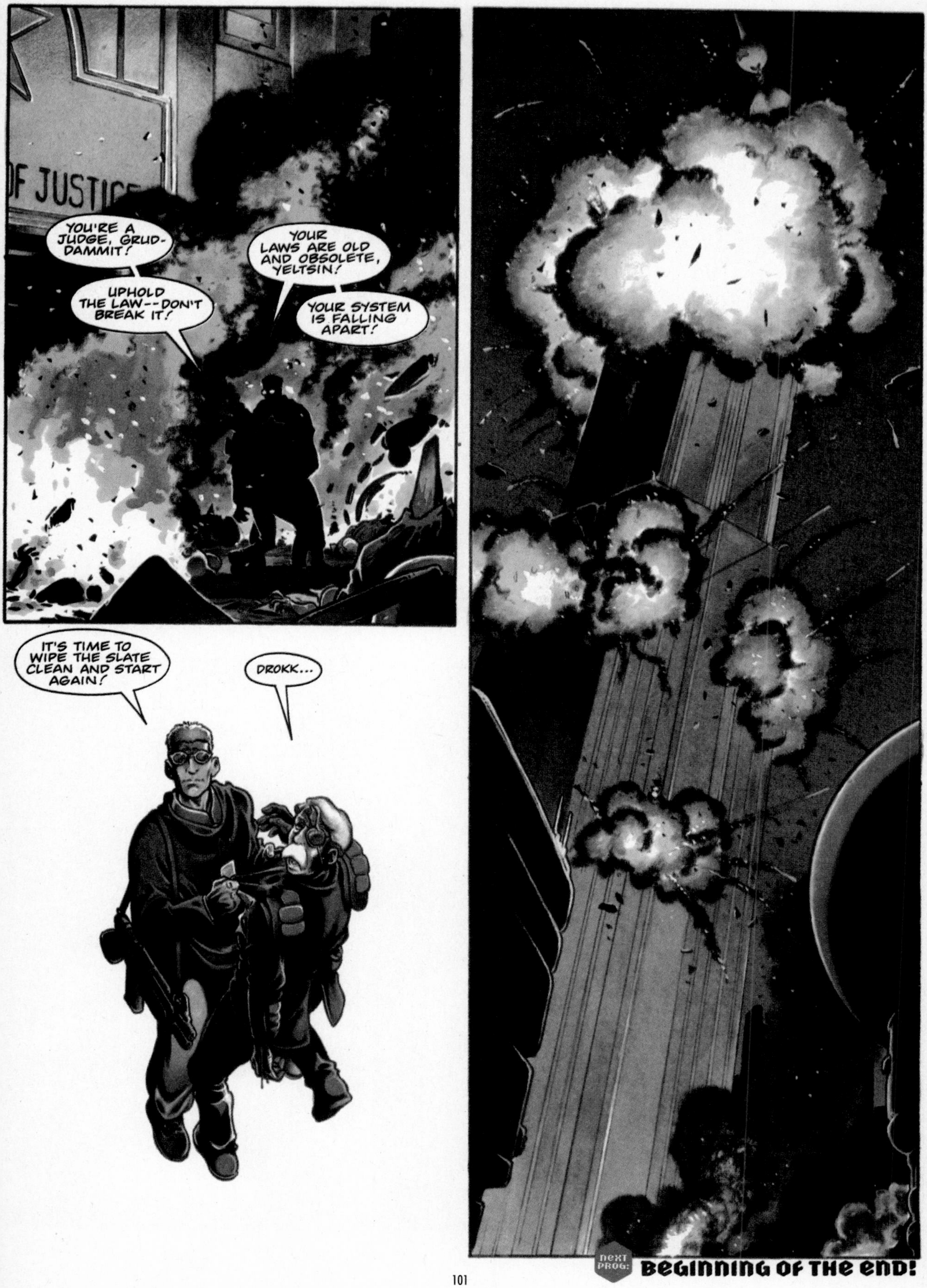
YOU'RE A JUDGE, GRUD-DAMMIT!
UPHOLD THE LAW--DON'T BREAK IT!
YOUR LAWS ARE OLD AND OBSOLETE, YELTSIN!
YOUR SYSTEM IS FALLING APART!
IT'S TIME TO WIPE THE SLATE CLEAN AND START AGAIN!
DROKK...

NEXT PROG: BEGINNING OF THE END!

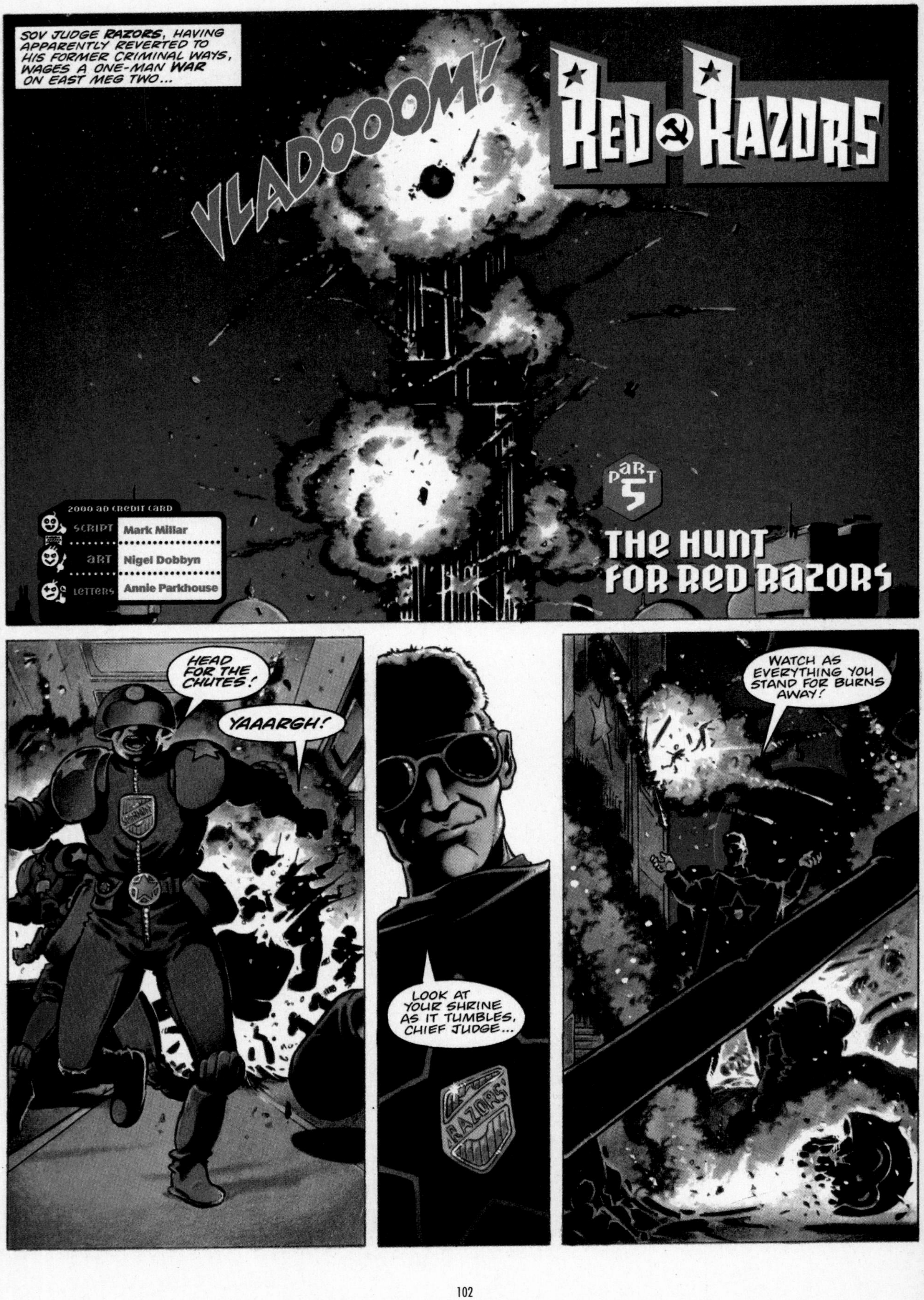
SOV JUDGE RAZORS, HAVING APPARENTLY REVERTED TO HIS FORMER CRIMINAL WAYS, WAGES A ONE-MAN WAR ON EAST MEG TWO...
VLADOOOM!
RED RAZORS
PART 5
THE HUNT FOR RED RAZORS
2000 AD CREDIT CARD
SCRIPT Mark Millar
ART Nigel Dobbyn
LETTERS Annie Parkhouse
HEAD FOR THE CHUTES!
YAAARGH!
LOOK AT YOUR SHRINE AS IT TUMBLES, CHIEF JUDGE...
RAZORS
WATCH AS EVERYTHING YOU STAND FOR BURNS AWAY!

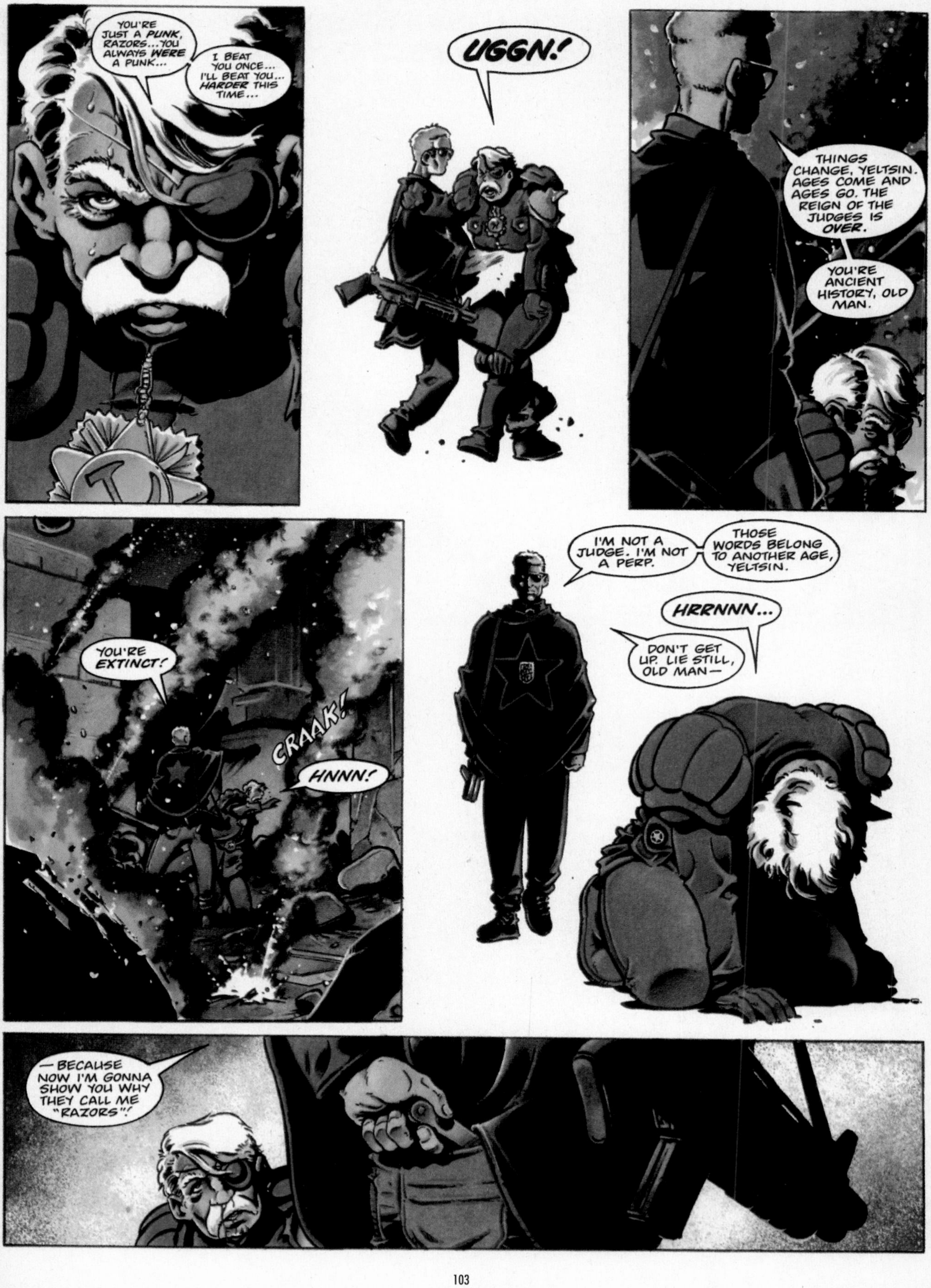

YOU'RE JUST A PUNK, RAZORS... YOU ALWAYS WERE A PUNK...
I BEAT YOU ONCE... I'LL BEAT YOU... HARDER THIS TIME...
UGGN!
THINGS CHANGE, YELTSIN. AGES COME AND AGES GO. THE REIGN OF THE JUDGES IS OVER.
YOU'RE ANCIENT HISTORY, OLD MAN.
YOU'RE EXTINCT!
CRAAK!
HNNN!
I'M NOT A JUDGE. I'M NOT A PERP.
THOSE WORDS BELONG TO ANOTHER AGE, YELTSIN.
HRRNNN...
DON'T GET UP. LIE STILL, OLD MAN—
—BECAUSE NOW I'M GONNA SHOW YOU WHY THEY CALL ME "RAZORS"!

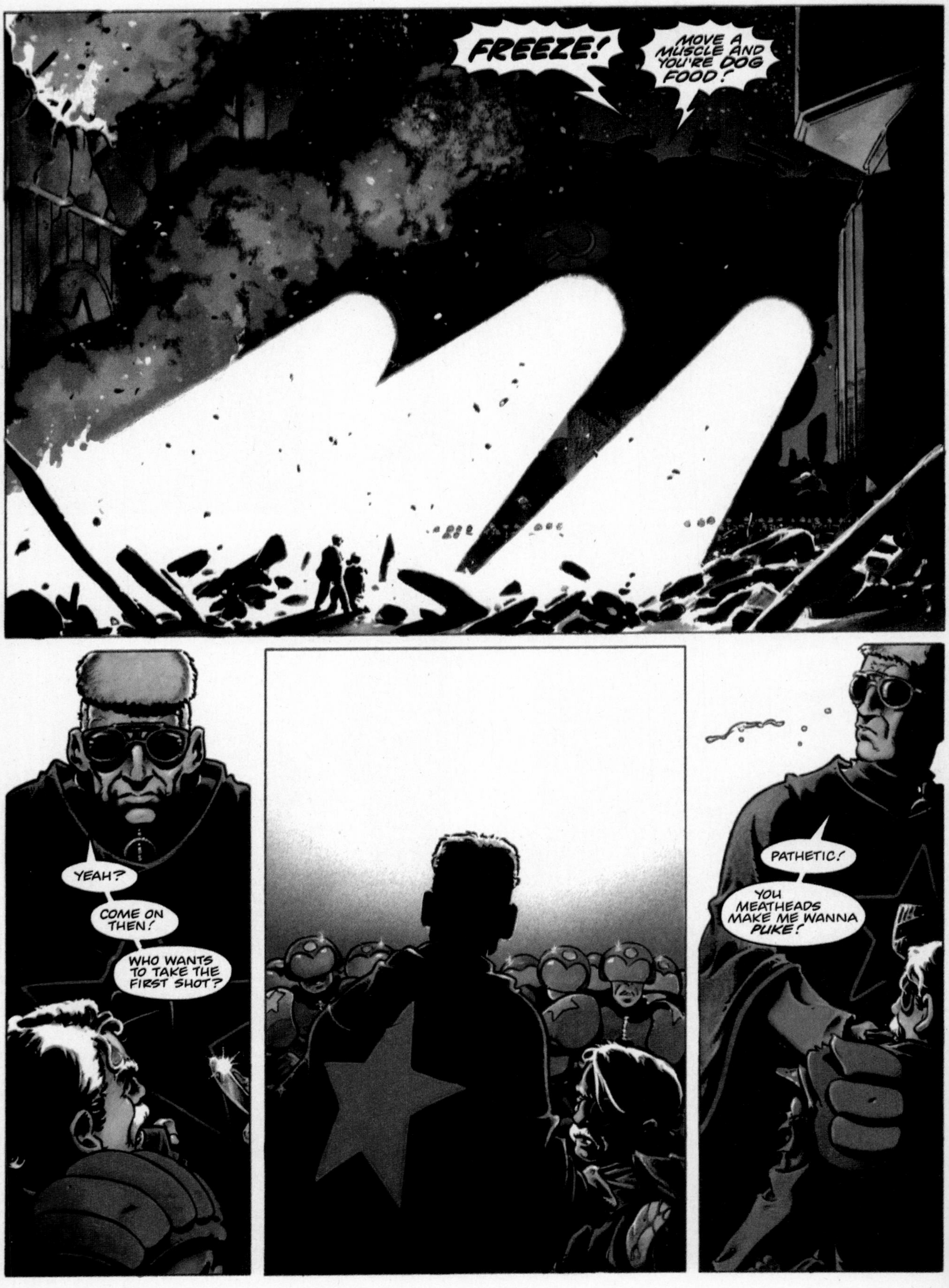
FREEZE!
MOVE A MUSCLE AND YOU'RE DOG FOOD!
YEAH?
COME ON THEN!
WHO WANTS TO TAKE THE FIRST SHOT?
PATHETIC!
YOU MEATHEADS MAKE ME WANNA PUKE!

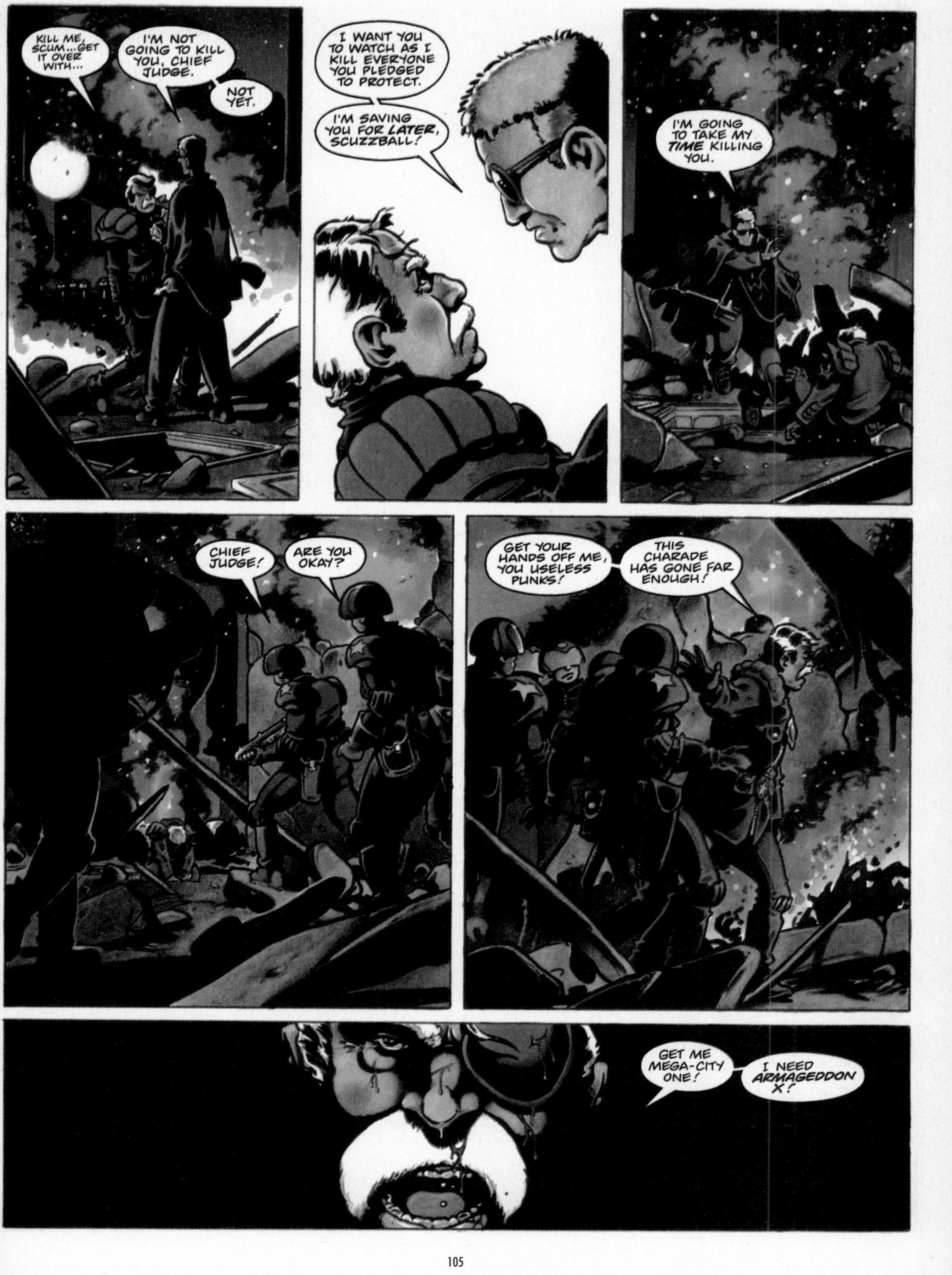

KILL ME, SCUM...GET IT OVER WITH...
I'M NOT GOING TO KILL YOU, CHIEF JUDGE.
NOT YET.
I WANT YOU TO WATCH AS I KILL EVERYONE YOU PLEDGED TO PROTECT.
I'M SAVING YOU FOR LATER, SCUZZBALL!
I'M GOING TO TAKE MY TIME KILLING YOU.
CHIEF JUDGE!
ARE YOU OKAY?
GET YOUR HANDS OFF ME, YOU USELESS PUNKS!
THIS CHARADE HAS GONE FAR ENOUGH!
GET ME MEGA-CITY ONE!
I NEED ARMAGEDDON X!

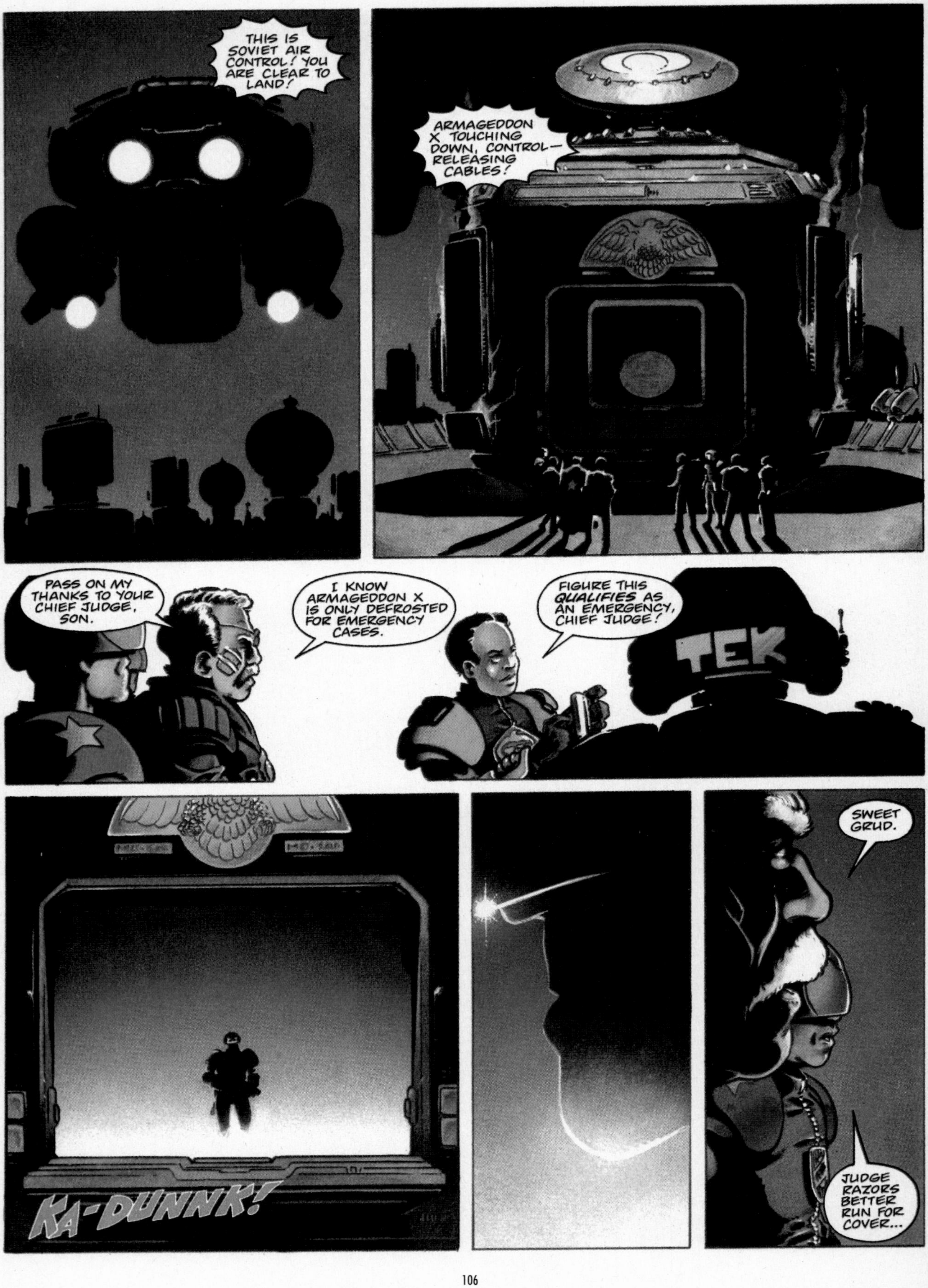

THIS IS SOVIET AIR CONTROL! YOU ARE CLEAR TO LAND!
ARMAGEDDON X TOUCHING DOWN, CONTROL-RELEASING CABLES!
PASS ON MY THANKS TO YOUR CHIEF JUDGE, SON.
I KNOW ARMAGEDDON X IS ONLY DEFROSTED FOR EMERGENCY CASES.
FIGURE THIS QUALIFIES AS AN EMERGENCY, CHIEF JUDGE!
TEK
KA-DUNNK!
SWEET GRUD.
JUDGE RAZORS BETTER RUN FOR COVER...

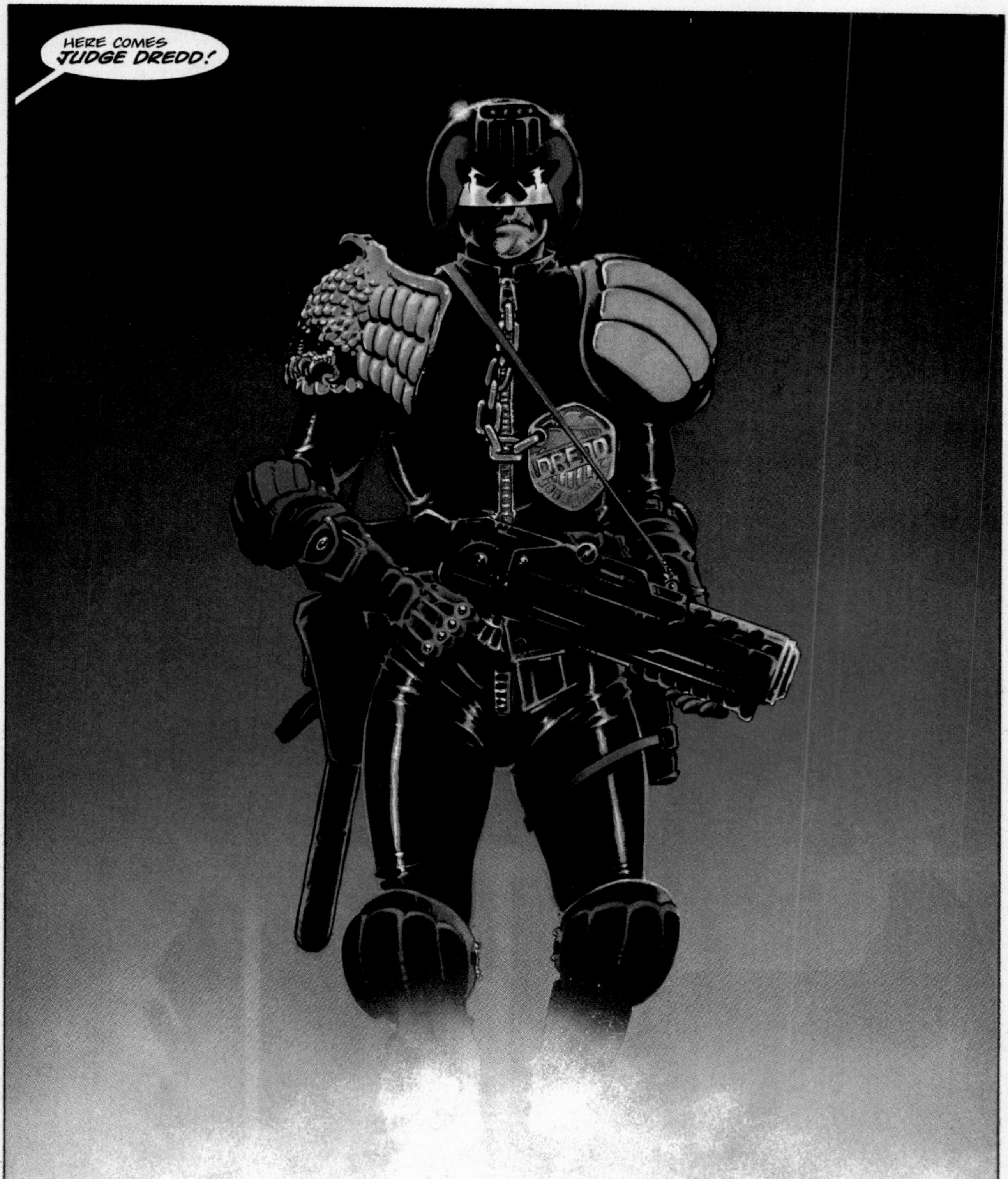
HERE COMES JUDGE DREDD!
ROBYN · 94

NEXT PROG: BACK FROM THE DREDD!

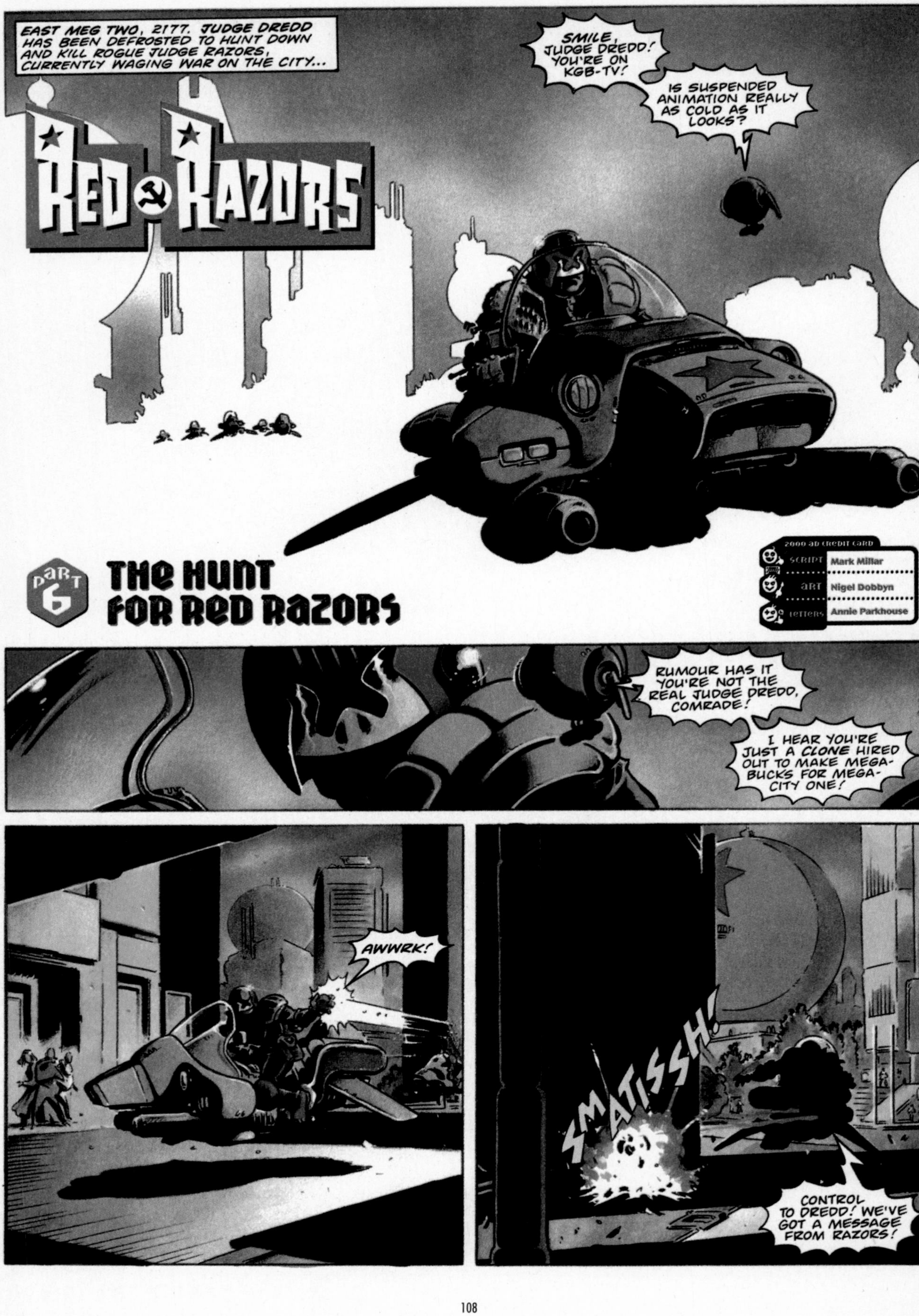

EAST MEG TWO, 2177. JUDGE DREDD HAS BEEN DEFROSTED TO HUNT DOWN AND KILL ROGUE JUDGE RAZORS, CURRENTLY WAGING WAR ON THE CITY...
RED RAZORS
SMILE, JUDGE DREDD! YOU'RE ON KGB-TV!
IS SUSPENDED ANIMATION REALLY AS COLD AS IT LOOKS?
PART 6
THE HUNT FOR RED RAZORS
2000 AD CREDIT CARD
SCRIPT Mark Millar
ART Nigel Dobbyn
LETTERS Annie Parkhouse
RUMOUR HAS IT YOU'RE NOT THE REAL JUDGE DREDD, COMRADE!
I HEAR YOU'RE JUST A CLONE HIRED OUT TO MAKE MEGA-BUCKS FOR MEGA-CITY ONE!
AWWRK!
SMATISSH!
CONTROL TO DREDD! WE'VE GOT A MESSAGE FROM RAZORS!

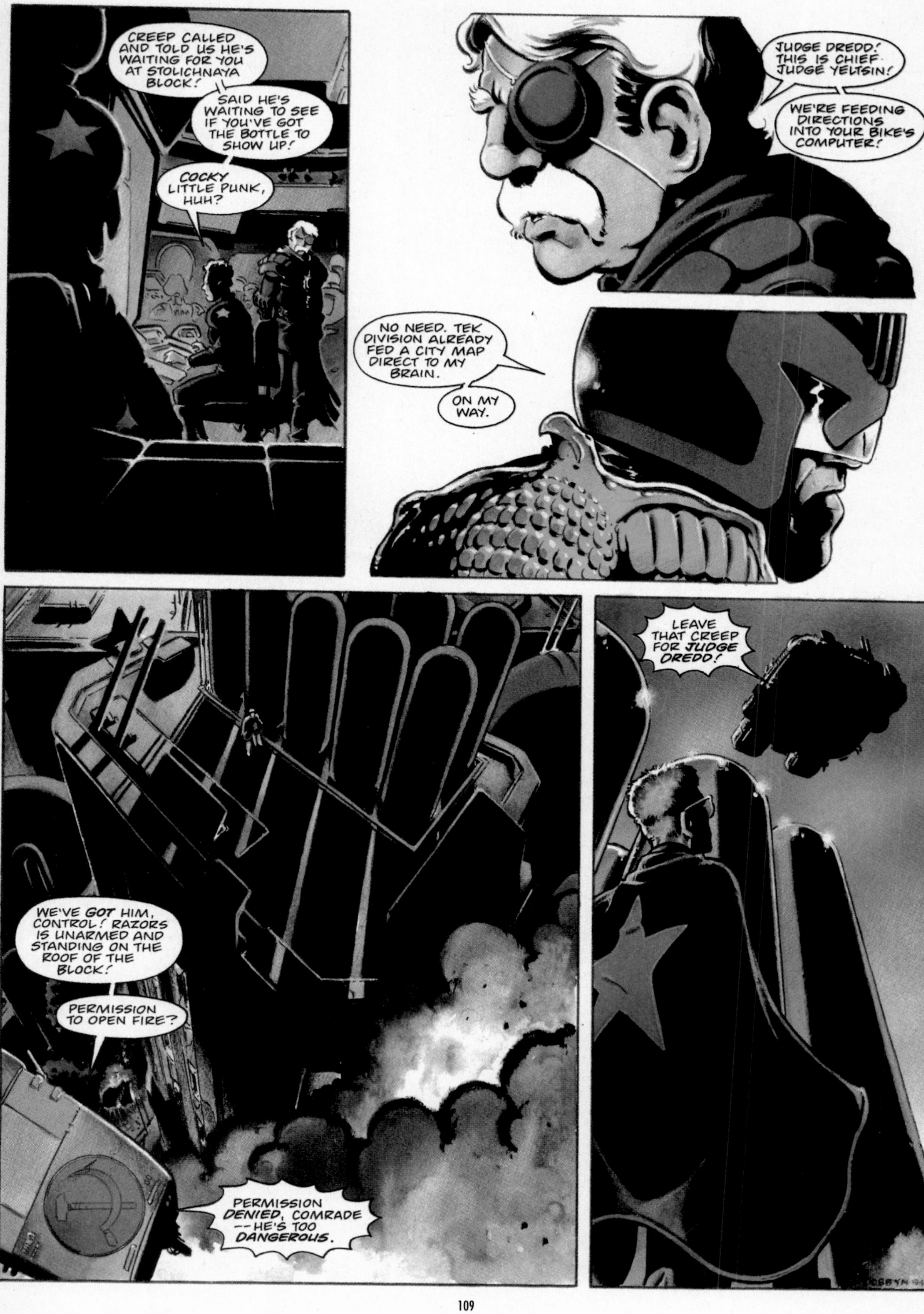
CREEP CALLED AND TOLD US HE'S WAITING FOR YOU AT STOLICHNAYA BLOCK!
SAID HE'S WAITING TO SEE IF YOU'VE GOT THE BOTTLE TO SHOW UP!
COCKY LITTLE PUNK, HUH?
JUDGE DREDD! THIS IS CHIEF JUDGE YELTSIN!
WE'RE FEEDING DIRECTIONS INTO YOUR BIKE'S COMPUTER!
NO NEED. TEK DIVISION ALREADY FED A CITY MAP DIRECT TO MY BRAIN.
ON MY WAY.
WE'VE GOT HIM, CONTROL! RAZORS IS UNARMED AND STANDING ON THE ROOF OF THE BLOCK!
PERMISSION TO OPEN FIRE?
PERMISSION DENIED, COMRADE -- HE'S TOO DANGEROUS.
LEAVE THAT CREEP FOR JUDGE DREDD!

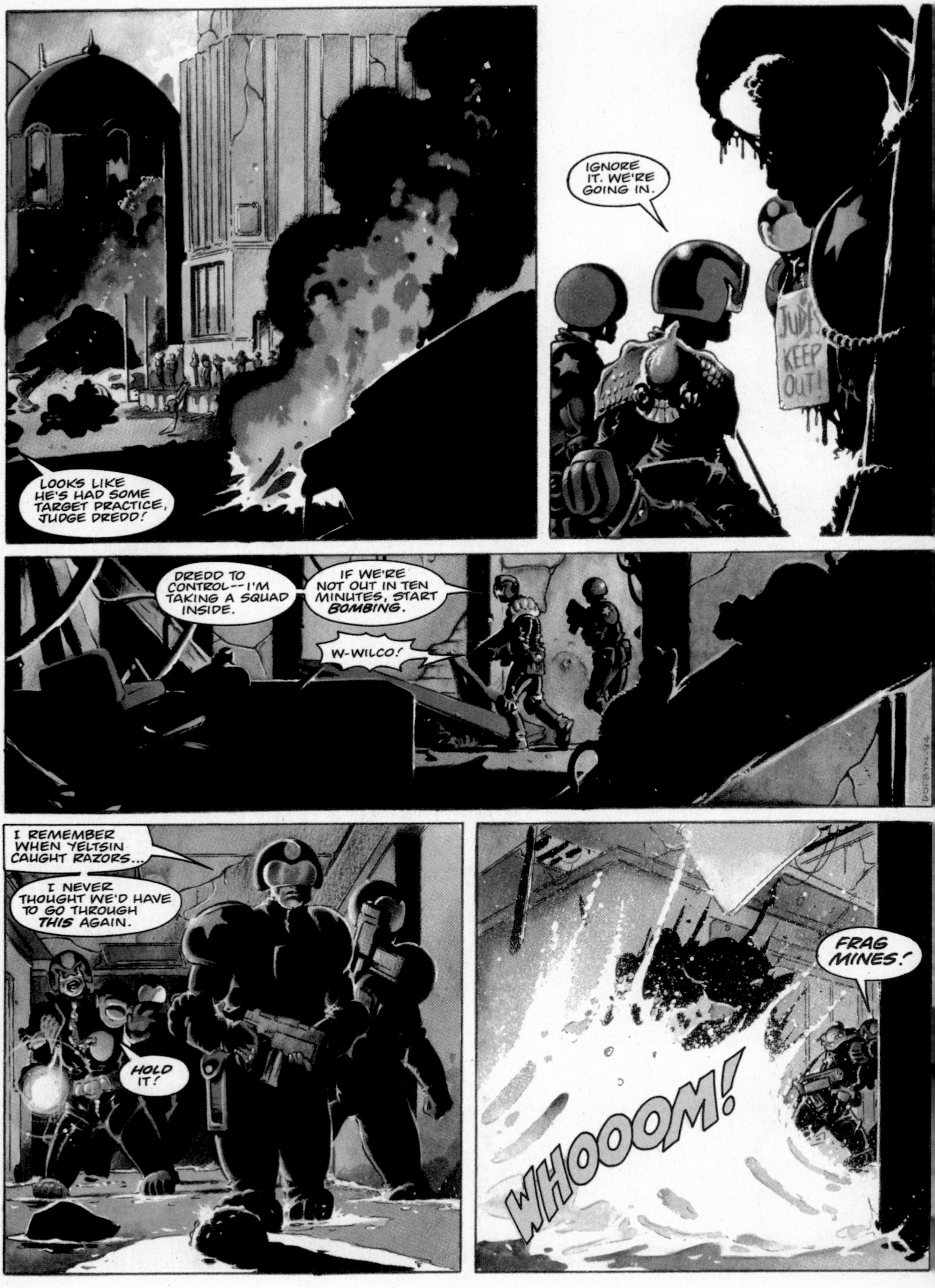
LOOKS LIKE HE'S HAD SOME TARGET PRACTICE, JUDGE DREDD!
IGNORE IT. WE'RE GOING IN.
KEEP OUT!
DREDD TO CONTROL--I'M TAKING A SQUAD INSIDE.
IF WE'RE NOT OUT IN TEN MINUTES, START BOMBING.
W-WILCO!
I REMEMBER WHEN YELTSIN CAUGHT RAZORS...
I NEVER THOUGHT WE'D HAVE TO GO THROUGH THIS AGAIN.
HOLD IT!
FRAG MINES!
WHOOOM!

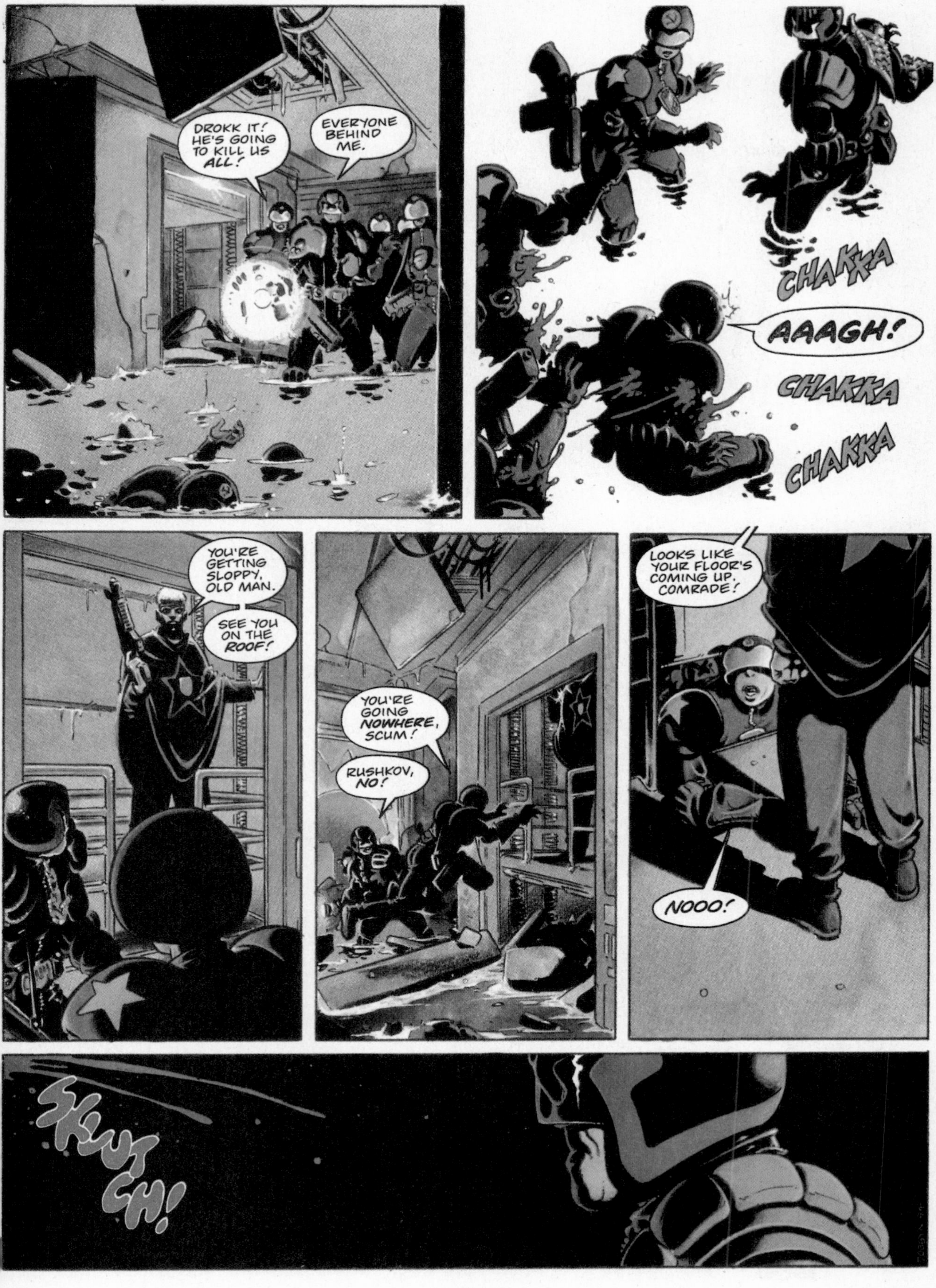
DROKK IT! HE'S GOING TO KILL US ALL!
EVERYONE BEHIND ME.
CHAKKA
AAAGH!
CHAKKA
CHAKKA
YOU'RE GETTING SLOPPY, OLD MAN.
SEE YOU ON THE ROOF!
YOU'RE GOING NOWHERE, SCUM!
RUSHKOV, NO!
LOOKS LIKE YOUR FLOOR'S COMING UP, COMRADE!
NOOO!
SKLUTCH!

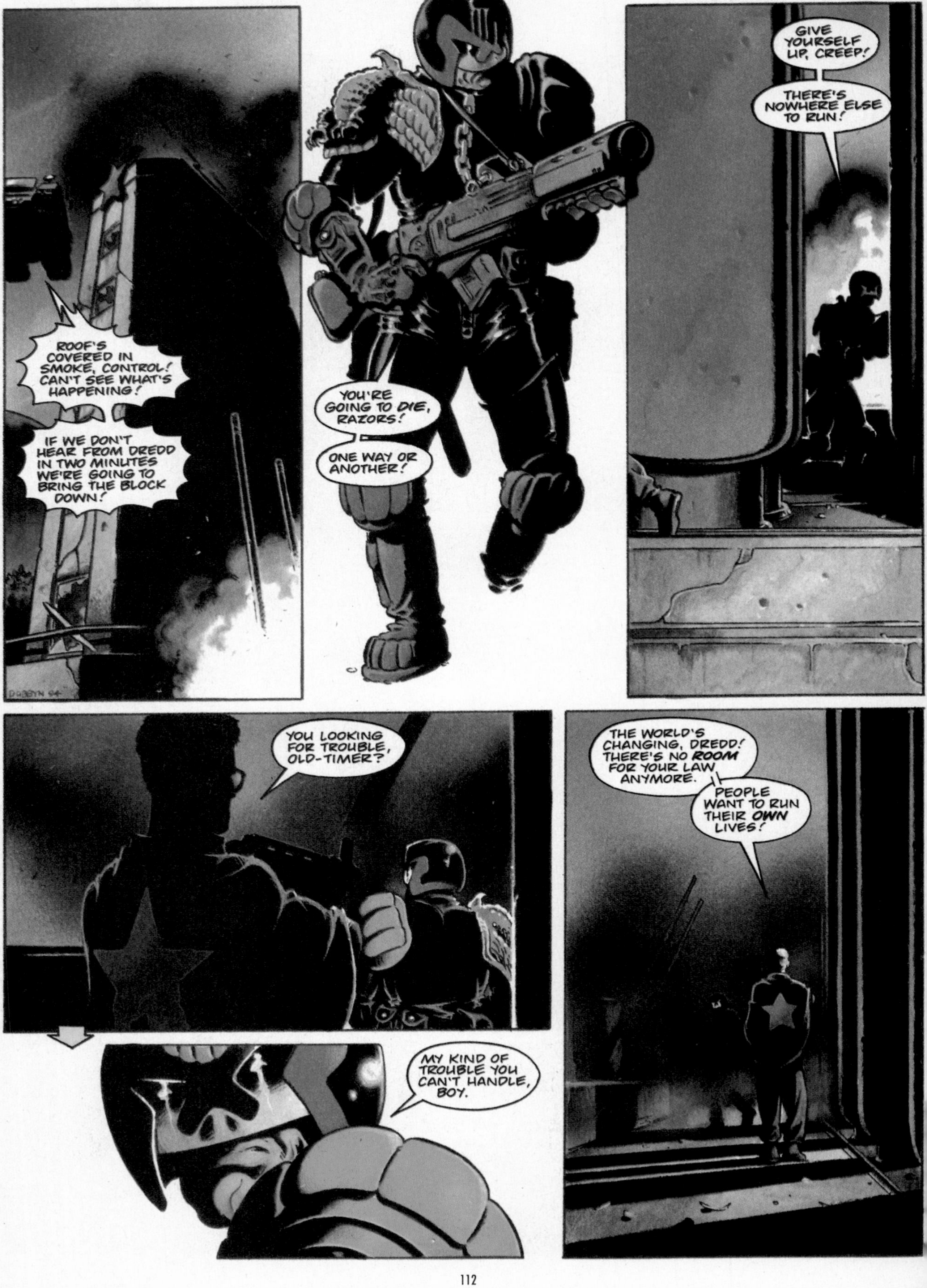

ROOF'S COVERED IN SMOKE, CONTROL! CAN'T SEE WHAT'S HAPPENING!
IF WE DON'T HEAR FROM DREDD IN TWO MINUTES WE'RE GOING TO BRING THE BLOCK DOWN!
DOBBYN 94
YOU'RE GOING TO DIE, RAZORS!
ONE WAY OR ANOTHER!
GIVE YOURSELF UP, CREEP!
THERE'S NOWHERE ELSE TO RUN!
YOU LOOKING FOR TROUBLE, OLD-TIMER?
MY KIND OF TROUBLE YOU CAN'T HANDLE, BOY.
THE WORLD'S CHANGING, DREDD! THERE'S NO ROOM FOR YOUR LAW ANYMORE.
PEOPLE WANT TO RUN THEIR OWN LIVES!

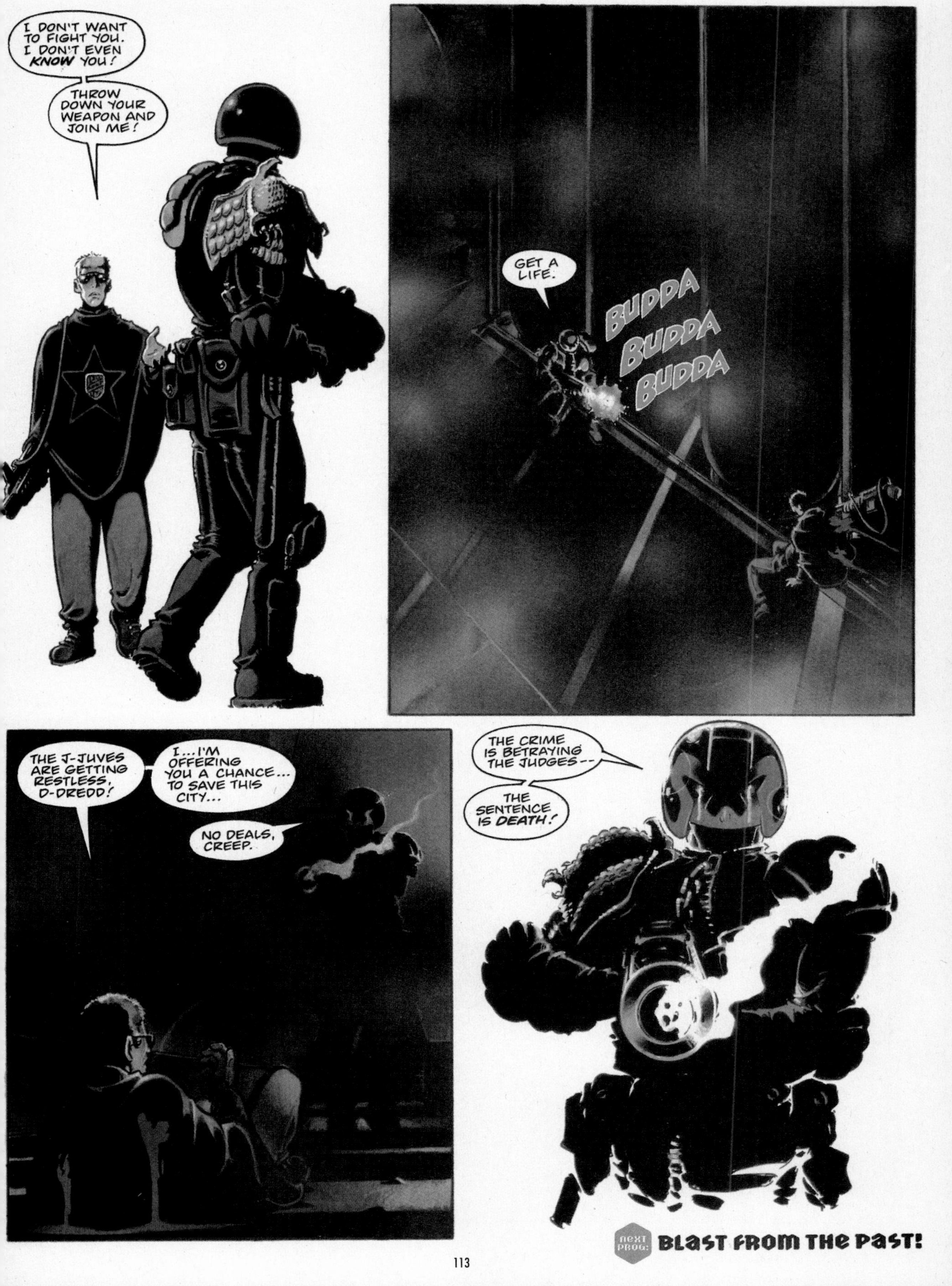
I DON'T WANT TO FIGHT YOU. I DON'T EVEN KNOW YOU!
THROW DOWN YOUR WEAPON AND JOIN ME!
GET A LIFE.
BUDDA BUDDA BUDDA
THE J-JUVES ARE GETTING RESTLESS, D-DREDD!
I...I'M OFFERING YOU A CHANCE... TO SAVE THIS CITY...
NO DEALS, CREEP.
THE CRIME IS BETRAYING THE JUDGES--
THE SENTENCE IS DEATH!
NEXT PROG: BLAST FROM THE PAST!

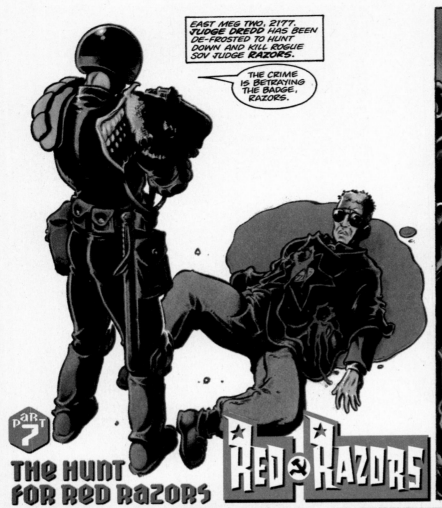

EAST MEG TWO, 2177. *JUDGE DREDD* HAS BEEN DE-FROSTED TO HUNT DOWN AND KILL ROGUE SOV JUDGE *RAZORS.*

THE CRIME IS BETRAYING THE BADGE, RAZORS.

PART 7

THE HUNT FOR RED RAZORS

THE SENTENCE IS *DEATH!*

ANY SIGN OF DREDD? HIS TEN MINUTES ARE UP!

CAN'T SEE A *THING* IN ALL THIS SMOKE...

COMMENCE FIRING! WE CAN'T TAKE ANY CHANCES!

FTOOOM!

DROKK!

2000 AD CREDIT CARD

SCRIPT | Mark Millar
ART | Nigel Dobbyn
LETTERS | Annie Parkhouse

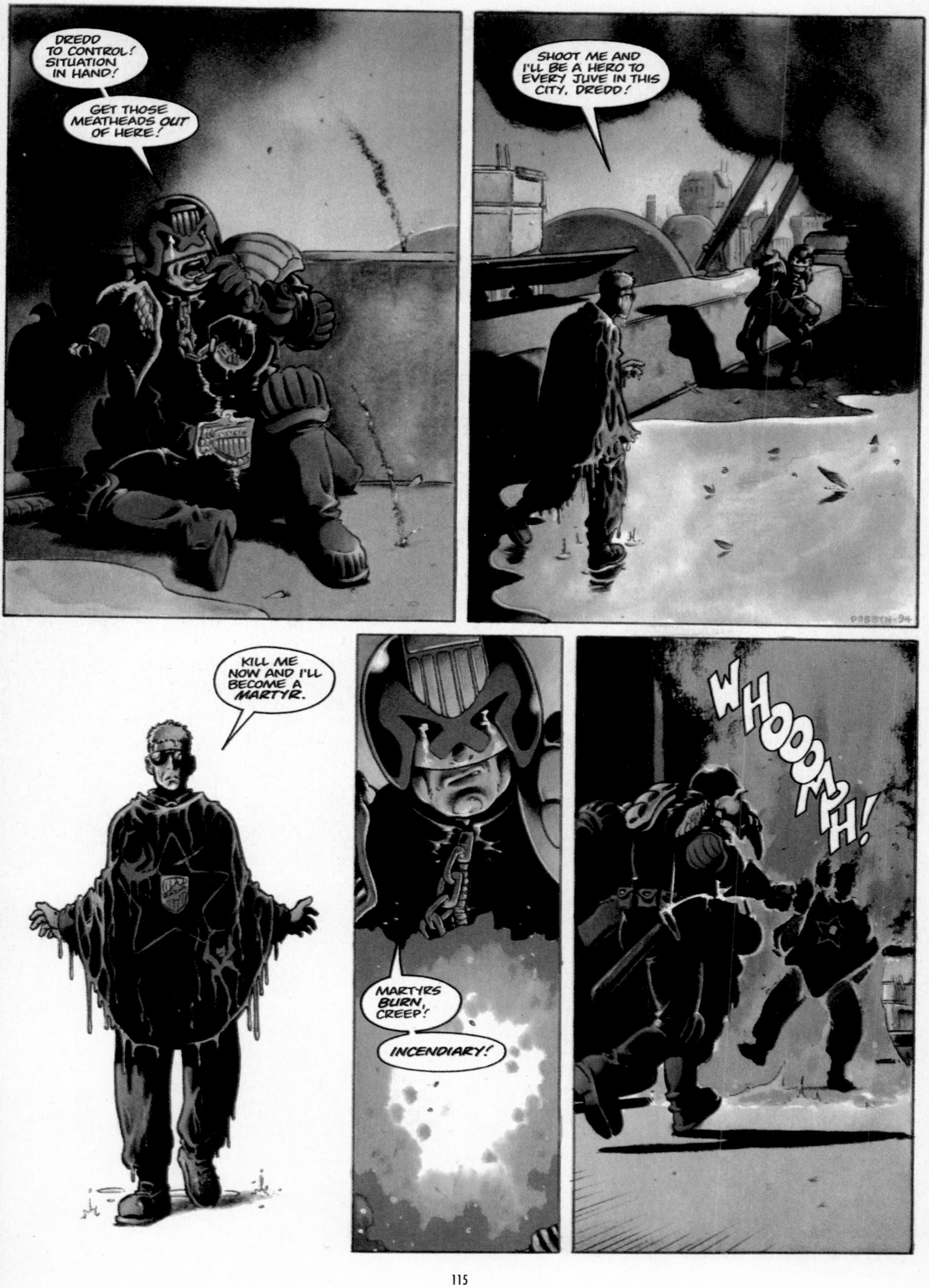
DREDD TO CONTROL! SITUATION IN HAND!
GET THOSE MEATHEADS OUT OF HERE!
SHOOT ME AND I'LL BE A HERO TO EVERY JUVE IN THIS CITY, DREDD!
DOBBYN-94
KILL ME NOW AND I'LL BECOME A MARTYR.
MARTYRS BURN, CREEP!
INCENDIARY!
WHOOOMPH!

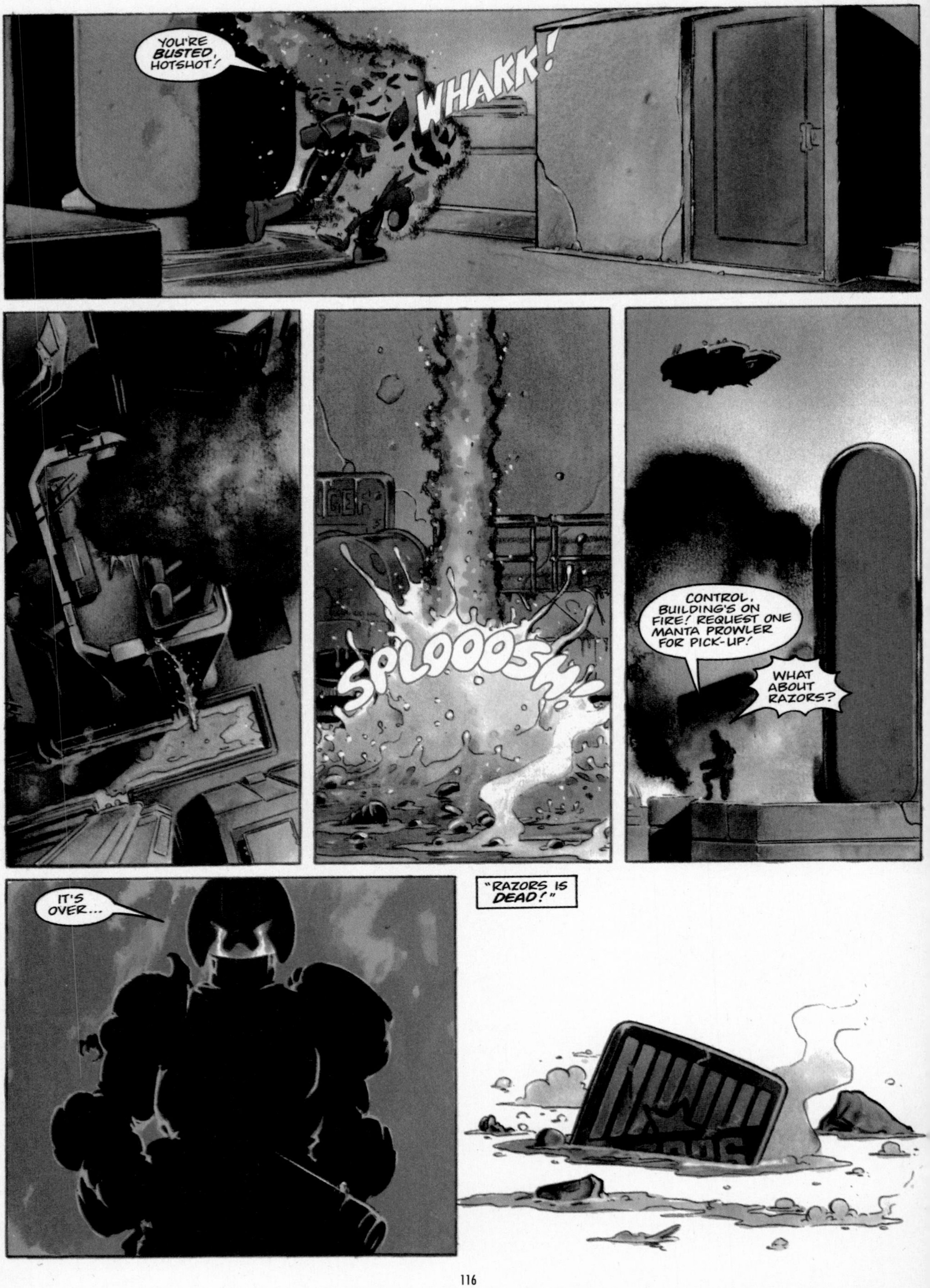
YOU'RE BUSTED, HOTSHOT!
WHAKK!
SPLOOOSH!
CONTROL, BUILDING'S ON FIRE! REQUEST ONE MANTA PROWLER FOR PICK-UP!
WHAT ABOUT RAZORS?
IT'S OVER...
"RAZORS IS DEAD!"

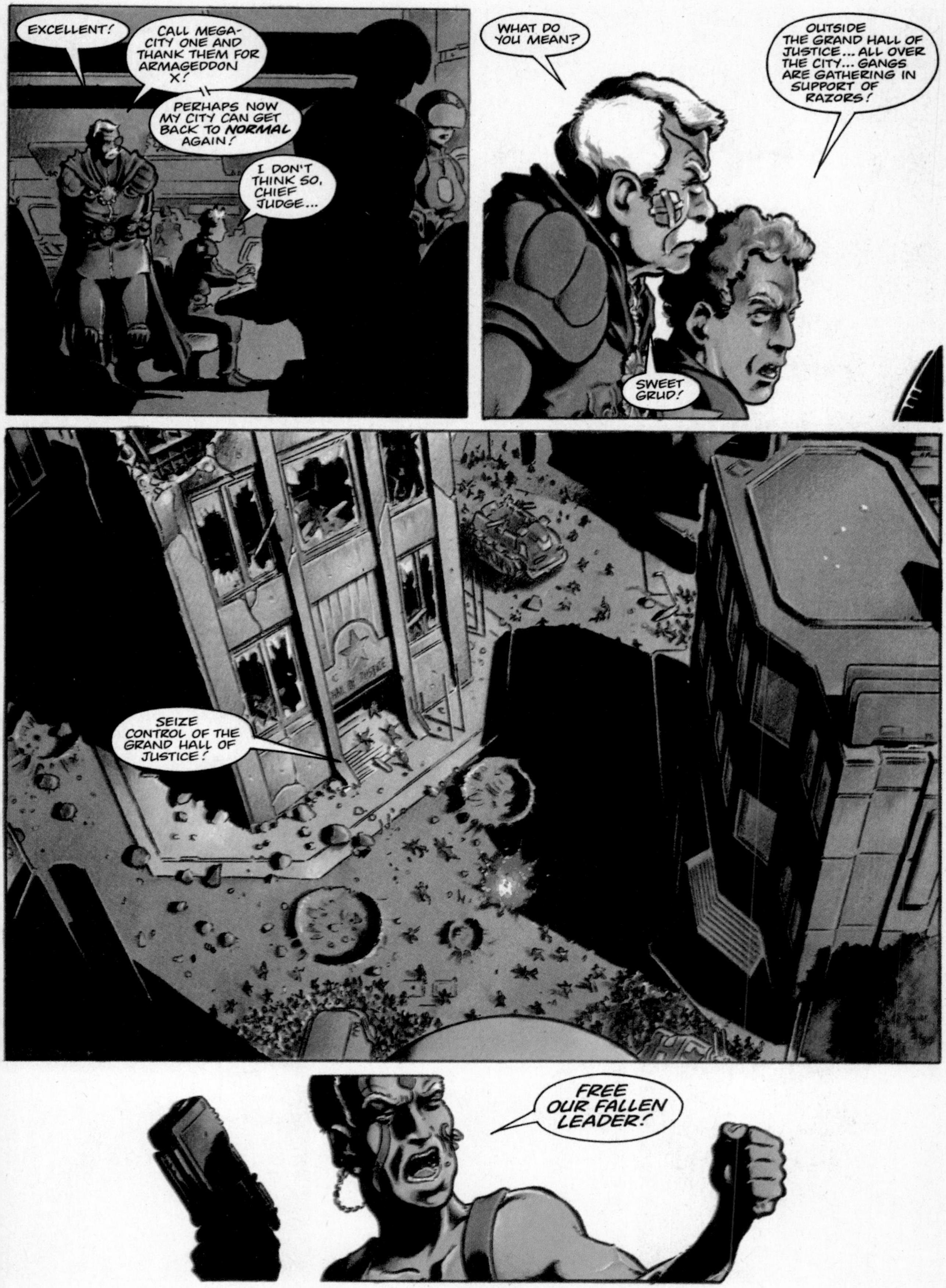
EXCELLENT!
CALL MEGA-CITY ONE AND THANK THEM FOR ARMAGEDDON X!
PERHAPS NOW MY CITY CAN GET BACK TO NORMAL AGAIN!
I DON'T THINK SO, CHIEF JUDGE...
WHAT DO YOU MEAN?
OUTSIDE THE GRAND HALL OF JUSTICE... ALL OVER THE CITY... GANGS ARE GATHERING IN SUPPORT OF RAZORS!
SWEET GRUD!
SEIZE CONTROL OF THE GRAND HALL OF JUSTICE!
FREE OUR FALLEN LEADER!

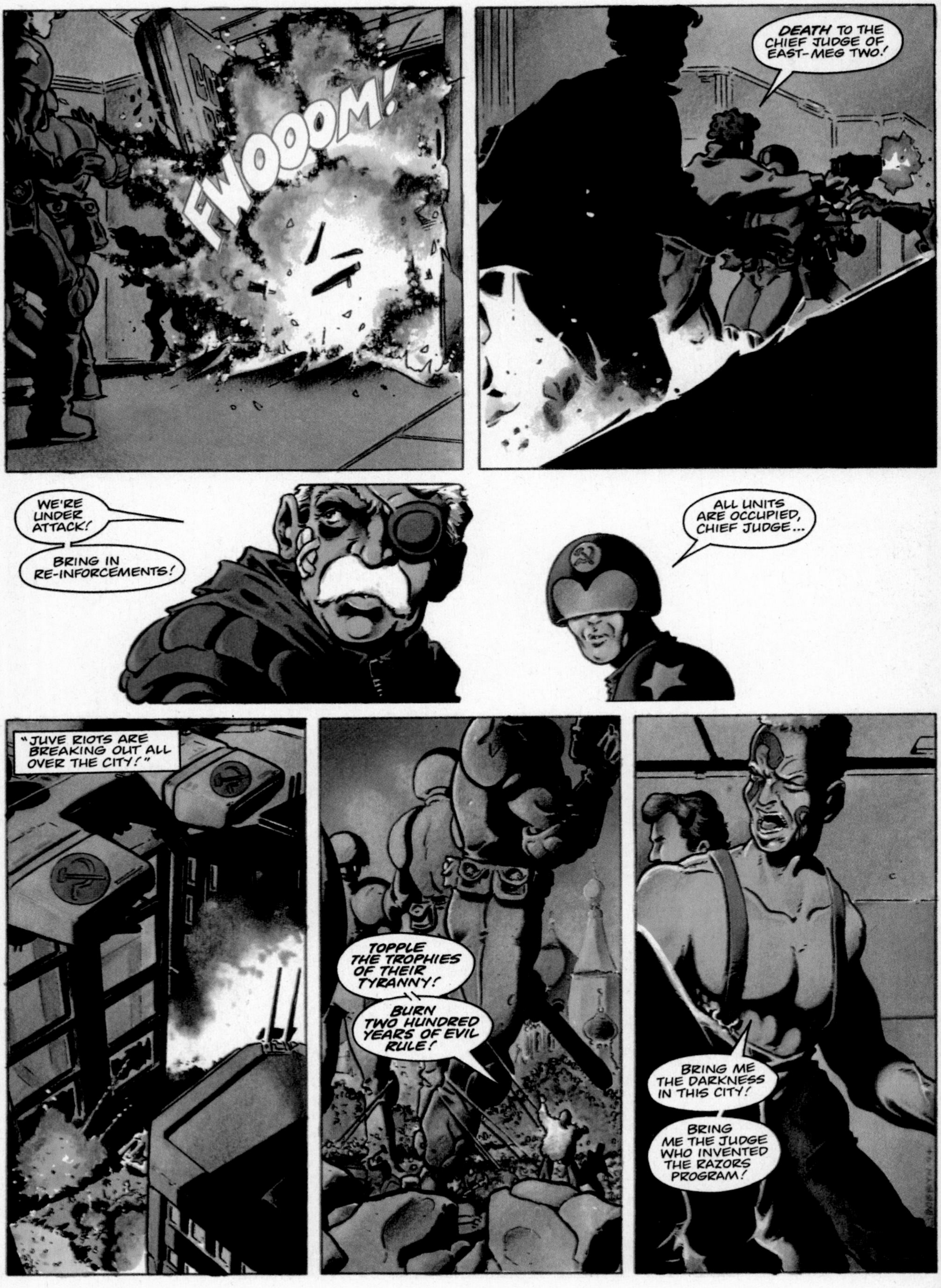
FWOOOM!
DEATH TO THE CHIEF JUDGE OF EAST-MEG TWO!
WE'RE UNDER ATTACK!
BRING IN RE-INFORCEMENTS!
ALL UNITS ARE OCCUPIED, CHIEF JUDGE...
"JUVE RIOTS ARE BREAKING OUT ALL OVER THE CITY!"
TOPPLE THE TROPHIES OF THEIR TYRANNY!
BURN TWO HUNDRED YEARS OF EVIL RULE!
BRING ME THE DARKNESS IN THIS CITY!
BRING ME THE JUDGE WHO INVENTED THE RAZORS PROGRAM!

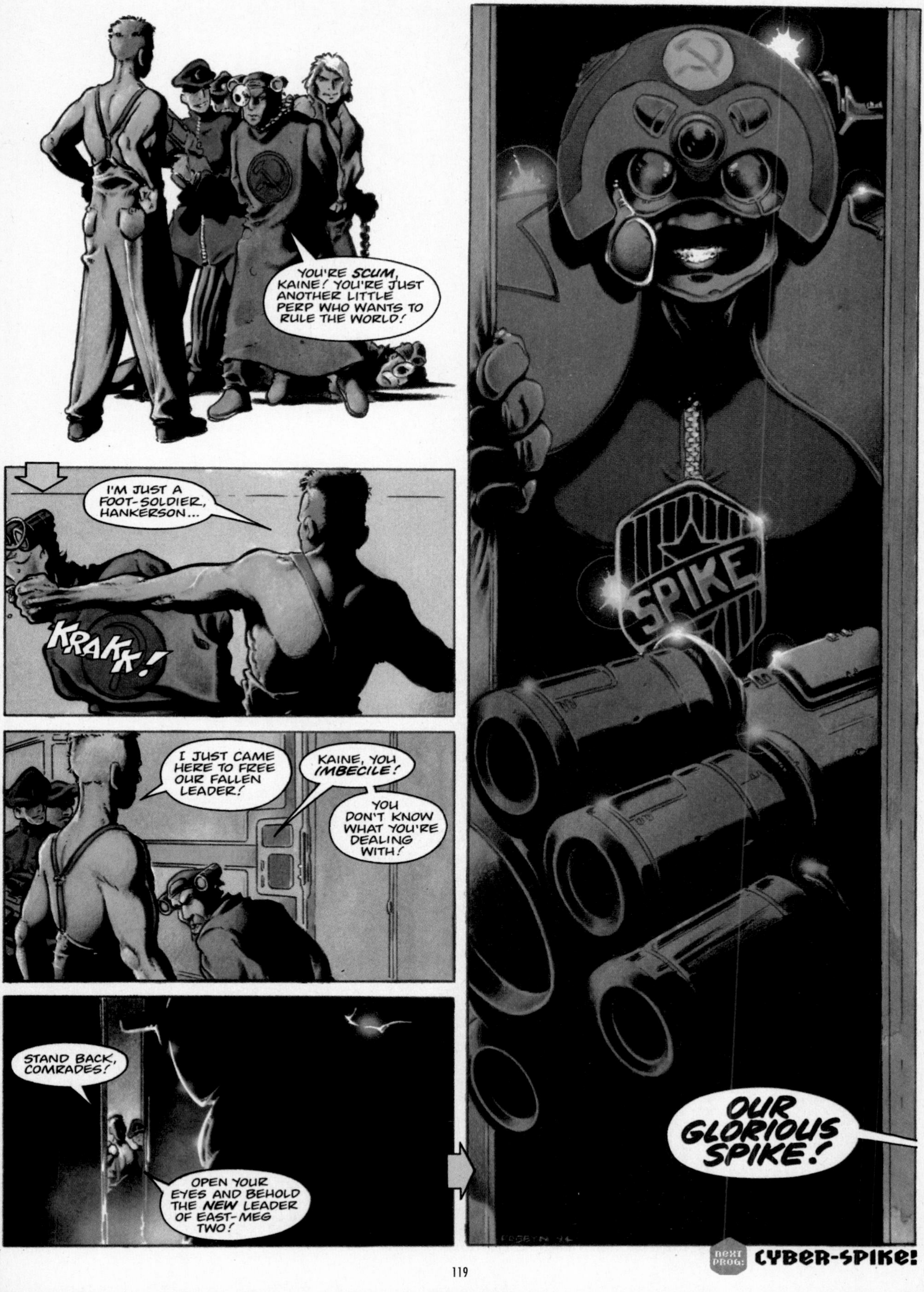
YOU'RE SCUM, KAINE! YOU'RE JUST ANOTHER LITTLE PERP WHO WANTS TO RULE THE WORLD!
I'M JUST A FOOT-SOLDIER, HANKERSON...
KRAKK!
I JUST CAME HERE TO FREE OUR FALLEN LEADER!
KAINE, YOU IMBECILE!
YOU DON'T KNOW WHAT YOU'RE DEALING WITH!
STAND BACK, COMRADES!
OPEN YOUR EYES AND BEHOLD THE NEW LEADER OF EAST-MEG TWO!
SPIKE
OUR GLORIOUS SPIKE!
NEXT PROG: CYBER-SPIKE!

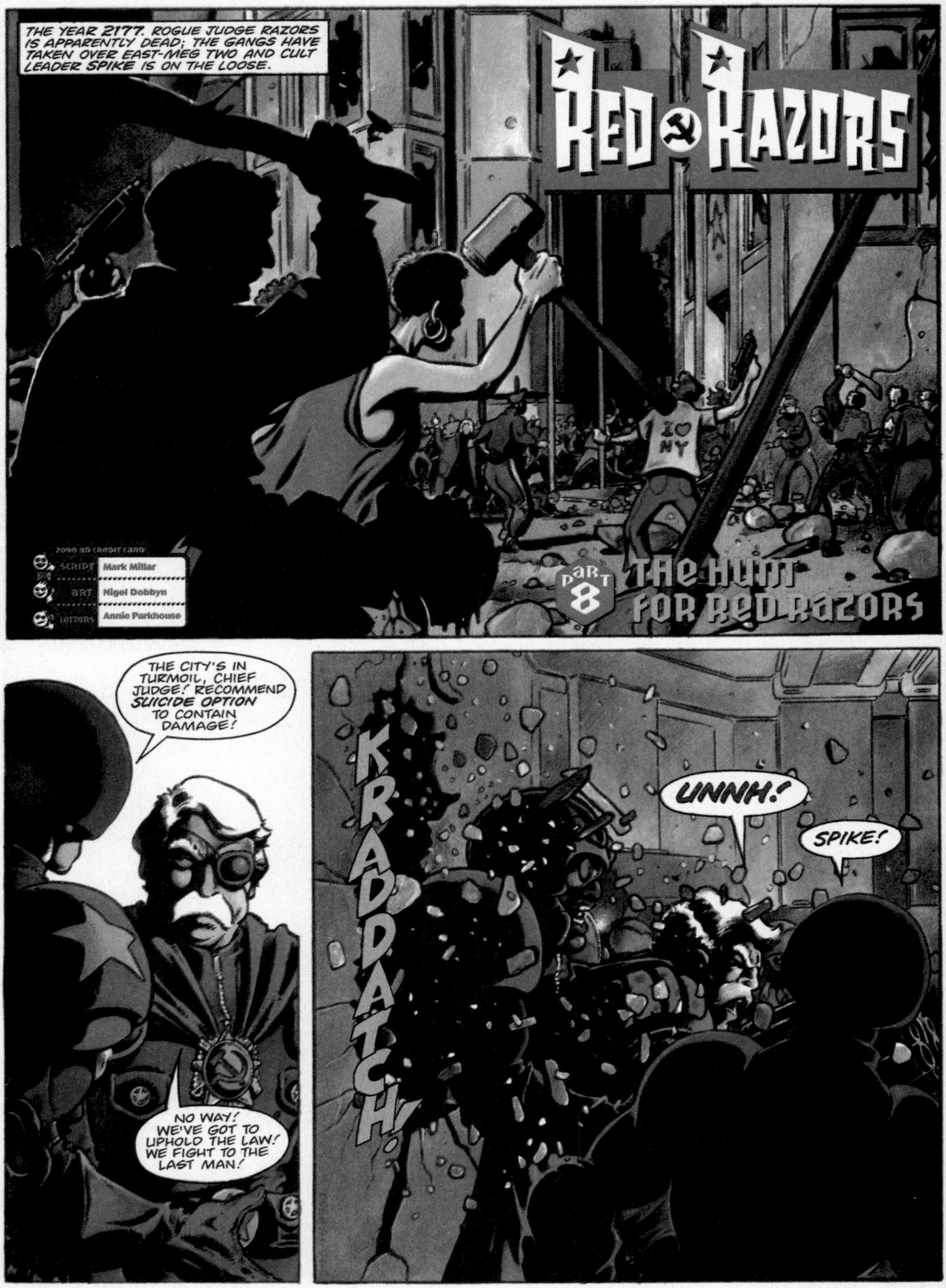
THE YEAR 2177. ROGUE JUDGE RAZORS IS APPARENTLY DEAD; THE GANGS HAVE TAKEN OVER EAST-MEG TWO AND CULT LEADER SPIKE IS ON THE LOOSE.
RED RAZORS
2000 AD CREDIT CARD
SCRIPT Mark Millar
ART Nigel Dobbyn
LETTERS Annie Parkhouse
PART 8 THE HUNT FOR RED RAZORS
I ♥ NY
THE CITY'S IN TURMOIL, CHIEF JUDGE! RECOMMEND SUICIDE OPTION TO CONTAIN DAMAGE!
NO WAY! WE'VE GOT TO UPHOLD THE LAW! WE FIGHT TO THE LAST MAN!
KRADDATCH!
UNNH!
SPIKE!

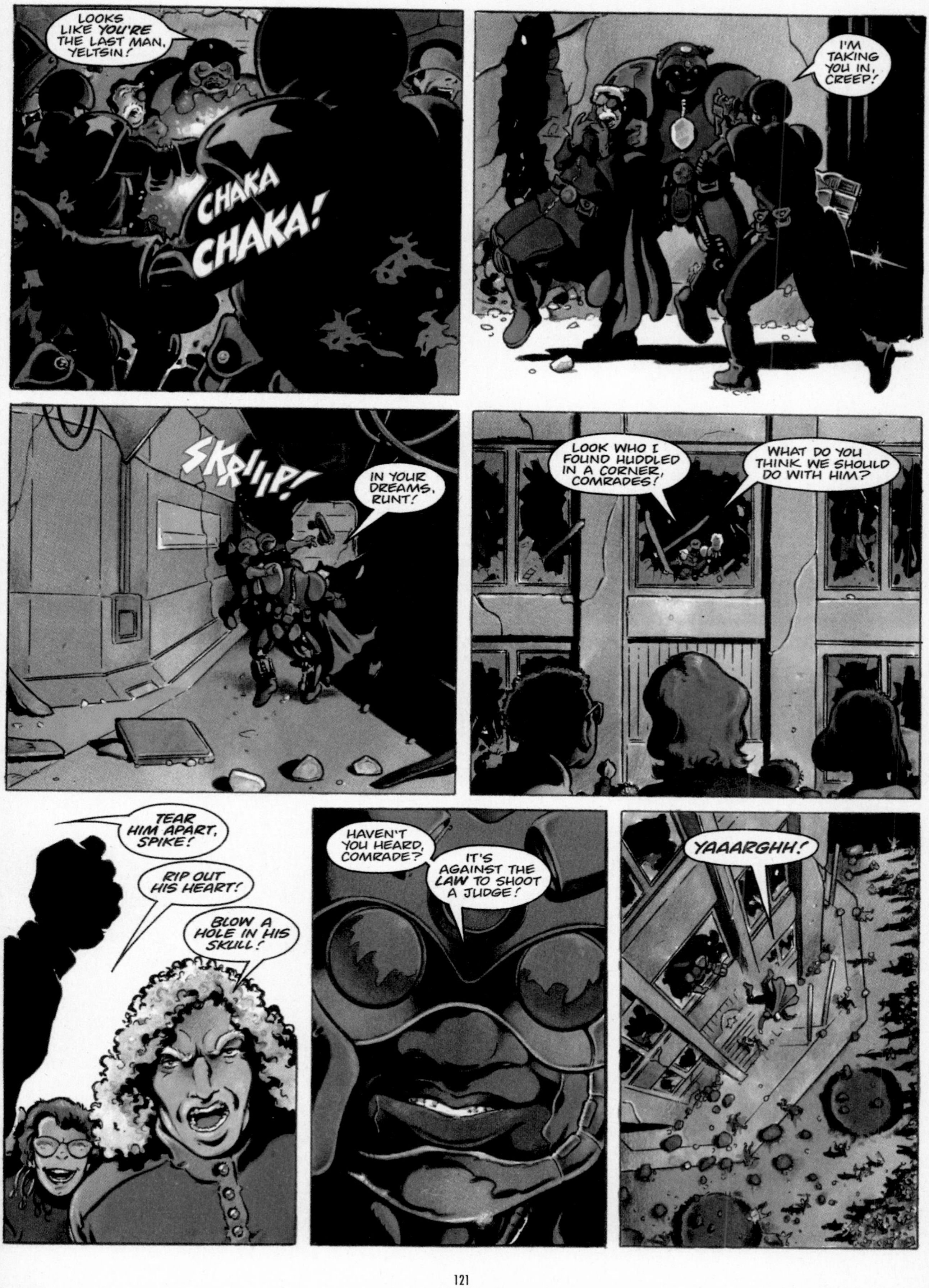

LOOKS LIKE YOU'RE THE LAST MAN, YELTSIN!
CHAKA CHAKA!
I'M TAKING YOU IN, CREEP!
SKRIIIIP!
IN YOUR DREAMS, RUNT!
LOOK WHO I FOUND HUDDLED IN A CORNER, COMRADES!
WHAT DO YOU THINK WE SHOULD DO WITH HIM?
TEAR HIM APART, SPIKE!
RIP OUT HIS HEART!
BLOW A HOLE IN HIS SKULL!
HAVEN'T YOU HEARD, COMRADE?
IT'S AGAINST THE LAW TO SHOOT A JUDGE!
YAAARGHH!

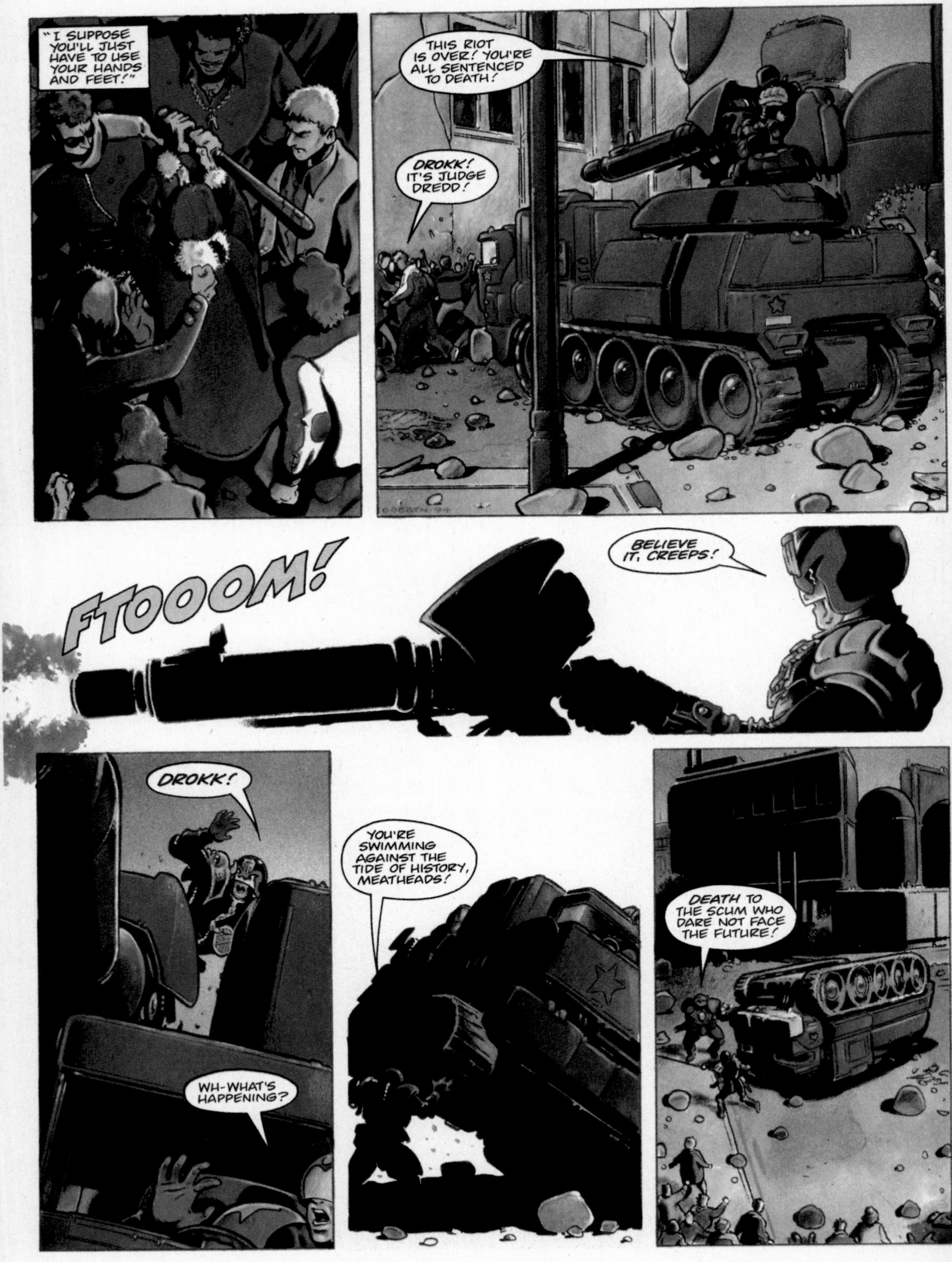
"I SUPPOSE YOU'LL JUST HAVE TO USE YOUR HANDS AND FEET!"
THIS RIOT IS OVER! YOU'RE ALL SENTENCED TO DEATH!
DROKK! IT'S JUDGE DREDD!
FTOOOM!
BELIEVE IT, CREEPS!
DROKK!
WH-WHAT'S HAPPENING?
YOU'RE SWIMMING AGAINST THE TIDE OF HISTORY, MEATHEADS!
DEATH TO THE SCUM WHO DARE NOT FACE THE FUTURE!

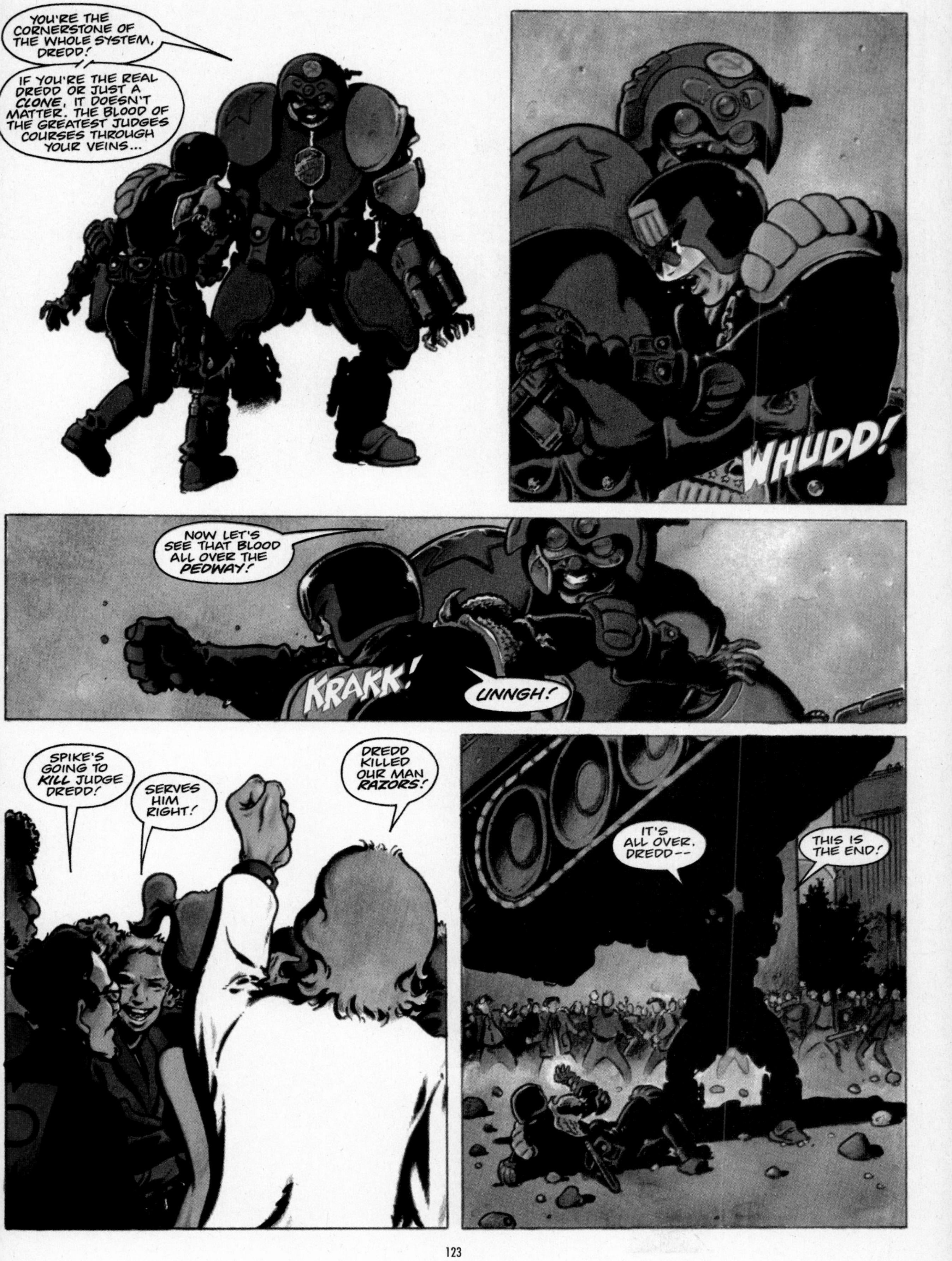
YOU'RE THE CORNERSTONE OF THE WHOLE SYSTEM, DREDD!
IF YOU'RE THE REAL DREDD OR JUST A CLONE, IT DOESN'T MATTER. THE BLOOD OF THE GREATEST JUDGES COURSES THROUGH YOUR VEINS...
WHUDD!
NOW LET'S SEE THAT BLOOD ALL OVER THE PEDWAY!
KRAKK!
UNNGH!
SPIKE'S GOING TO KILL JUDGE DREDD!
SERVES HIM RIGHT!
DREDD KILLED OUR MAN RAZORS!
IT'S ALL OVER, DREDD--
THIS IS THE END!

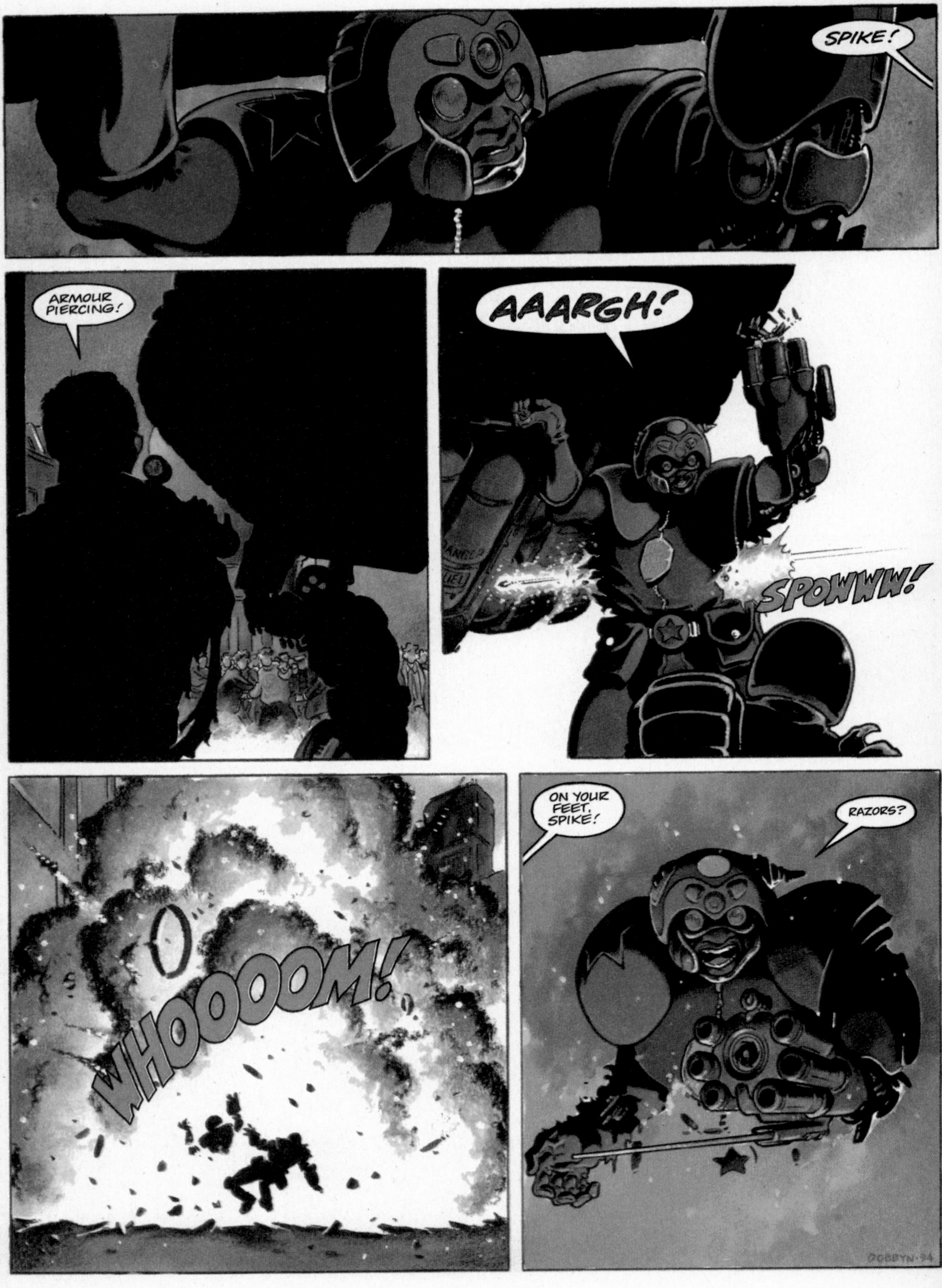
SPIKE!
ARMOUR PIERCING!
AAARGH!
SPOWWW!
WHOOOOM!
ON YOUR FEET, SPIKE!
RAZORS?
DOBBYN·94

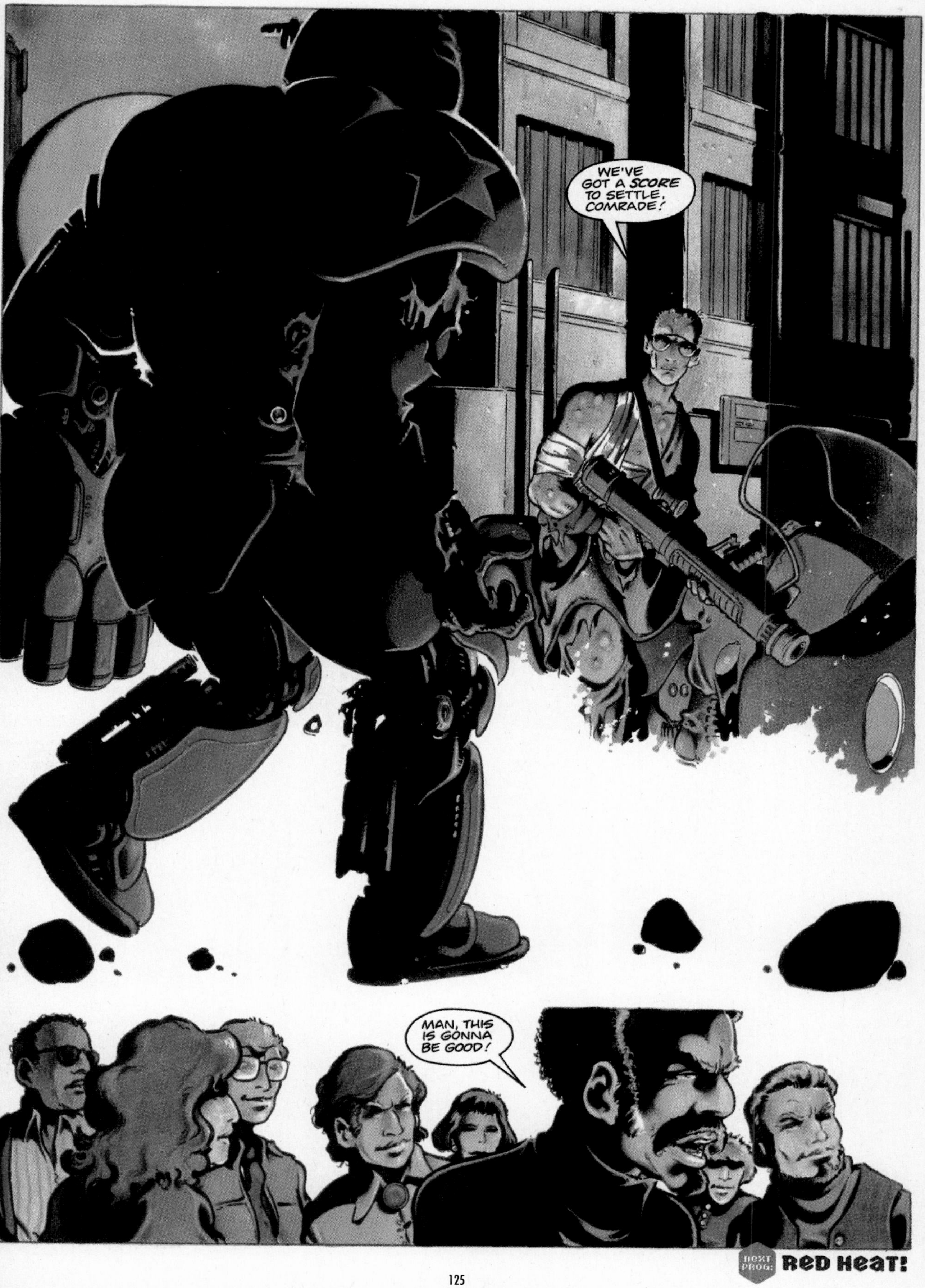
WE'VE GOT A SCORE TO SETTLE, COMRADE!
MAN, THIS IS GONNA BE GOOD!
NEXT PROG: RED HEAT!

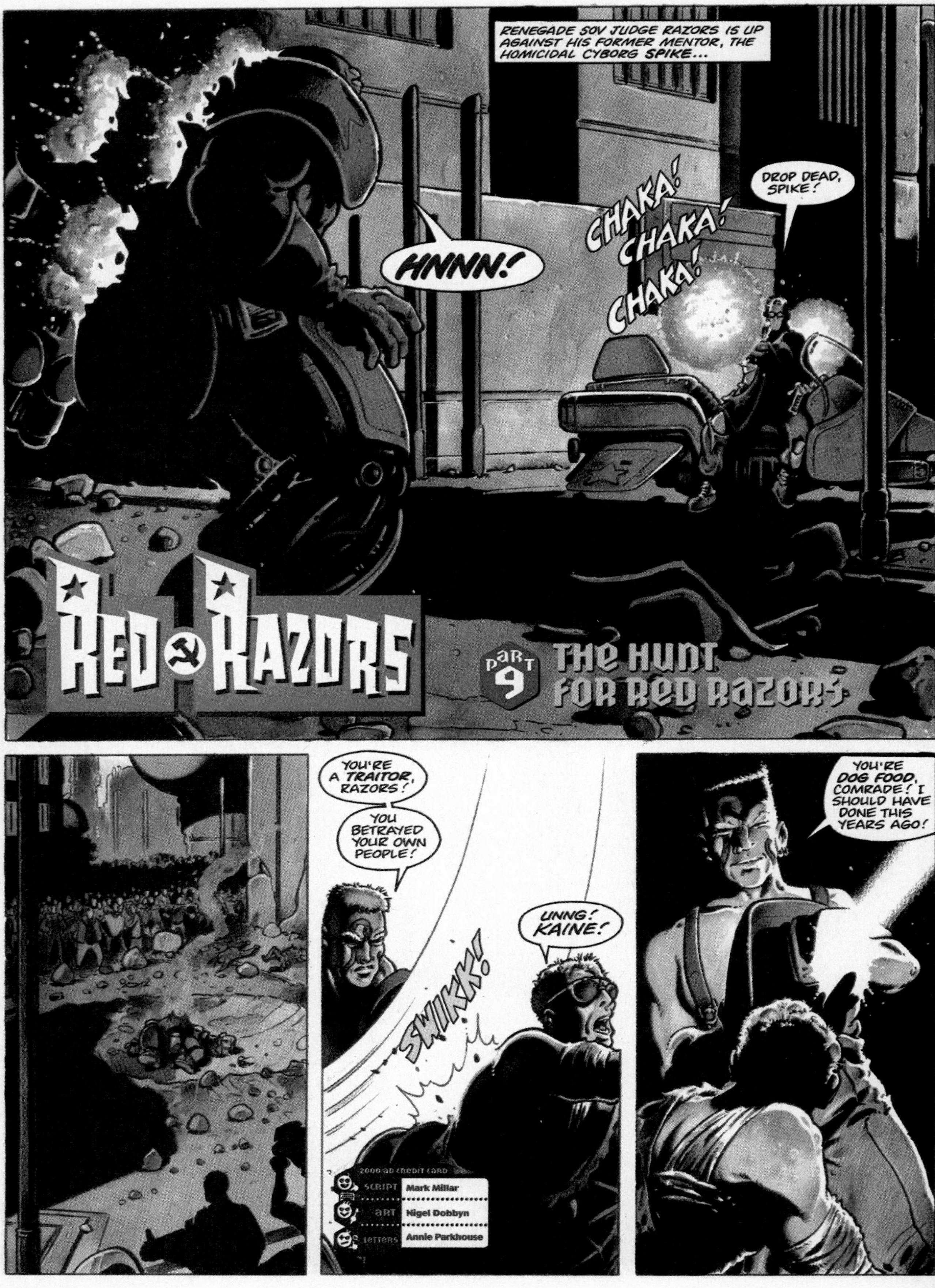
RENEGADE SOV JUDGE RAZORS IS UP AGAINST HIS FORMER MENTOR, THE HOMICIDAL CYBORG SPIKE...
HNNN!
CHAKA! CHAKA! CHAKA!
DROP DEAD, SPIKE!
RED RAZORS
PART 9 THE HUNT FOR RED RAZORS
YOU'RE A TRAITOR, RAZORS!
YOU BETRAYED YOUR OWN PEOPLE!
UNNG! KAINE!
SWIKK!
2000 AD CREDIT CARD
SCRIPT Mark Millar
ART Nigel Dobbyn
LETTERS Annie Parkhouse
YOU'RE DOG FOOD, COMRADE! I SHOULD HAVE DONE THIS YEARS AGO!

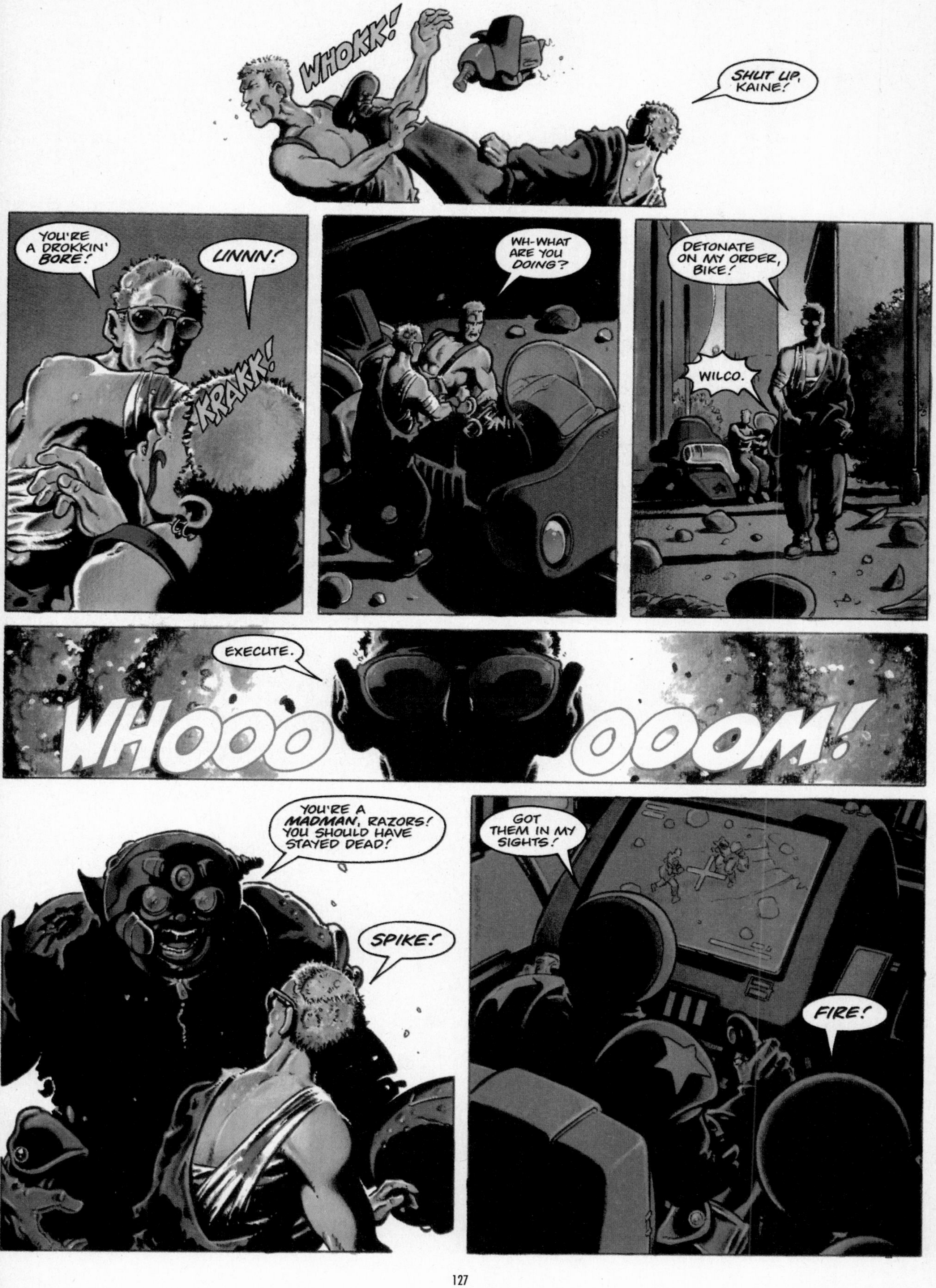
WHOKK!
SHUT UP, KAINE!
YOU'RE A DROKKIN' BORE!
UNNN!
KRAKK!
WH-WHAT ARE YOU DOING?
DETONATE ON MY ORDER, BIKE!
WILCO.
EXECUTE.
WHOOOOOOM!
YOU'RE A MADMAN, RAZORS! YOU SHOULD HAVE STAYED DEAD!
SPIKE!
GOT THEM IN MY SIGHTS!
FIRE!

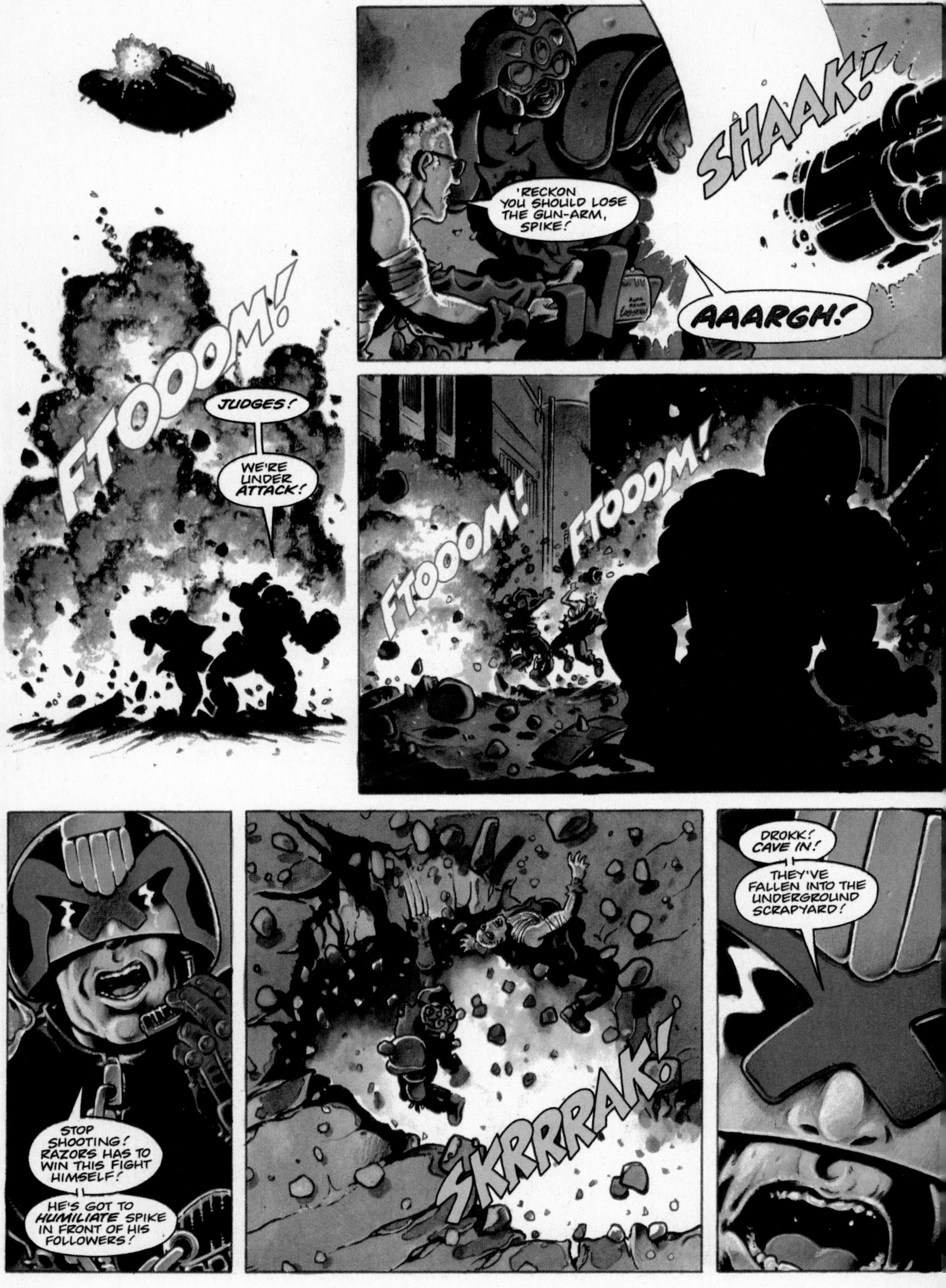
'RECKON YOU SHOULD LOSE THE GUN-ARM, SPIKE!
SHAAK!
AAARGH!
FTOOOM!
JUDGES!
WE'RE UNDER ATTACK!
FTOOOM!
FTOOOM!
STOP SHOOTING! RAZORS HAS TO WIN THIS FIGHT HIMSELF!
HE'S GOT TO HUMILIATE SPIKE IN FRONT OF HIS FOLLOWERS!
SKRRRAK!
DROKK! CAVE IN!
THEY'VE FALLEN INTO THE UNDERGROUND SCRAPYARD!

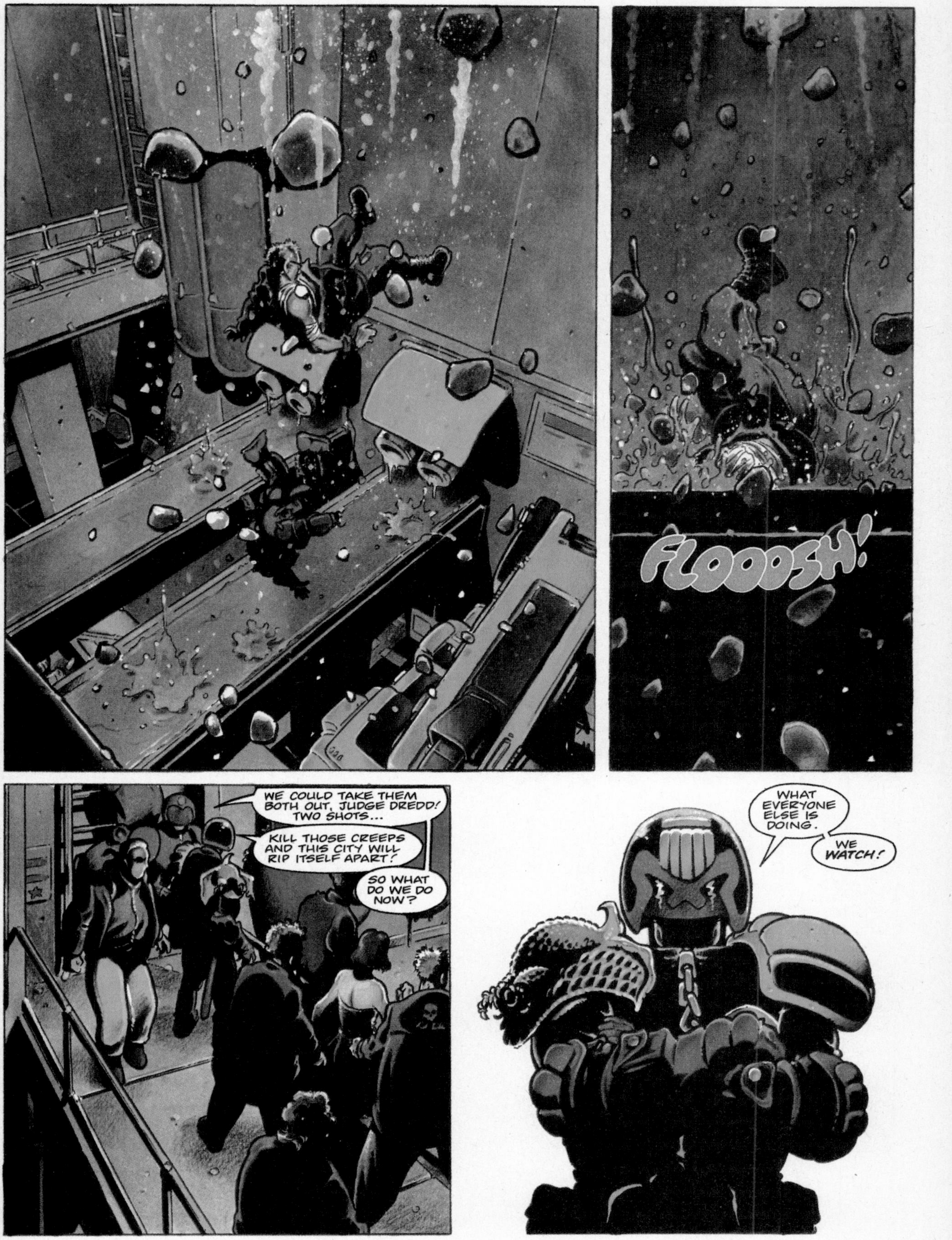
FLOOOSH!
WE COULD TAKE THEM BOTH OUT, JUDGE DREDD! TWO SHOTS...
KILL THOSE CREEPS AND THIS CITY WILL RIP ITSELF APART!
SO WHAT DO WE DO NOW?
WHAT EVERYONE ELSE IS DOING.
WE WATCH!

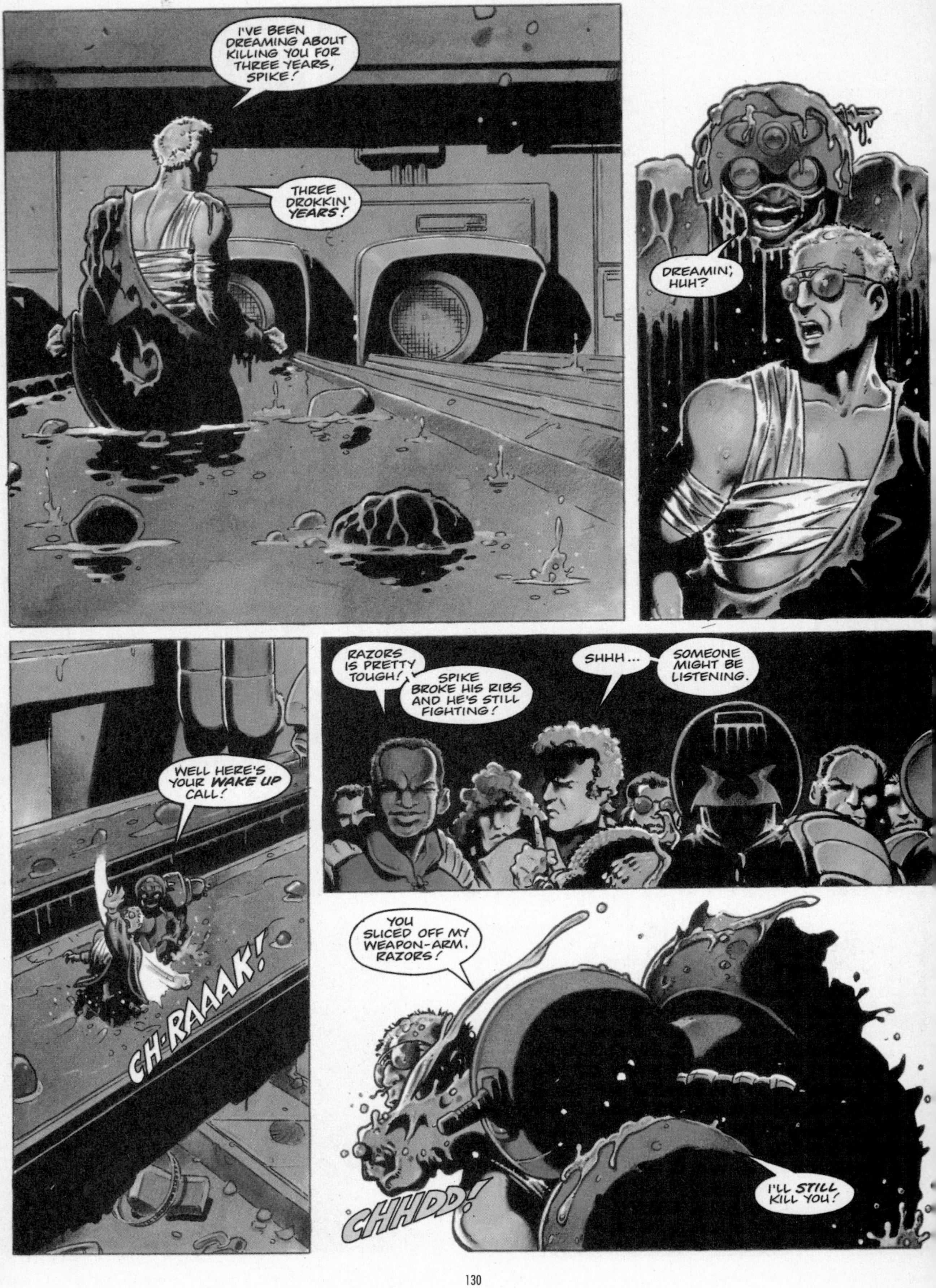
I'VE BEEN DREAMING ABOUT KILLING YOU FOR THREE YEARS, SPIKE!
THREE DROKKIN' YEARS!
DREAMIN', HUH?
WELL HERE'S YOUR WAKE UP CALL!
CH-RAAAK!
RAZORS IS PRETTY TOUGH!
SPIKE BROKE HIS RIBS AND HE'S STILL FIGHTING!
SHHH...
SOMEONE MIGHT BE LISTENING.
YOU SLICED OFF MY WEAPON-ARM, RAZORS!
CHHDD!
I'LL STILL KILL YOU!

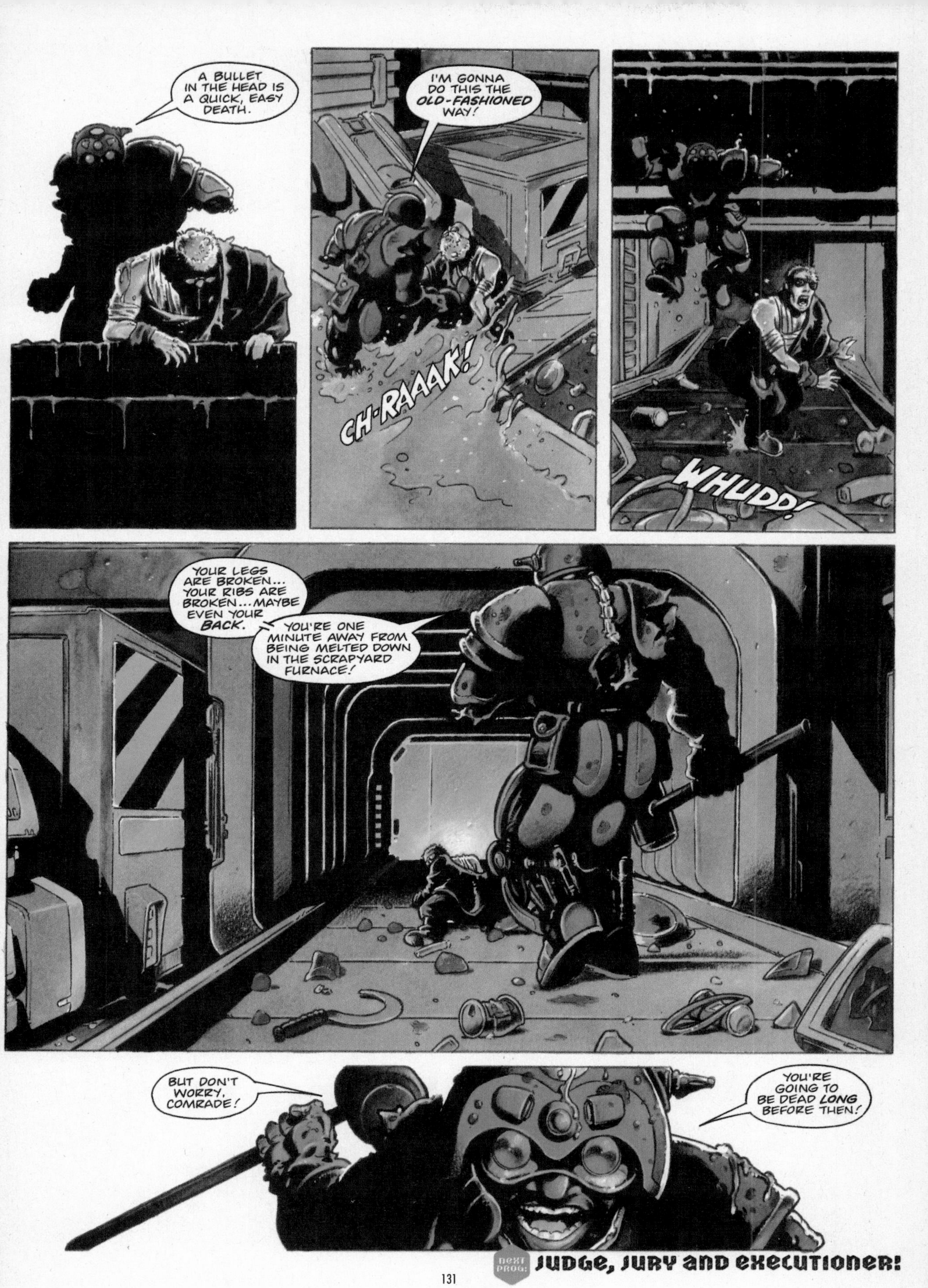
A BULLET IN THE HEAD IS A QUICK, EASY DEATH.
I'M GONNA DO THIS THE OLD-FASHIONED WAY!
CH-RAAAK!
WHUDD!
YOUR LEGS ARE BROKEN... YOUR RIBS ARE BROKEN...MAYBE EVEN YOUR BACK.
YOU'RE ONE MINUTE AWAY FROM BEING MELTED DOWN IN THE SCRAPYARD FURNACE!
BUT DON'T WORRY, COMRADE!
YOU'RE GOING TO BE DEAD LONG BEFORE THEN!
NEXT PROG: JUDGE, JURY AND EXECUTIONER!

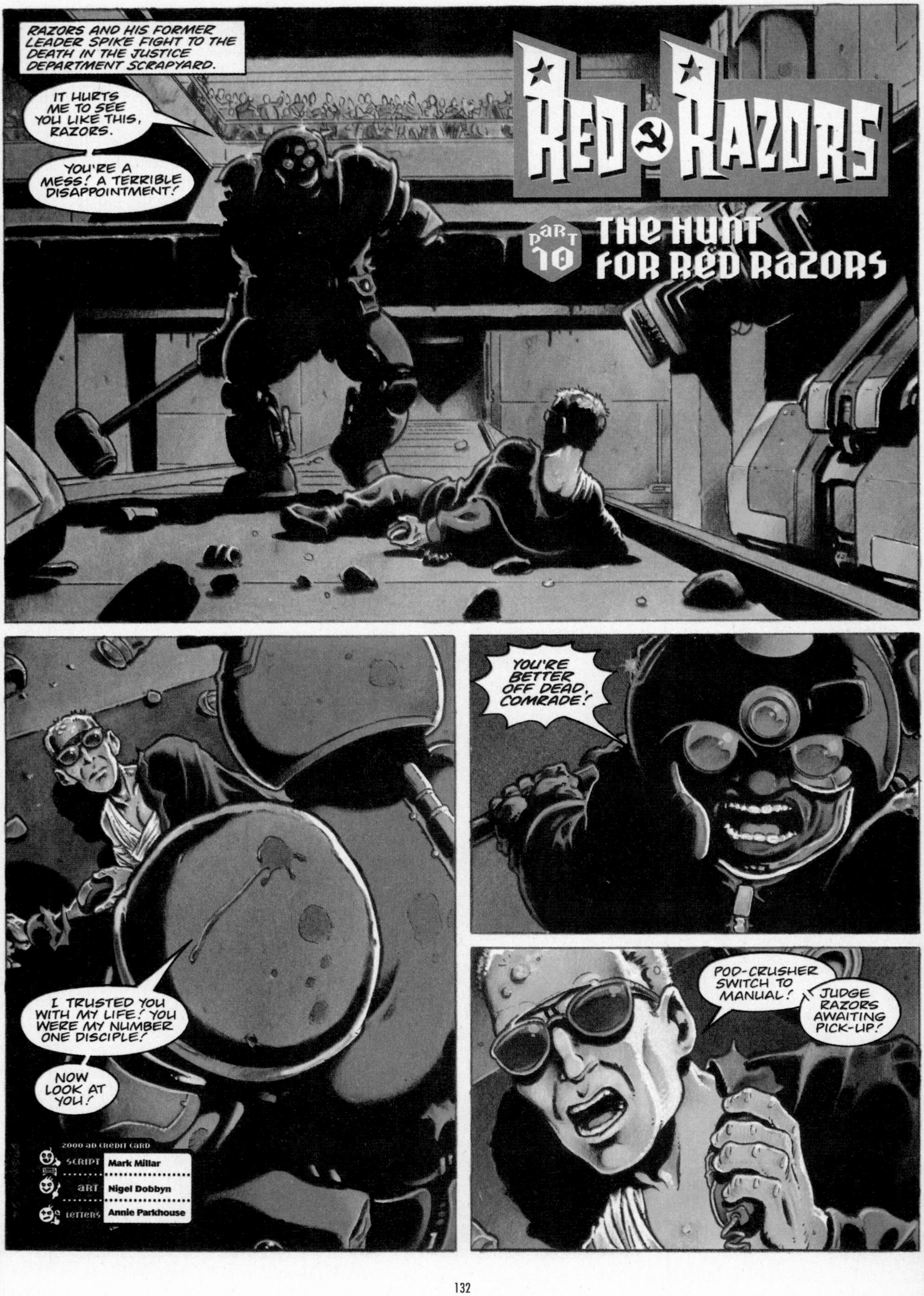
RAZORS AND HIS FORMER LEADER SPIKE FIGHT TO THE DEATH IN THE JUSTICE DEPARTMENT SCRAPYARD.
IT HURTS ME TO SEE YOU LIKE THIS, RAZORS.
YOU'RE A MESS! A TERRIBLE DISAPPOINTMENT!
RED RAZORS
PART 10 THE HUNT FOR RED RAZORS
I TRUSTED YOU WITH MY LIFE! YOU WERE MY NUMBER ONE DISCIPLE!
NOW LOOK AT YOU!
2000 AD CREDIT CARD
SCRIPT Mark Millar
ART Nigel Dobbyn
LETTERS Annie Parkhouse
YOU'RE BETTER OFF DEAD, COMRADE!
POD-CRUSHER SWITCH TO MANUAL!
JUDGE RAZORS AWAITING PICK-UP!

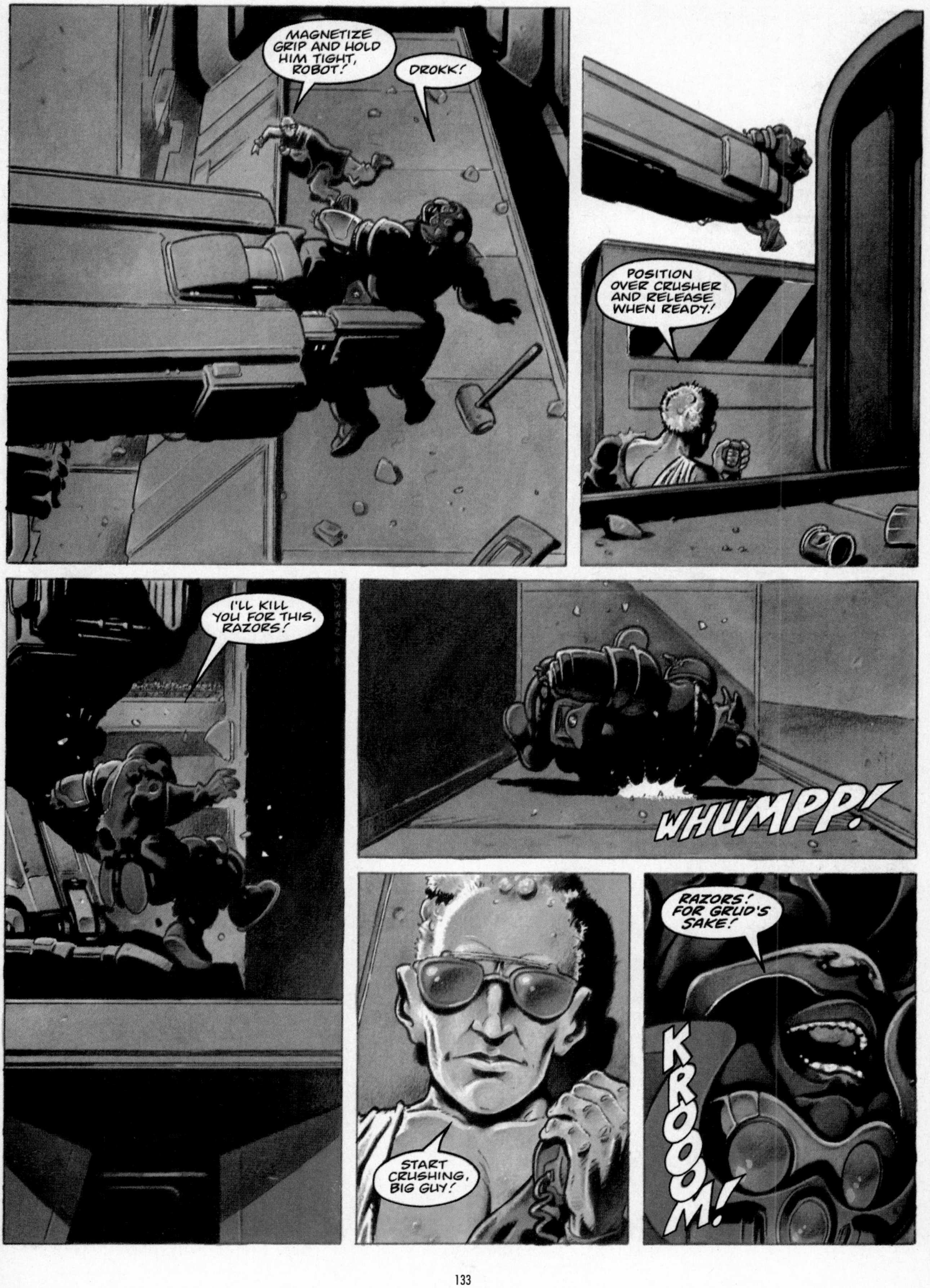

MAGNETIZE GRIP AND HOLD HIM TIGHT, ROBOT!
DROKK!
POSITION OVER CRUSHER AND RELEASE WHEN READY!
I'LL KILL YOU FOR THIS, RAZORS!
WHUMPP!
START CRUSHING, BIG GUY!
RAZORS! FOR GRUD'S SAKE!
KROOOM!

IT'S KILLING ME! I'M GOING TO DIE!

THAT'S THE IDEA, PUNK!

HOPE IT HURTS!

R-ENNNK!

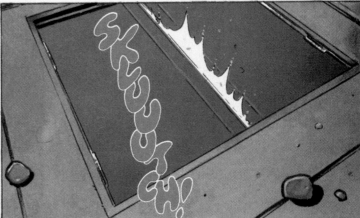

SKUUUGH!

SWEET GRUD! SPIKE'S DEAD!

I DON'T BELIEVE IT!

WHAT A WIMP!

OKAY! SOMEBODY CUFF 'IM!

WHRRRR

PLONK!

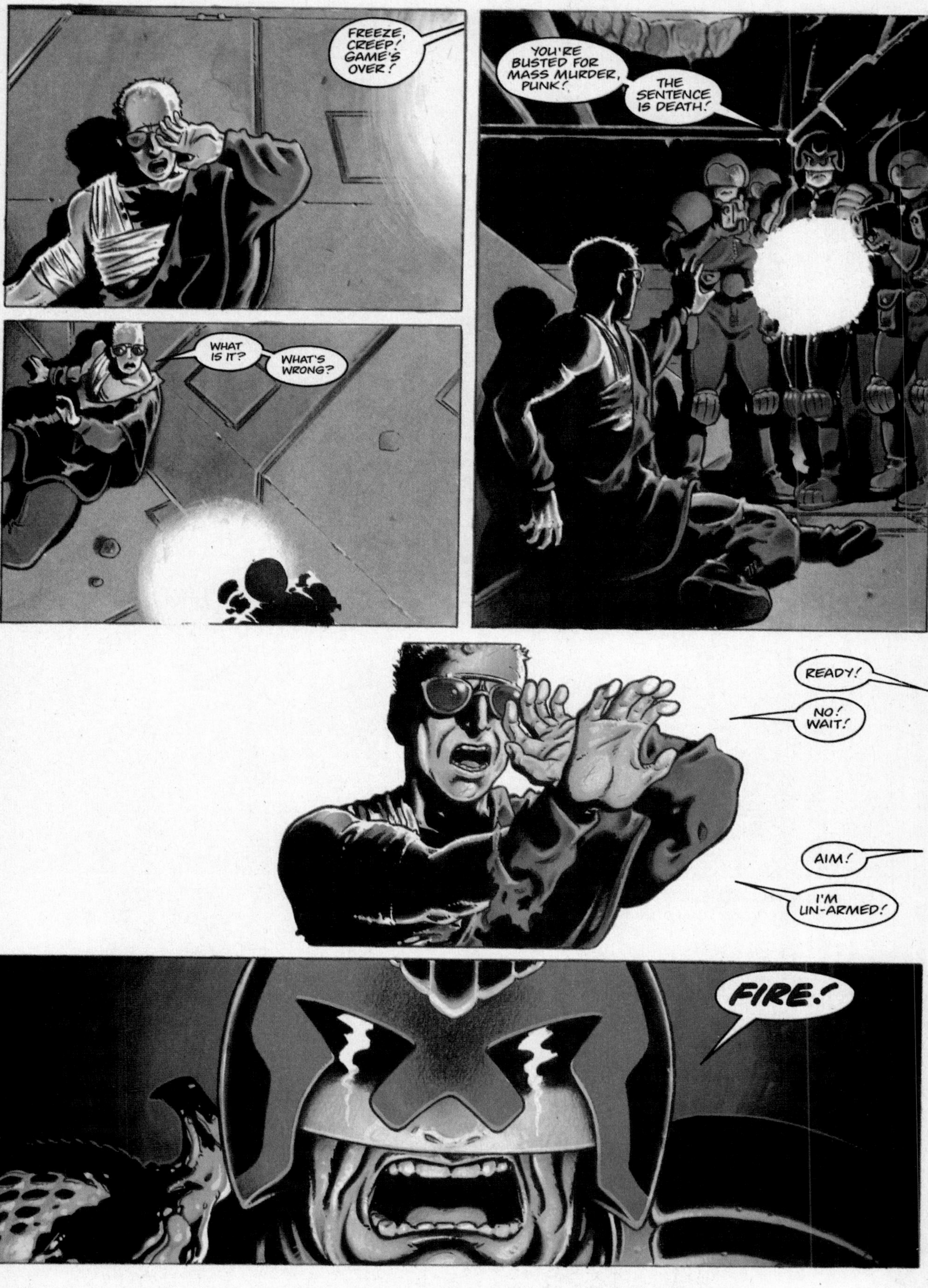
FREEZE, CREEP! GAME'S OVER!
YOU'RE BUSTED FOR MASS MURDER, PUNK!
THE SENTENCE IS DEATH!
WHAT IS IT?
WHAT'S WRONG?
READY!
NO! WAIT!
AIM!
I'M UN-ARMED!
FIRE!

CHOOM CHOOM CHOOM CHOOM CHOOM

HOLD YOUR FIRE!

IS HE STILL ALIVE?

HE LOOKS LIKE HE'S TWITCHING!

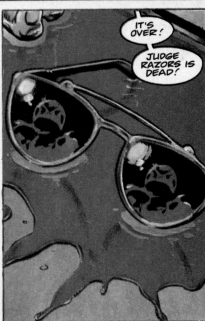

IT'S OVER!

JUDGE RAZORS IS DEAD!

THE GRAND HALL OF JUSTICE. JUDGE HANKERSON ADDRESSES THE SENIOR JUDGES.

JUDGE DREDD HAS RETURNED TO MEGA-CITY ONE!

THE CRISIS IS OVER!

JUDGE RAZORS HAS BEEN EXECUTED AND THE GANGS ARE LOST WITHOUT THEIR LEADERS!

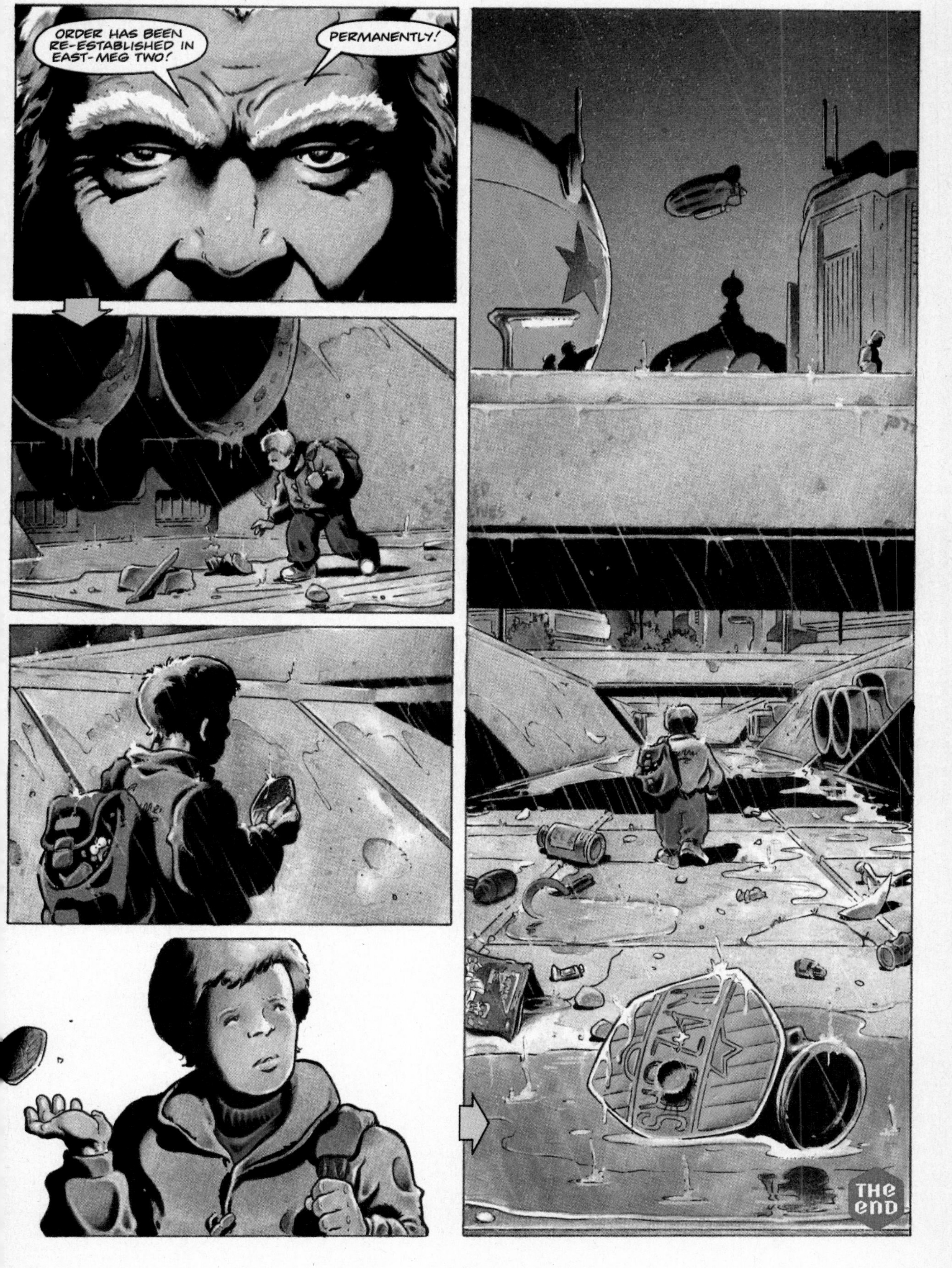
ORDER HAS BEEN RE-ESTABLISHED IN EAST-MEG TWO!
PERMANENTLY!
THE END

RITES OF PASSAGE

Script: Mark Millar

Art: Nigel Dobbyn

Colors: Dondie Cox

Letters: Ellie de Ville

Originally published in *2000 AD* Prog 971

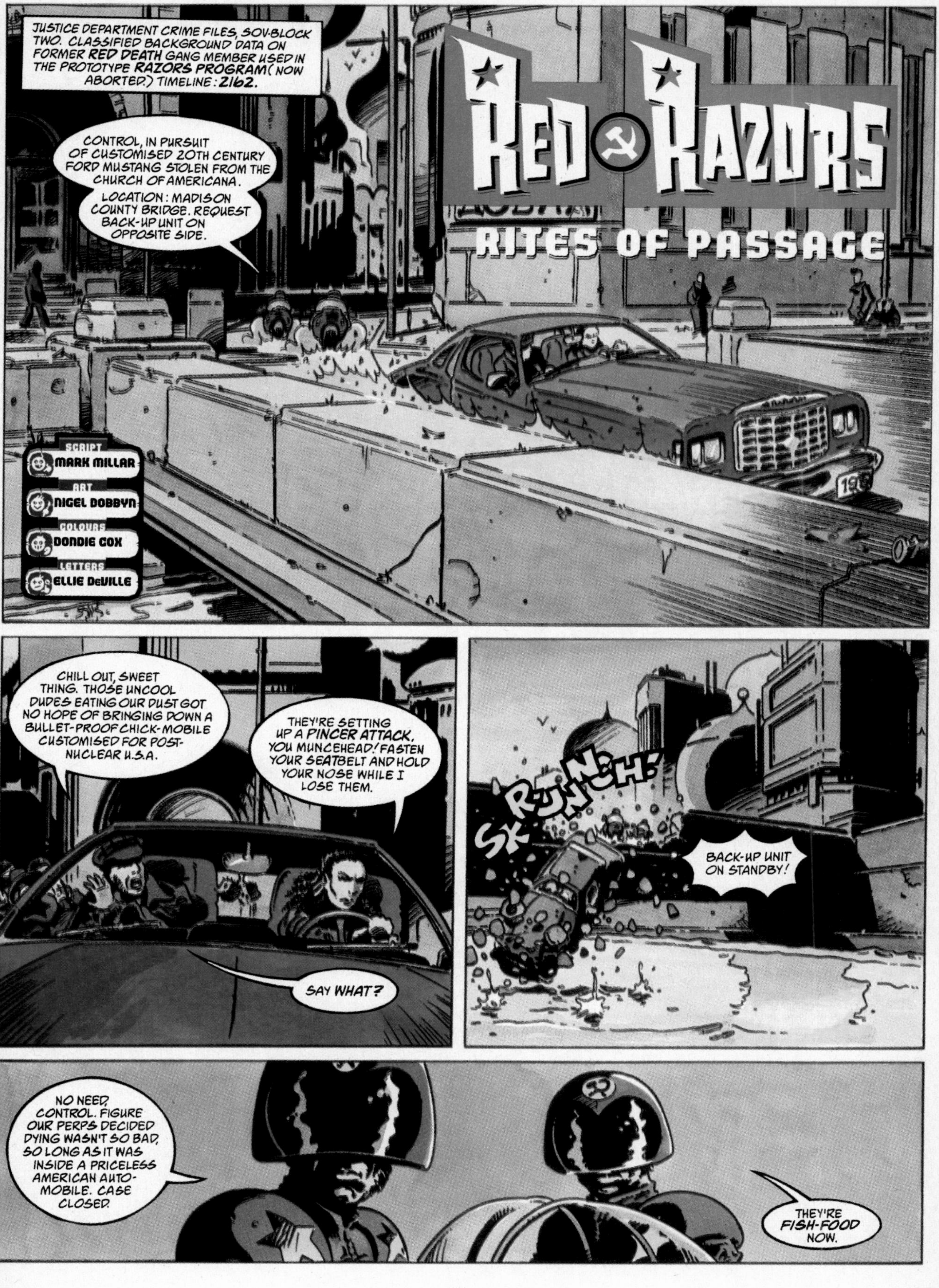
JUSTICE DEPARTMENT CRIME FILES, SOV-BLOCK TWO. CLASSIFIED BACKGROUND DATA ON FORMER RED DEATH GANG MEMBER USED IN THE PROTOTYPE RAZORS PROGRAM (NOW ABORTED) TIMELINE: 2162.
RED RAZORS
RITES OF PASSAGE
CONTROL, IN PURSUIT OF CUSTOMISED 20TH CENTURY FORD MUSTANG STOLEN FROM THE CHURCH OF AMERICANA.
LOCATION: MADISON COUNTY BRIDGE. REQUEST BACK-UP UNIT ON OPPOSITE SIDE.
SCRIPT MARK MILLAR
ART NIGEL DOBBYN
COLOURS DONDIE COX
LETTERS ELLIE DeVILLE
CHILL OUT, SWEET THING. THOSE UNCOOL DUDES EATING OUR DUST GOT NO HOPE OF BRINGING DOWN A BULLET-PROOF CHICK-MOBILE CUSTOMISED FOR POST-NUCLEAR U.S.A.
THEY'RE SETTING UP A PINCER ATTACK, YOU MUNCEHEAD! FASTEN YOUR SEATBELT AND HOLD YOUR NOSE WHILE I LOSE THEM.
SAY WHAT?
SKRUNCH!
BACK-UP UNIT ON STANDBY!
NO NEED, CONTROL. FIGURE OUR PERPS DECIDED DYING WASN'T SO BAD, SO LONG AS IT WAS INSIDE A PRICELESS AMERICAN AUTO-MOBILE. CASE CLOSED.
THEY'RE FISH-FOOD NOW.

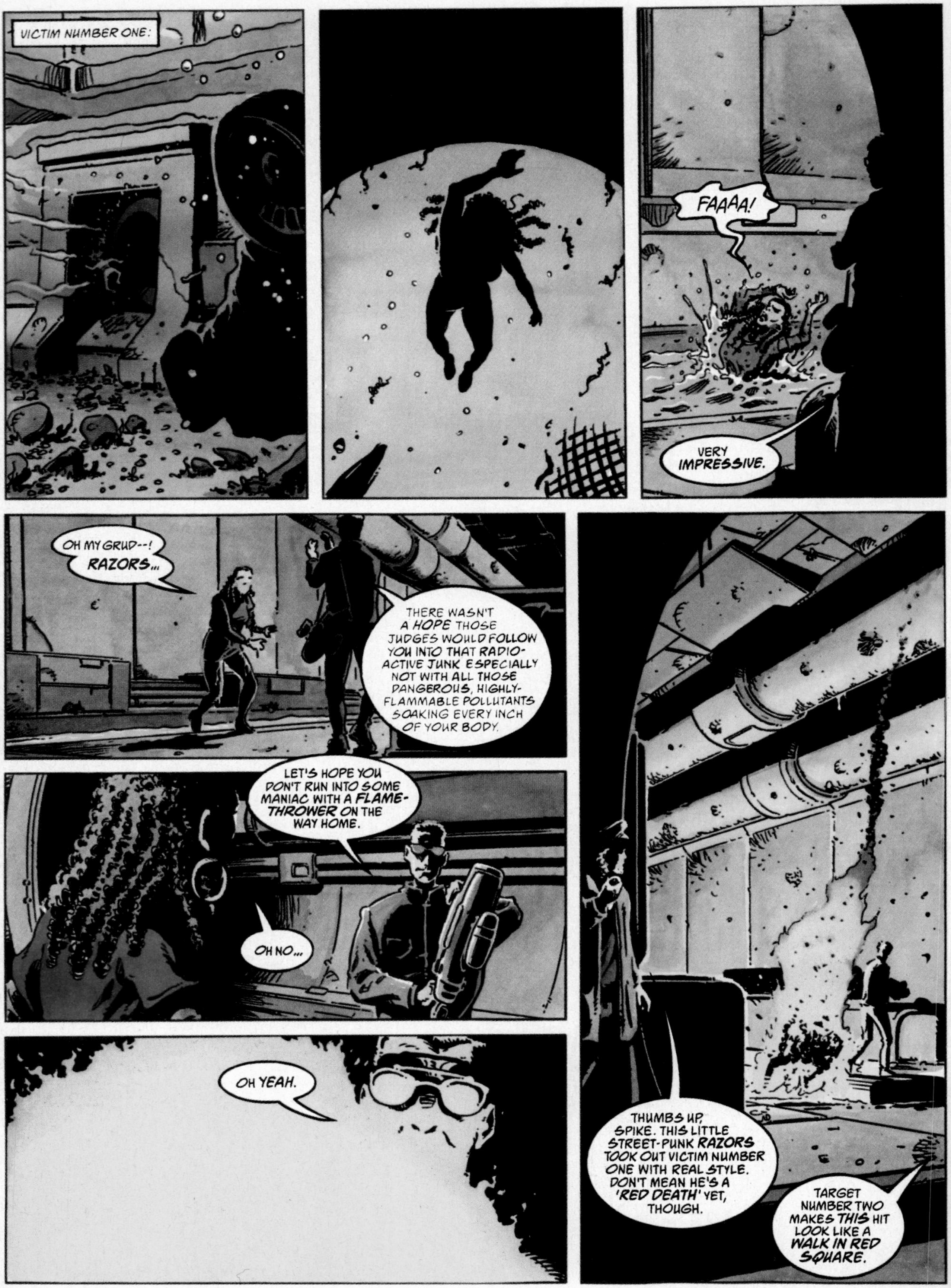
VICTIM NUMBER ONE:
FAAAA!
VERY IMPRESSIVE.
OH MY GRUD--! RAZORS...
THERE WASN'T A HOPE THOSE JUDGES WOULD FOLLOW YOU INTO THAT RADIO-ACTIVE JUNK ESPECIALLY NOT WITH ALL THOSE DANGEROUS, HIGHLY-FLAMMABLE POLLUTANTS SOAKING EVERY INCH OF YOUR BODY.
LET'S HOPE YOU DON'T RUN INTO SOME MANIAC WITH A FLAME-THROWER ON THE WAY HOME.
OH NO...
OH YEAH.
THUMBS UP, SPIKE. THIS LITTLE STREET-PUNK RAZORS TOOK OUT VICTIM NUMBER ONE WITH REAL STYLE. DON'T MEAN HE'S A 'RED DEATH' YET, THOUGH.
TARGET NUMBER TWO MAKES THIS HIT LOOK LIKE A WALK IN RED SQUARE.

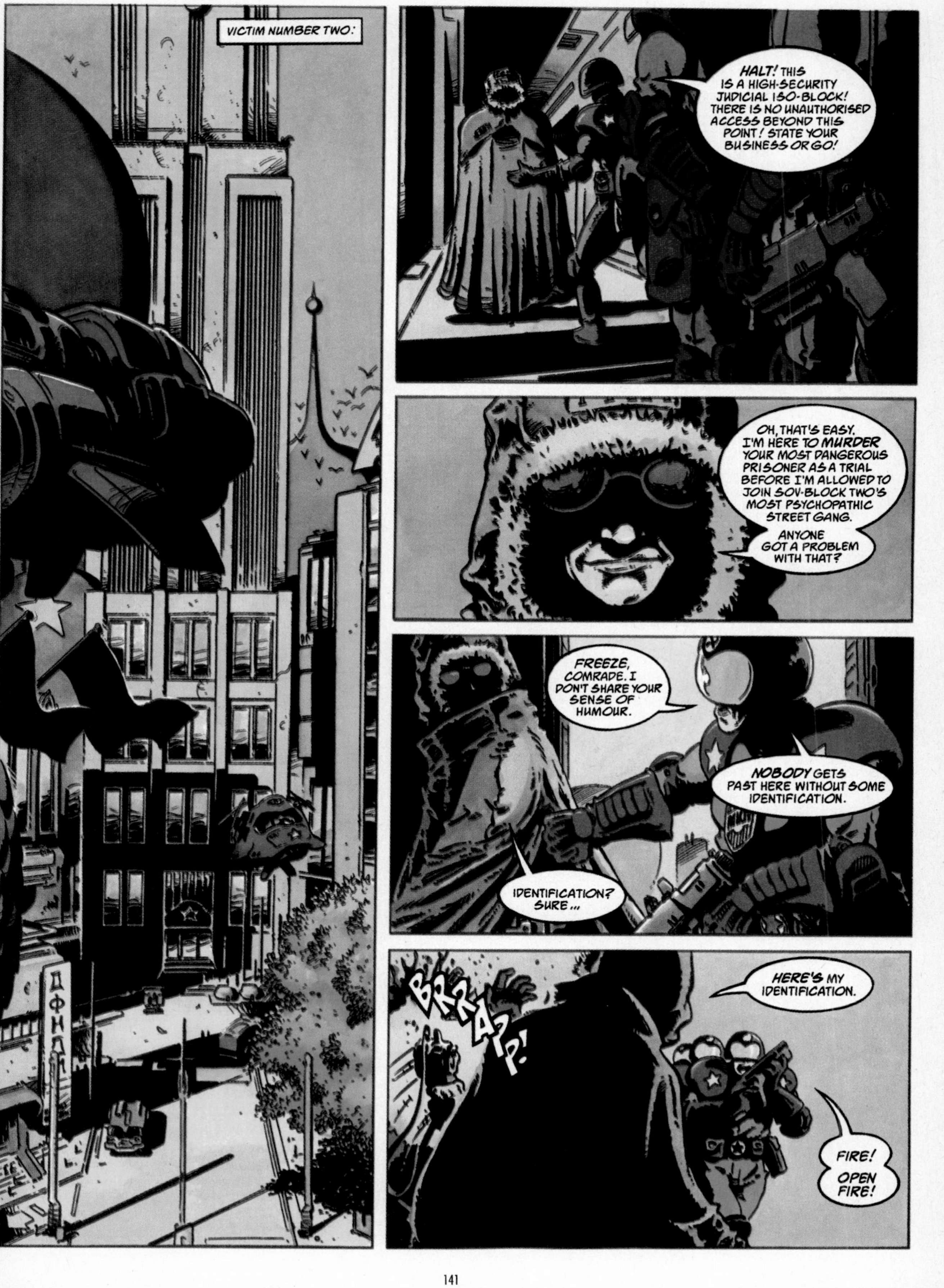
VICTIM NUMBER TWO:
HALT! THIS IS A HIGH-SECURITY JUDICIAL ISO-BLOCK! THERE IS NO UNAUTHORISED ACCESS BEYOND THIS POINT! STATE YOUR BUSINESS OR GO!
OH, THAT'S EASY. I'M HERE TO MURDER YOUR MOST DANGEROUS PRISONER AS A TRIAL BEFORE I'M ALLOWED TO JOIN SOV-BLOCK TWO'S MOST PSYCHOPATHIC STREET GANG.
ANYONE GOT A PROBLEM WITH THAT?
FREEZE, COMRADE. I DON'T SHARE YOUR SENSE OF HUMOUR.
NOBODY GETS PAST HERE WITHOUT SOME IDENTIFICATION.
IDENTIFICATION? SURE...
BRRRAPP!
HERE'S MY IDENTIFICATION.
FIRE! OPEN FIRE!

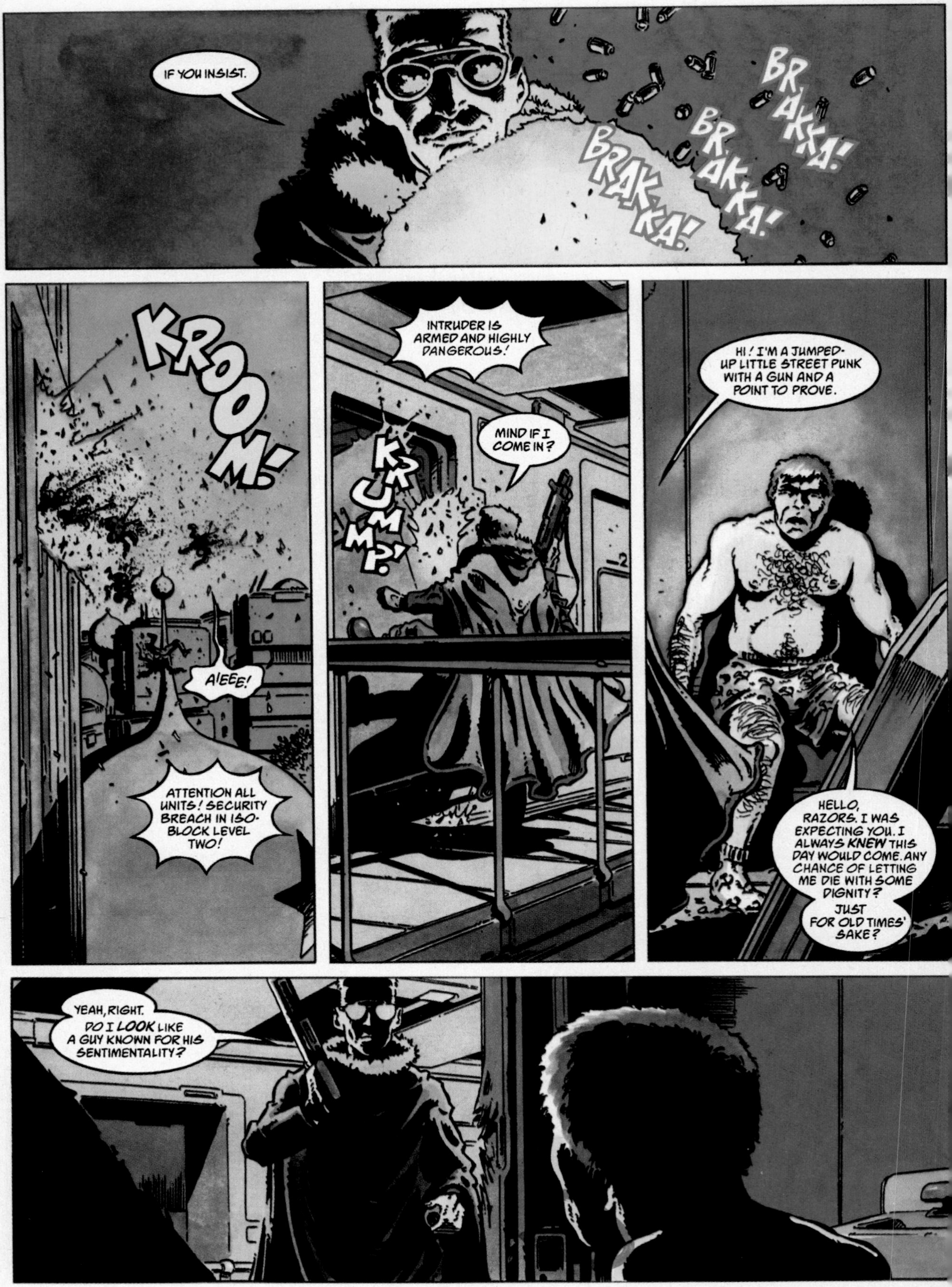
IF YOU INSIST.
BRAKKA!
BRAKKA!
BRAKKA!
KROOM!
AIEEE!
ATTENTION ALL UNITS! SECURITY BREACH IN ISO-BLOCK LEVEL TWO!
INTRUDER IS ARMED AND HIGHLY DANGEROUS!
MIND IF I COME IN?
KRUMMP!
HI! I'M A JUMPED-UP LITTLE STREET PUNK WITH A GUN AND A POINT TO PROVE.
HELLO, RAZORS. I WAS EXPECTING YOU. I ALWAYS KNEW THIS DAY WOULD COME. ANY CHANCE OF LETTING ME DIE WITH SOME DIGNITY?
JUST FOR OLD TIMES' SAKE?
YEAH, RIGHT. DO I LOOK LIKE A GUY KNOWN FOR HIS SENTIMENTALITY?

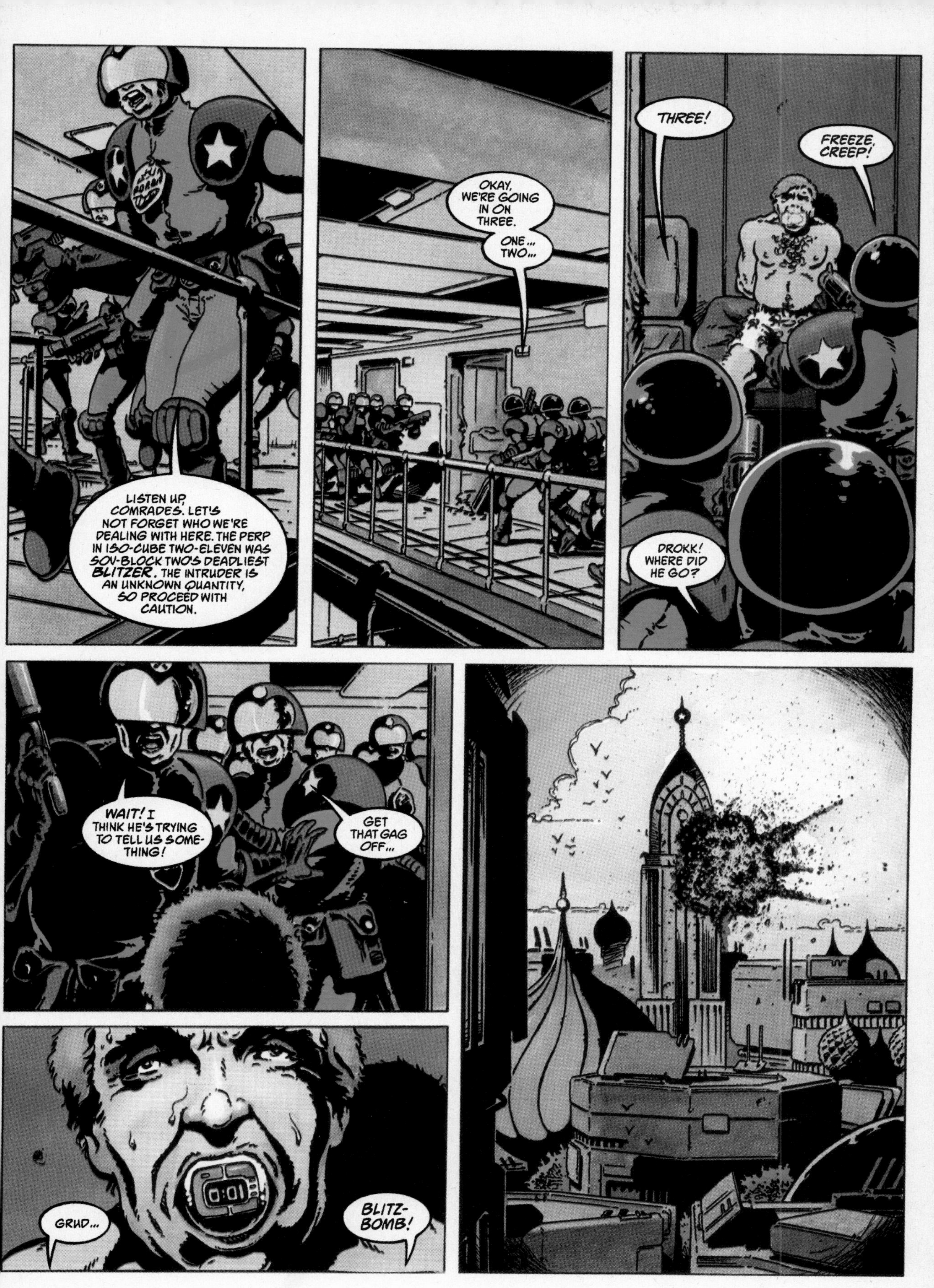
LISTEN UP, COMRADES. LET'S NOT FORGET WHO WE'RE DEALING WITH HERE. THE PERP IN ISO-CUBE TWO-ELEVEN WAS SOV-BLOCK TWO'S DEADLIEST BLITZER. THE INTRUDER IS AN UNKNOWN QUANTITY, SO PROCEED WITH CAUTION.
OKAY, WE'RE GOING IN ON THREE.
ONE... TWO...
THREE!
FREEZE, CREEP!
DROKK! WHERE DID HE GO?
WAIT! I THINK HE'S TRYING TO TELL US SOME-THING!
GET THAT GAG OFF...
GRUD...
BLITZ-BOMB!

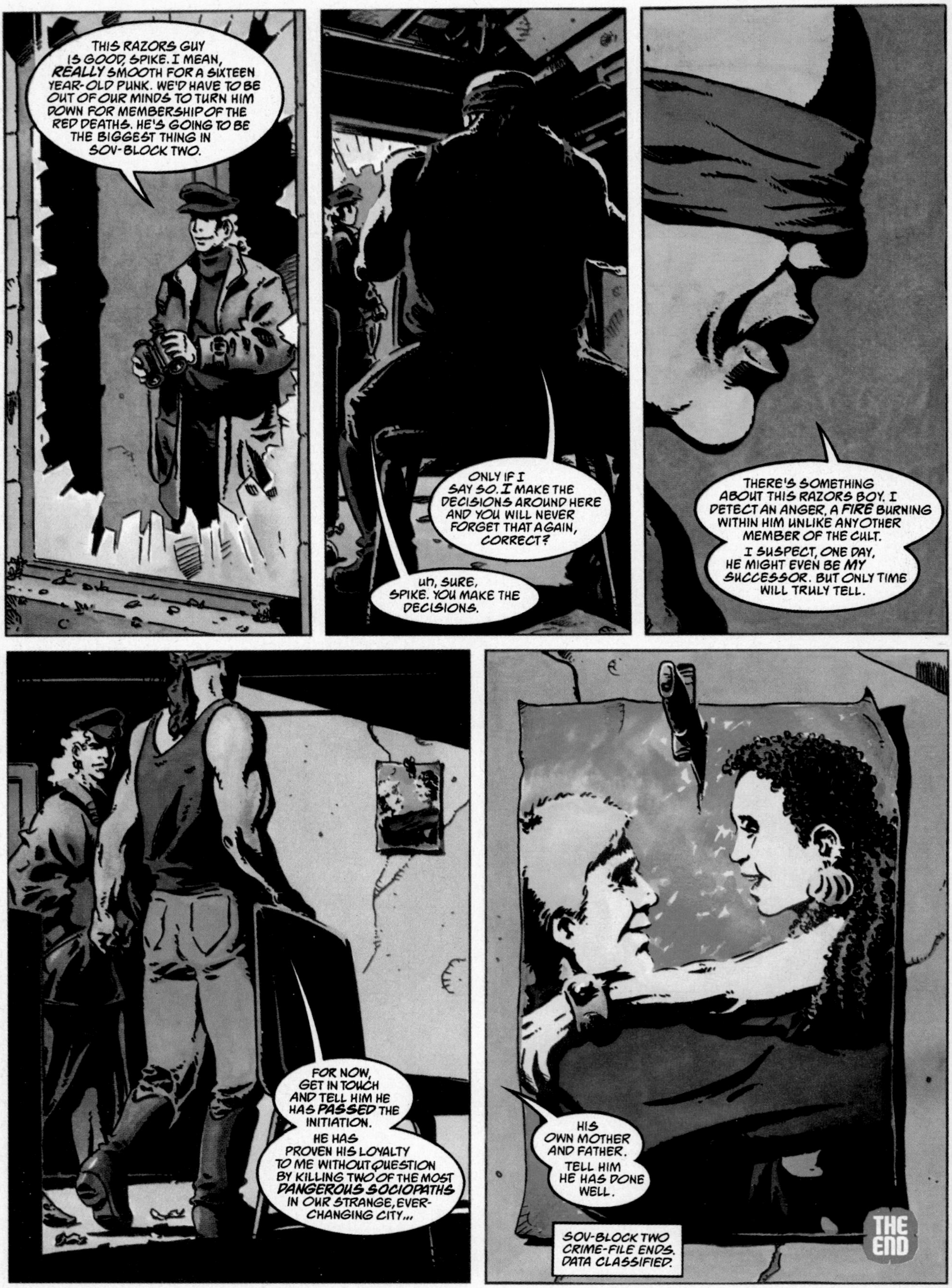
THIS RAZORS GUY IS GOOD, SPIKE. I MEAN, REALLY SMOOTH FOR A SIXTEEN YEAR-OLD PUNK. WE'D HAVE TO BE OUT OF OUR MINDS TO TURN HIM DOWN FOR MEMBERSHIP OF THE RED DEATHS. HE'S GOING TO BE THE BIGGEST THING IN SOV-BLOCK TWO.
ONLY IF I SAY SO. I MAKE THE DECISIONS AROUND HERE AND YOU WILL NEVER FORGET THAT AGAIN, CORRECT?
UH, SURE, SPIKE. YOU MAKE THE DECISIONS.
THERE'S SOMETHING ABOUT THIS RAZORS BOY. I DETECT AN ANGER, A FIRE BURNING WITHIN HIM UNLIKE ANY OTHER MEMBER OF THE CULT.
I SUSPECT, ONE DAY, HE MIGHT EVEN BE MY SUCCESSOR. BUT ONLY TIME WILL TRULY TELL.
FOR NOW, GET IN TOUCH AND TELL HIM HE HAS PASSED THE INITIATION.
HE HAS PROVEN HIS LOYALTY TO ME WITHOUT QUESTION BY KILLING TWO OF THE MOST DANGEROUS SOCIOPATHS IN OUR STRANGE, EVER-CHANGING CITY...
HIS OWN MOTHER AND FATHER.
TELL HIM HE HAS DONE WELL.
SOV-BLOCK TWO CRIME-FILE ENDS. DATA CLASSIFIED.
THE END